SO-AJY-096

XML™:
A Primer,
2nd Edition

XML™: A Primer, 2nd Edition

Simon St.Laurent

M&T Books

An imprint of IDG Books Worldwide, Inc.

Foster City, CA ■ Chicago, IL ■ Indianapolis, IN ■ New York, NY

XML™: A Primer, 2nd Edition

Published by
M&T Books
An imprint of IDG Books Worldwide, Inc.
919 E. Hillsdale Blvd., Suite 400
Foster City, CA 94404
www.idgbooks.com (IDG Books Worldwide Web site)

Copyright © 1999 by Simon St. Laurent. All rights reserved. No part of this book, including interior design, cover design, and icons, may be reproduced or transmitted in any form, by any means (electronic, photocopying, recording, or otherwise) without the prior written permission of the publisher.

ISBN: 0-7645-3310-X

Printed in the United States of America

10 9 8 7 6 5 4 3 2 1

1P/QZ/QZ/ZZ/FC

Distributed in the United States by IDG Books Worldwide, Inc.

Distributed by CDG Books Canada Inc. for Canada; by Transworld Publishers Limited in the United Kingdom; by IDG Norge Books for Norway; by IDG Sweden Books for Sweden; by Woodslane Pty. Ltd. for Australia; by Woodslane (NZ) Ltd. for New Zealand; by TransQuest Publishers Pte Ltd. for Singapore, Malaysia, Thailand, Indonesia, and Hong Kong; by ICG Muse, Inc. for Japan; by Norma Comunicaciones S.A. for Colombia; by Intersoft for South Africa; by Eyrolles for France; by International Thomson Publishing for Germany, Austria and Switzerland; by Distribuidora Cuspide for Argentina; by Livraria Cultura for Brazil; by Ediciones ZETA S.C.R. Ltda. for Peru; by WS Computer Publishing Corporation, Inc., for the Philippines; by Contemporanea de Ediciones for Venezuela; by Express Computer Distributors for the Caribbean and West Indies; by Micronesia Media Distributor, Inc. for Micronesia; by Grupo Editorial Norma S.A. for Guatemala; by Chips Computadoras S.A. de C.V. for Mexico; by Editorial Norma de Panama S.A. for Panama; by American Bookshops for Finland. Authorized Sales Agent: Anthony Rudkin Associates for the Middle East and North Africa.

For general information on IDG Books Worldwide's books in the U.S., please call our Consumer Customer Service department at 800-762-2974. For reseller information, including discounts and premium sales, please call our Reseller Customer Service department at 800-434-3422.

For information on where to purchase IDG Books Worldwide's books outside the U.S., please contact our International Sales department at 317-596-5530 or fax 317-596-5692.

For consumer information on foreign language translations, please contact our Customer Service department at 800-434-3422, fax 317-596-5692, or e-mail rights@idgbooks.com.

For information on licensing foreign or domestic rights, please phone +1-650-655-3109.

For sales inquiries and special prices for bulk quantities, please contact our Sales department at 650-655-3200 or write to the address above.

For information on using IDG Books Worldwide's books in the classroom or for ordering examination copies, please contact our Educational Sales department at 800-434-2086 or fax 317-596-5499.

For press review copies, author interviews, or other publicity information, please contact our Public Relations department at 650-655-3000 or fax 650-655-3299.

For authorization to photocopy items for corporate, personal, or educational use, please contact Copyright Clearance Center, 222 Rosewood Drive, Danvers, MA 01923, or fax 978-750-4470.

Library of Congress Cataloging-in-Publication Data

St. Laurent, Simon.
    XML : a primer / by Simon St. Laurent. -- 2nd ed.
      p. cm.
    ISBN 0-7645-3310-X (alk. paper)
    1. XML (Document markup language) I. Title.
QA76.76.H94S72 1999
005.72'2--dc21   99-15723
                           CIP

LIMIT OF LIABILITY/DISCLAIMER OF WARRANTY: THE PUBLISHER AND AUTHOR HAVE USED THEIR BEST EFFORTS IN PREPARING THIS BOOK. THE PUBLISHER AND AUTHOR MAKE NO REPRESENTATIONS OR WARRANTIES WITH RESPECT TO THE ACCURACY OR COMPLETENESS OF THE CONTENTS OF THIS BOOK AND SPECIFICALLY DISCLAIM ANY IMPLIED WARRANTIES OF MERCHANTABILITY OR FITNESS FOR A PARTICULAR PURPOSE. THERE ARE NO WARRANTIES WHICH EXTEND BEYOND THE DESCRIPTIONS CONTAINED IN THIS PARAGRAPH. NO WARRANTY MAY BE CREATED OR EXTENDED BY SALES REPRESENTATIVES OR WRITTEN SALES MATERIALS. THE ACCURACY AND COMPLETENESS OF THE INFORMATION PROVIDED HEREIN AND THE OPINIONS STATED HEREIN ARE NOT GUARANTEED OR WARRANTED TO PRODUCE ANY PARTICULAR RESULTS, AND THE ADVICE AND STRATEGIES CONTAINED HEREIN MAY NOT BE SUITABLE FOR EVERY INDIVIDUAL. NEITHER THE PUBLISHER NOR AUTHOR SHALL BE LIABLE FOR ANY LOSS OF PROFIT OR ANY OTHER COMMERCIAL DAMAGES, INCLUDING BUT NOT LIMITED TO SPECIAL, INCIDENTAL, CONSEQUENTIAL, OR OTHER DAMAGES.

Trademarks: All brand names and product names used in this book are trade names, service marks, trademarks, or registered trademarks of their respective owners. IDG Books Worldwide is not associated with any product or vendor mentioned in this book.

is a registered trademark under exclusive license to IDG Books Worldwide, Inc. from International Data Group, Inc.

is registered trademark of IDG Books Worldwide, Inc.

ABOUT IDG BOOKS WORLDWIDE

Welcome to the world of IDG Books Worldwide.

IDG Books Worldwide, Inc., is a subsidiary of International Data Group, the world's largest publisher of computer-related information and the leading global provider of information services on information technology. IDG was founded more than 30 years ago by Patrick J. McGovern and now employs more than 9,000 people worldwide. IDG publishes more than 290 computer publications in over 75 countries. More than 90 million people read one or more IDG publications each month.

Launched in 1990, IDG Books Worldwide is today the #1 publisher of best-selling computer books in the United States. We are proud to have received eight awards from the Computer Press Association in recognition of editorial excellence and three from Computer Currents' First Annual Readers' Choice Awards. Our best-selling ...For Dummies® series has more than 50 million copies in print with translations in 31 languages. IDG Books Worldwide, through a joint venture with IDG's Hi-Tech Beijing, became the first U.S. publisher to publish a computer book in the People's Republic of China. In record time, IDG Books Worldwide has become the first choice for millions of readers around the world who want to learn how to better manage their businesses.

Our mission is simple: Every one of our books is designed to bring extra value and skill-building instructions to the reader. Our books are written by experts who understand and care about our readers. The knowledge base of our editorial staff comes from years of experience in publishing, education, and journalism — experience we use to produce books to carry us into the new millennium. In short, we care about books, so we attract the best people. We devote special attention to details such as audience, interior design, use of icons, and illustrations. And because we use an efficient process of authoring, editing, and desktop publishing our books electronically, we can spend more time ensuring superior content and less time on the technicalities of making books.

You can count on our commitment to deliver high-quality books at competitive prices on topics you want to read about. At IDG Books Worldwide, we continue in the IDG tradition of delivering quality for more than 30 years. You'll find no better book on a subject than one from IDG Books Worldwide.

John Kilcullen
Chairman and CEO
IDG Books Worldwide, Inc.

Steven Berkowitz
President and Publisher
IDG Books Worldwide, Inc.

Eighth Annual Computer Press Awards ≥1992

Ninth Annual Computer Press Awards ≥1993

Tenth Annual Computer Press Awards ≥1994

Eleventh Annual Computer Press Awards ≥1995

IDG is the world's leading IT media, research and exposition company. Founded in 1964, IDG had 1997 revenues of $2.05 billion and has more than 9,000 employees worldwide. IDG offers the widest range of media options that reach IT buyers in 75 countries representing 95% of worldwide IT spending. IDG's diverse product and services portfolio spans six key areas including print publishing, online publishing, expositions and conferences, market research, education and training, and global marketing services. More than 90 million people read one or more of IDG's 290 magazines and newspapers, including IDG's leading global brands — Computerworld, PC World, Network World, Macworld and the Channel World family of publications. IDG Books Worldwide is one of the fastest-growing computer book publishers in the world, with more than 700 titles in 36 languages. The "...For Dummies®" series alone has more than 50 million copies in print. IDG offers online users the largest network of technology-specific Web sites around the world through IDG.net (http://www.idg.net), which comprises more than 225 targeted Web sites in 55 countries worldwide. International Data Corporation (IDC) is the world's largest provider of information technology data, analysis and consulting, with research centers in over 41 countries and more than 400 research analysts worldwide. IDG World Expo is a leading producer of more than 168 globally branded conferences and expositions in 35 countries including E3 (Electronic Entertainment Expo), Macworld Expo, ComNet, Windows World Expo, ICE (Internet Commerce Expo), Agenda, DEMO, and Spotlight. IDG's training subsidiary, ExecuTrain, is the world's largest computer training company, with more than 230 locations worldwide and 785 training courses. IDG Marketing Services helps industry-leading IT companies build international brand recognition by developing global integrated marketing programs via IDG's print, online and exposition products worldwide. Further information about the company can be found at www.idg.com.   1/24/99

Credits

Acquisitions Editor
Ann Lush

Development Editor
Barbra Guerra

Technical Editor
Ethan Cerami

Copy Editor
Amy Eoff

Book Designer
Kurt Krames

Production
York Graphic Services

Proofreading and Indexing
York Production Services

About the Author

Simon St. Laurent is a Web developer, network administrator, computer book author, and XML troublemaker living in Ithaca, New York. His books include *Building XML Applications, Inside XML DTDs: Scientific and Technical, Dynamic HTML: A Primer, Cookies,* and *Sharing Bandwidth.* In his spare time, he writes open-source Java code for XML processing, available at `http://www.simonstl.com`.

For Tracey, my sweetest dream

Preface

Extensible Markup Language (XML) has been hyped and hyped and hyped in the press. This second edition of *XML: A Primer* shows you the reality of XML, exploring its current reality as well as several possible future directions.

Who Should Read This Book

This book is for anyone who's just getting started with XML. Its biases lean toward the document side of information processing, but those interested in using XML to exchange raw data should find useful information as well. HTML developers have a head start, coming to XML with an understanding of basic markup, but I hope that anyone with a basic understanding of the Web will be able to understand this book. It's definitely a primer — you won't find extended explanations of some of XML's odder corners or code samples for programmers — but you should get a thorough grounding in XML markup.

How This Book Is Organized

The first edition of this book was originally organized to give developers with some experience in HTML the quickest possible route to learning XML. This bias still exists to some extent, although I hope that developers with other backgrounds will feel free to skip through chapters as they find it convenient to do so.

The first three chapters provide an introduction to basic XML. Chapter 1 focuses on HTML, the still-dominant means of transferring information over the Web. Chapter 2 explores tools for presenting information, style sheets that supplement markup so that the markup can focus on content. Chapter 3 covers the basics of XML syntax and introduces parsers, a key foundation tool for XML.

The next six chapters move into the territory of document type definitions (DTDs), the more complex but also more powerful part of XML. Chapter 4 prepares you for the work ahead by describing some of the tasks involved in data modeling, and Chapter 5 provides you with the toolkit needed to build XML DTDs. Chapters 6, 7, 8, and 9 present XML DTDs, built step by step. Chapter 9 should be of particular interest to programmers.

The next two chapters cover XLink and XPointer, two much-delayed but very promising additions to the XML toolkit. These two standards should help build the next-generation Web's navigation, with implications that move far beyond that narrow field.

Chapters 12 and 13 wrap up the book by exploring the impact of XML on several technological fields, including the developing of Web browsers and client-server infrastructures.

Icons Used in This Book

Most of this book is the usual mix of text and pictures, but frequently throughout the book, some important information stands out, and so is put into a tip, a reference, or, most important of all, a warning.

Note

Notes provide extra details about the topic being discussed, which not everyone may find as exciting as I do. Notes provide extra information that may be useful but isn't critical.

Tip

Tips are the kind of information that often doesn't make it into traditional documentation, but are learned through hard experience. Tips are appropriate to every situation, but can be real time-savers when they appear.

Caution

Warning icons are *important.* You may not think there's a problem, but ordinary-seeming actions can have dire consequences. Read the warnings to avoid potential catastrophes.

 Cross-Reference

Every now and then I mention something that's better discussed elsewhere. Cross-references send you to a place where you can find further information about a topic that may be useful.

Acknowledgments

I'd like to thank Tracey Cranston St.Laurent for keeping me going even on the darkest winter days. Ann Lush, my editor, had rare confidence in the first edition and saw this edition through as well. Thanks to Barbra Guerra and Amy Eoff for managing the editorial chores, and to Ethan Cerami for his technical comments on this book and for our general discussions about putting XML to use. Finally, I'd like to thank the XML community — particularly the members of the XML-dev, XML-L, and xlxp-dev mailing lists — for providing this crazy new markup language with an interesting and lively home.

Contents at a Glance

Contents

Introduction to the Second Edition

XML has been a standard (a W3C Recommendation) for a year now, and that year has seen an enormous amount of interest and many significant product announcements. XML has gone from the dream of a small group in the SGML community to a reality that many of us working on the Web — in distributed computing, in databases, and in a surprising number of other computing fields — have to deal with every day. XML is still getting started — much like Java, the hype still outweighs the actual implementations, though the tool set is constantly improving.

When I wrote the first edition of this book, XML seemed destined for greatness on the Web. Unfortunately, the much slower base of browser development has held that vision back. Microsoft's Internet Explorer 5 will likely be the first browser with "real" XML support, arriving 14 months after the standard became official. Netscape's next version of its browser is only available in a preview version, called Gecko. Neither browser has support for XML's linking facilities (XLink), which are still in development at the W3C. As a result, while XML's future on the Web remains promising, the tools for creating Web sites in XML are still experimental. This book remains largely focused, as it was in the first edition, on the needs of Web developers using a new approach to their old tools, but I've tried to make clearer both the implications of using XML and the limitations that currently apply to using XML as a format for transmitting information to users over the Web.

A different community of users — developers working on data-centric applications — has become a key early-adopter community for XML. Java developers in particular, but developers of all types have started poking at this latest arrival and putting it to work in projects requiring document and data interchange. The document-management community, especially vendors of document repositories, are busily creating new tools for storing, processing, and managing XML documents. The promise of XML at present rests largely with these "behind-the-scenes" developers, and I've tried to include more information relevant to their needs. This is still not a book on developing software for XML — it definitely aims at document authors and managers rather than programmers — but I've done my best to include useful pointers to heavier-duty information that developers can use to get started with XML.

Most of what I said in the Introduction to the first edition of this book (below) remains accurate. XML still offers a unique combination of flexibility, simplicity, and human- and machine-readability. The creators of those early parsers and processors are still bold pioneers, and many of them have continued to innovate even as more people have joined the project. While I wish it were time to abandon hand-coding XML, this book remains focused on that practice, still waiting for friendlier editors to arrive. Fortunately, Internet Explorer now provides XML validation services, reducing the need to install a parser and run it from the command line, a task that frustrated many readers of the first edition. XML itself is about the same as it was when I wrote the first edition, but I hope that it has grown easier and more approachable, and that this book still serves as a solid introduction to the many possibilities it opens.

Introduction to the First Edition

XML, to a certain extent, is HTML (HyperText Markup Language) "done right". XML (eXtensible Markup Language) offers a unique combination of flexibility, simplicity, and readability by both humans and machines. HTML developers who have spent years cursing the strange formatting quirks of HTML and the extreme difficulty of converting anything from HTML are in for a treat. XML gives developers the ability to create and manipulate their own tags and works smoothly with Cascading Style Sheets to enable developers to create pages that are as elegantly presented as they are structured. Programmers can build simple parsers to read XML data (or, better, reuse parsers built by others), making it an excellent format for interchanging data.

If you're an HTML developer who's interested in XML, you're in the right place. This book attempts to explain XML in terms that any reasonably experienced HTML developer can understand. Although some of the concepts may be difficult, XML itself is really quite approachable. Unlike the Standard Generalized Markup Language (SGML), its behemoth predecessor, XML uses a reasonably concise syntax that can provide developers with an enormous amount of power — without the learning curve associated with SGML. Although XML is, in a sense, SGML-lite, I've done my best to avoid describing XML from an SGML perspective.

Because much of the best literature (and experience) available on creating document type definitions (DTDs) and using marked-up documents has come from the SGML community, I've pointed out some of the many differences between SGML and XML. If you don't know or care about SGML, you can safely ignore all such information. Still, it won't hurt to learn a bit about SGML, if you have the time and interest.

I have great hopes for XML. XML seems to me the best tool for accomplishing great things with markup, a significant improvement over both HTML and SGML. It has more flexibility than HTML, without the mind-numbing complexity of SGML. XML holds the promise of markup that both humans and machines can interpret, making it easy for developers to debug their documents and for programmers to build systems around them. Although the "paperless office" has been just over the horizon for the last 20 years, XML, in combination with ubiquitous networking, may finally provide the tools needed to make that a reality. (Don't hold your breath, though; old habits die very slowly.) The simplicity of XML makes it useful for small projects, whereas its clear structures make it useful for larger projects. XML can be massaged, manipulated, processed, fragmented, and rebuilt far more easily than previous formats.

Unfortunately, at press time, there aren't many tools available that work with XML. This book has been written around some of the few tools available—Tim Bray's Lark, Microsoft's MSXML, Norbert Mikula's NXP, and Peter Murray-Rust's Jumbo, all of which deserve praise as bold pioneers. James Clark's NSGMLSU (part of his SP package) deserves honorable mention as a powerful parser, albeit one from the more staid world of SGML. The two leading browsers, Microsoft's Internet Explorer and Netscape Communicator, offer feeble support for XML and no support, respectively. Nonetheless, both companies have made public commitments to providing support and hopefully will make good on those commitments in a reasonably short time.

This book definitely focuses on hand-coding XML. Although I certainly hope that hand-coding will be quickly replaced by rapidly evolving tools, hand-coded XML will be around for a short while at least. It took a while for the HTML toolset to grow, and undoubtedly XML will have its growing pains as well. Even though many SGML tools are available and can be applied to XML development, their price ranges and target market seem to stay well above the broader audience for XML. With time, prices will fall, and tools will become more powerful, just as they have in every other area of computing.

This book is a primer and not a complete guide to all things XML. The document type definitions need applications built around them for them to be useful, and most of the tools presented can give only a basic idea of XML's potential. I fully expect that "graduates" of this book will be eager to move on to the next great thing. With any luck, those graduates (and people who have read other books as well) will spread the word about XML, building an XML community as rich and varied as the HTML community is now.

Chapter 1

Let Data Be Data

XML promises to transform the basic structure of the Web, moving beyond HTML and replacing it with a stronger, more extensible architecture. It promises to return the Web to content-based structures instead of the format-based structures imposed by designers frustrated by the immaturity of Web-design tools. It may also free the Web from the tyranny of browser developers by ending their monopoly on element development and implementation. At the same time, XML promises application developers, whether or not they work on the Web, an extremely convenient format for storing many different kinds of information.

The World Wide Web Consortium — or W3C — at (`http://www.w3.org`) moved far ahead of the commercial browser developers with a very promising new approach to markup. XML, the Extensible Markup Language, makes it possible for developers to create their own mutually interoperable dialects of markup languages, including but not limited to HTML. The use of XML might bring about a cease-fire in the browser wars between Netscape and Microsoft as added features shift to a component model rather than a single bloated program, and may even encourage the appearance of new browsing technologies. More immediately, it allows developers to create markup structures based on logical content rather than formatting. This will make it easier for humans and computers to search for specific content-based information within a document instead of just searching the entire text of a page. XML, in concert with style technologies, will allow authors to create beautiful pages that are easily managed, and give developers a new level of control over their information combined with enormous flexibility.

The WYSIWYG Disaster

The first word processor I used was a very simple text editor. I thought it was really amazing how the screen could move around my cursor point to make my 40-column screen display most of an 80-column page, but for the most part it was only good for doing homework and writing other similarly boring documents that I printed out on my lovely dot-matrix printer. After working with computers for a few years, programming them and cursing them, I gave up and bought an electric typewriter. It let me do some pretty fancy things, like underline text without having to enter bizarre escape codes. There wasn't a good way to type boldface text, but I didn't have to worry about wasting acres of paper because of a typo in a strange code. The typewriter gave me what-you-see-is-what-you-get (WYSIWYG) in a classical ink-on-paper kind of way.

I stuck with my typewriter for a couple of years until I discovered the Macintosh. I hated the Mac when it first came out, because every magazine I got covered an expensive machine I didn't own. It didn't even have a decent programming package. But when I encountered the Mac again about four years later, I was thrilled. It was actually fun to write papers, because I could toggle all the style information, write in multiple columns, and even use 72-point type once in a while. It didn't look very good on my ImageWriter, but it was pretty amazing compared to my old dot-matrix computer text. I turned in papers with headlines, bibliographies that used proper italics, multiple columns, and even a picture or two. Writing wasn't just about spewing out sentences anymore. I could create headlines, subheads, tables, footnotes, and use all kinds of other formatting to give even a short paper a set of structures that made it look smart.

Using styles made it even easier to apply a set of formatting tools once, then call it up as a named set. It seemed like magic.

Ten years later I still format my documents with headings and subheads. Fortunately, I'm not as concerned about footnotes, but I've developed a new problem: it's hard to reuse my old documents. When I was writing papers for a grade it didn't matter very much — I wrote the paper, turned it in, and never thought about it again. Now I spend my days working with piles of information written years ago by people thousands of miles away — converting the files into the same word-processing format is the least of my worries. Instead of editing material, I frequently find myself spending hours reformatting it, and not because I love doing so. A whole generation that grew up abusing tabs and spaces (typewriter habits die hard) has created documents that can't be cut and pasted into other documents because everything breaks. Line breaks come out totally wrong, text gets shoved to the left or right, tables collapse, and even simple things like line spacing cause problems. The same magic formatting that made it so easy to create documents that looked exactly the way they should is now creating massive problems.

Other, more subtle problems exist as well. All those years when I thought I was creating headlines and subheads, I wasn't really. I was creating text that was formatted like a headline. I might even have called the style "headline," but to the computer it was just another collection of letters with no intrinsic meaning. WYSIWYG changed people, too. People who probably shouldn't have been allowed to graduate from a fifth-grade art class started using 30 fonts on a page. After the novelty wore off, many of them adopted a more conservative approach to formatting but always with the declared intention of making their documents look precisely the way they wanted them. Designers became accustomed to specifying placement to thousandths of an inch — as if anyone can see differences measured in such a small increment.

Before WYSIWYG, documents were undoubtedly ugly, but they had a few other virtues that went unnoticed. There were moves afoot to create document-management and document-markup systems that would allow computers to efficiently manage large libraries of documents. Plain text, dull though it may be, is much easier to manage than the output of the average word processor or desktop publishing program. These document-management tools were also very new in the early days of WYSIWYG, and they didn't become affordable or readily available until long after users had become accustomed to systems that used paper-based media. The final printout of a document always remained the ultimate goal of most of the design programs on the market.

The HTML Explosion

When the World Wide Web first received widespread attention in 1994, a small army of amateur and professional designers set out to create the most exciting pages they could. Many left quickly; accustomed to full WYSIWYG environments, they were disappointed by the dearth of HTML formatting tools. The strange differences between browsers made it difficult to predict what any page would look like, and corporate users demanded a level of layout control over their electronic documents that was similar to the control they had over paper documents. For a while, these complaints nearly throttled HTML development. Like many Internet technologies before it, HTML was spread by enthusiasts who were working for fun and because HTML was interesting. HTML was simple enough to learn in a day or two, and it offered a whole new reading and authoring experience. The momentum generated by these early enthusiasts and the press coverage they received gave HTML the potential to become the next big thing.

For the Web to become an economically viable marketplace, however, HTML had to change to meet user demands. Designers and their employers wanted to be able to create pages that looked precisely the way they wanted them, and they wanted to have a level of control comparable to that provided by the average desktop publishing system. An often explosive browser war (where the designers were frequent casualties) led to more powerful, though incompatible, dialects of HTML, which the W3C has more or less knitted together into HTML 4.0. HTML still isn't exactly a simple page-layout system for the average user, but the tools have become a lot more convenient. Web design has become a specialty of designers and communications specialists the world over, making it possible for companies and individuals to create sophisticated, if not always visually pleasing, sites.

Tables were a huge step forward for HTML design, though their widespread usage subverted many strongly-held opinions about the proper application of tables. Designers applied tables to create documents that bore some resemblance to the traditional grid systems used in many print designs, using them in many situations that went well beyond the normal tabular display of information in rows and columns. Continuing improvements in image-map technology made it easy for frustrated designers to create their own point-and-click interfaces when HTML just couldn't produce what they needed. Frames and pop-up windows let developers focus on elements instead of having to rebuild entire screens of information every time they wanted to change something. The <FONT> tag made it possible to specify text presentation much more precisely than structure-based formatting had allowed. The escalating competition between Microsoft and Netscape added all kinds of tools to the palette as the companies fought for market share and mind share. Netscape created <BLINK>, and Microsoft countered with <MARQUEE>. Both companies created extensions to the elements and the attributes of HTML, confusing developers and requiring enormous expenditures of time and equipment to check sites in multiple browsers. Worse still, neither company implemented tags in exactly the same way. Spacing varied, colors could change, and carefully aligned elements would scatter across a page.

Note

If the constant bickering over standards and vendors' apparent disinterest in complying with them bothers you, explore the Web Standards Project (`http://www.webstandards.org`). HTML's semi-standard nature and vendors' partial implementations of other standards, including CSS and XML itself, has driven a significant group of Web developers to take up arms in defense of standards.

At the same time, the number of pages on large Web sites exploded. Sites routinely grew to include 10,000 pages or more, organized loosely in hierarchical schemes concocted by developers who knew little about hypertext and even less about organization. Many sites were organized according to chaotic directory structures built by developers who were originally conditioned by the structures of FTP archives and gopher sites, the predecessors of the Web. Large sites presented continual difficulties to the managers who had to keep up with them and the users who attempted to read them. Navigating hypertext is a strange art form all its own, a blend of organizational skill, memory, good design, and sheer luck. Designing it can be even more difficult. Search engines arrived to help users find their way, but it quickly became clear that librarians, even those with massive computing power available, could never keep up with the explosive growth of this new medium.

Automated tools appeared as crawlers and robots began searching the enormous swamp of Web documents. Some merely indexed titles, whereas more sophisticated ones began to index the entire contents of a page. AltaVista (`http://www.altavista.com`), a search engine originally created by Digital to demonstrate and promote its Alpha processor, brought a brute force approach to the Web, applying multiple processors that shared gigabytes of memory and enormous bandwidth, to indexing the Web. Although Alta-Vista and the many other search engines can and do provide a service, they work on the broadest of criteria: the complete contents of a document. We've managed to confer a lot of intelligence on search engines, even letting them identify languages and handle word forms, but we're still a very long way from teaching them to read, categorize, and organize documents without us having to specify which part is which. For the most part, the formatting information that humans use to recognize key parts of a document is discarded by the search engines.

This combination of volume and increasing complexity of formatting led developers to wonder if there might be a better way to do markup. HTML has come a long way, quickly, but the limitations of a markup language designed for formatting are beginning to chafe. As the browser wars move into a new phase, designers are beginning to demand an alternative to letting the browser determine the presentation of individual tags. The limitations of search engines become more apparent every time the Web doubles in size. Finally, as the Web grows more omnipresent, the limitations of HTML for presenting information that doesn't easily fit the standard text and graphics model are becoming more pressing. Developers need to be able to create their own tag vocabularies, and they need to be able to do so in a way that works with their customers' browsers.

Back to the Origins: Structure and SGML

When Tim Berners-Lee created HTML in 1991, he based it in part on a more powerful but vastly more complex markup language called SGML, the Standard Generalized Markup Language. SGML had been around in various forms for 20 years, but its complexity had hobbled its adoption by organizations outside of publishing, government, and large-scale information processing. SGML markup, management, and processing were specialized skills, mastered by a small group of government, corporate, and academic users.

Developers who complain that the HTML standards are developing too slowly should look back at the tortured pace of SGML's development. First conceived in the late 1960s, the Generalized Markup Language (GML) was created at IBM in 1969 by researchers coincidentally named Goldfarb, Mosher, and Lorris. Charles Goldfarb went on to chair the American National Standards Institute (ANSI) committee on Computer Languages for the Processing of Text in 1978, after GML had become an important standard in publishing. In 1980, the committee released its first working draft, and by 1983 the sixth working draft was adopted by users including the Internal Revenue Service and the Department of Defense, which mandated that its largest contractors use SGML as well. In 1984, the committee expanded into a group of collaborating committees developing standards for the International Organization for Standardization (ISO) as well as ANSI. In 1986, eight years into the standards process, SGML became ISO 8879:1986. Work on SGML continues, of course. A group of committees evaluates changes regularly, including projects on scripted style sheets, multimedia, link extensions, and a variety of document-management issues.

Note

To see the SGML specification in its full flower (almost – a few modifications have been made over the years), take a look at what amounts to the SGML bible: Charles F. Goldfarb's *The SGML Handbook* (Oxford University Press, 1992).

Unlike HTML, SGML doesn't specify how text should be presented. SGML is not a formatting language, nor even a particular markup language. SGML is a specification that allows people to create their own markup languages. It specifies content identifiers that make it easy to format text consistently and which enable document-management systems to locate information quickly. SGML is well-suited for projects that involve large quantities of similarly structured data, such as catalogs, manuals, listings, transcripts, and statistical abstracts. SGML is a favorite of the federal government, as well as IBM and other large companies. It makes it easy for a centralized team to develop specifications for data structures, to create a Document Type Definition (DTD) that can then be applied to documents throughout the organization.

More importantly, in many cases documents created with SGML are easy to port to different formats. Because SGML uses content-based markup rather than format-based markup, it's easy to change the formatting rules, depending on whether a document is being output to a dot-matrix line printer, a laser printer, a four-color press, a CD-ROM, a Web site, or even audio speakers. Design teams determine formatting that can work with or follow up the work of the original DTD designers to present information in different styles that are appropriate to particular output media. Computerized storage systems can also treat the documents as small databases, querying them with searches based on content tags and index information. Companies that use the same information repeatedly — for proposals, for instance — can benefit greatly from having prefabricated text ready to be dropped into new documents. It doesn't make the writing any better, but it does make it easier to manage.

HTML's Roots

Most of what SGML contributed to HTML was syntax: a markup language that used the now familiar <TAG ATTRIBUTE= "VALUE"> Content here </TAG> style. Some of SGML's intent to separate content from formatting survived as well, as evidenced by the wildly divergent interpretations of common tags by different browsers. By describing elements with terms like <EM> for emphasis and <ADDRESS> for address information, Berners-Lee created a simple formatting language that was flexible enough to handle many different kinds of information. The <H1> through <H6> tags spoke of levels of headings, providing a somewhat natural structure to documents. The <HEAD> and <BODY> tags separated meta-information (the <TITLE>, at first) from the visible text of a document. Most important, the <A HREF="destination.html"> anchor tags provided a simple yet powerful structure for hypertext links.

HTML did a wonderful job of simplifying SGML and putting markup into the hands of amateurs, a necessary move for broadening markup's appeal. Ironically, Tim Berners-Lee never really intended for users to have to enter codes by hand. The initial experiments at CERN used a simple markup processor that managed the codes invisibly. While HTML remained a small collection of tags with only a few attributes, this friendly model made it easy for authors to get started using the Web to exchange papers and share information.

As we've seen, however, HTML was ill-suited to a world that had been spoiled by the control WYSIWYG tools had already given designers. Although it was clear that hyperlinks and the Web's incredible ease of use were good things, there were rumblings from the start about what these academics had done to create a useless formatting language. At the beginning of the browser wars, it was clear that HTML's extremely simple original formatting tools were not going to be accepted in the long run by designers and developers who wanted to create documents on the Web that were as detailed (allowing for screen resolution) as documents on paper. The inherent flexibility of simple standards lacked appeal. Tags whose sole duty was formatting sprawled across the HTML landscape, with <B> and <I> and eventually <FONT> receiving much more use than <EM> or <ADDRESS>. Designers hand-crafted HTML, mixing and matching tags to achieve the precise appearance they wanted without regard to document structure. Because the HTML tags were used only to specify formatting, with no alternative formatting structures, HTML was doomed to life as a formatting language instead of a structured framework for documents. All the problems categorized earlier began to grow, springing from fundamental flaws in the originally brilliant nature of HTML.

20% of SGML's Complexity, 80% of its Capacity: The Emergence of XML

The creators of the original Web standards and their successor organization, the W3C, scrambled to catch up to the commercial browser developers for a while. "Netscape extensions" provided designers with controls that the early versions of HTML had lacked and fueled the phenomenal growth of Netscape. Only recently has the W3C caught up to the browser developers and cut them off at the pass, with the next set of powerful standards. Cascading Style Sheets (CSS) was the first blow. CSS makes it possible for designers to declare their formatting intentions for a document without having to cook up a tortured mix of tags and graphics. CSS frees tags from the burden of carrying formatting information and permits them to carry content information once again. By providing a complete vocabulary for describing formatting (more complete, in fact, than is possible with HTML 4.0), CSS provides a styling tool that can work with HTML or any other markup language.

Once a formatting standard was available that didn't interfere with the markup, it became possible for the W3C to create a markup standard that took advantage of the flexibility of SGML. XML emphasizes the importance of content information by making it possible for designers to create and manage their own sets of elements, without necessarily stumbling into "tag soup." Designers can apply these sets in concert with CSS to create tags that produce formatting if they like, but the main emphasis is on managing content, including hypertext links, which are receiving considerable enhancements themselves. XML arose from the concerns of the SGML Editorial Review Board at the W3C which felt that HTML was heading in the wrong direction. To improve the situation, they proposed a markup language that could work in concert with exsiting Web technologies, using some of the tools developed for use with HTML, while moving forward with more manageable techniques. XML provides a subset of SGML functionality rather than just a set of tags that use SGML syntax. It remains a simplification (and there is some grumbling from SGML users about how gross a simplification it may be), but it promises to restore the initial promise of the Web, adding a little more complexity in an attempt to simplify the complicated mess that is the current state of Web-page creation. One measure of how strongly this has succeeded is the W3C's plans for the next generation of HTML (available at http://www.w3.org/MarkUp/Activity.html), which should result in the breakdown of the currently enormous HTML project, into a number of smaller modules defined using XML.

XML is under the control of the XML Working Group at the W3C, the descendant of the SGML Editorial Review Board. The XML Working Group (`http://www.w3.org/XML/`) controls most of the specifications directly relating to XML: XML syntax, extended linking for XML, and XML fragment use. At the same time, other Working Groups at the W3C control support standards like the Document Object Model (DOM), Cascading Style Sheets (CSS), Extensible Style Language (XSL), and standards that complement or apply XML, like Mathematical Markup Language (MathML), Synchronized Multimedia Integration Language (SMIL), and Resource Description Framework (RDF). While this part of this alphabet soup is under the control of the W3C, many other applications of XML — with their own acronyms, of course — are under the control of other organizations, corporations, and individuals. The implementation of XML, as is typical with the W3C, is up to vendors, though hopefully developers will stick closely to the standards.

XML implementations have taken a while to appear. While the W3C Recommendation for XML 1.0 syntax (effectively, the official standard) appeared in February 1998, most of the support for XML is still at the level where programmers can use it, but regular HTML developers can't do much with it. This situation is changing slowly, with Microsoft providing fairly sophisticated support in

Internet Explorer 5 and Netscape's Mozilla project providing significant support in its latest builds. Because of the problems of the installed base (people don't always upgrade their browsers), however, it may be a while before everyone has access to XML-enabled viewers, XML editors, and other XML applications.

In this book, we'll take a close look at the tools XML provides and how developers can apply them to common tasks. HTML developers should find much of the information familiar, although much of the content (creating DTDs, for instance) will be fairly alien. This book isn't targeted at SGML developers, but readers familiar with SGML should find many familiar concepts integrated with the concepts from the wilder world of the Web. Although the book focuses on creating documents with XML, we'll also cover techniques for managing XML and integrating it with other Web technologies. Software developers have also been a key market for XML, and many of the projects discussed here may add pieces to software developers as well. XML may seem abstract at first, but its practical implications should become more evident as you proceed through the book and try the examples. We'll see how sets of XML documents can be treated like databases even though they are very unlike the previous generations of strictly hierarchical or tabular structures, and we'll explore the new architectures for documents and data that XML makes possible.

Chapter 2

Separating Content from Presentation: Markup and Styles

Before we move on to XML's potential for modeling content, a brief examination of how XML gets us out of the presentation nightmares of HTML is in order. Although I pointed out some of HTML's inadequacies in the previous chapter, HTML has popularized markup in general, and its existing structures deserve a full examination. In particular, we'll be looking at the way HTML was used before style sheets (browser versions 3.0 and earlier) and after (versions 4 and later.) By looking at HTML from the perspective of XML, you should understand what's to come without being too put off by the brave new world of XML. Style Sheets are also important to both projects. Style sheets free markup from the formatting structures that have complicated HTML for so long, allowing markup to focus on content and re-use rather than presentation.

Note

If you're not concerned with presentation and don't come from a Web development background, you may want to skip this chapter and move right into modeling content with XML. The information in this chapter is most appropriate to applications of XML that are intended for human reading such as Web pages or printed documents, and not really for other uses where XML is used to connect computers and databases rather than people. The section on XSL transformations is useful in those contexts (though highly unstable at present), but it's probably better to read ahead and then return when and if you need that material.

HTML is one of many applications of SGML. The W3C uses an SGML Document Type Definition (DTD) to provide a formal definition of the rules for creating HTML documents. A DTD is available for each of the versions of HTML that have appeared, although some HTML elements (for example, the BR element that indicates line breaks) are hard to express meaningfully in the more tightly structured world of SGML. HTML's syntax has always tended toward the loose and forgiving end of SGML's many possibilities. For example, closing tags have traditionally been optional. Only recently, with the development of HTML creation tools, has closing every tag become common (and many of those tools still can't close tags).

Browsers have long been tolerant of a variety of syntactical usages; they could usually figure where one element ended and another began, even though they often would display them slightly differently based on the particular syntax used. This variety of syntax produced a wide range of results—browsers often displayed documents in ways that looked completely different from what the document looked like on other browsers. Combined with the loose definitions for how browsers should format particular tags, this syntactical flexibility kept many designers up nights as they struggled to recreate the same formatting in multiple browsers, never finding the half-broken tag that was causing them grief.

HTML Roots: Old, Original Specifications

Before there were tables, frames, font tags, client-side image maps, and all the other magical tools that HTML now has, there was a small set of tags that provided formatting based on the structures of the average academic paper. (The Web, after all, was created by CERN as a place for physicists to exchange their findings.) HTML, unlike SGML, had definite formatting intentions for its tags, but they weren't as specific as those available in the typical WYSIWYG word processor or desktop publishing package.

Nested under the opening HTML tag are the two major pieces of an HTML document: the HEAD element and the BODY element, each of which carries a different kind of information. The HEAD element contains data about the document — like the TITLE, the BASE element that can set the base URL for all hyperlinks in the document, and the META elements. The META elements can contain information — also called metadata because it's data about data — about the author of the document, the organization that created it, keywords for search engines to find, and information that page-creation and document-management software can use to keep track of a page's place in the broader organization of a site. The LINK tag, which may also appear in the HEAD element, connects the document to external resources like style sheets.

Note

In this chapter (and pretty much throughout the book) I use the common uppercase versions of HTML element names, like BODY instead of body and HTML instead of html. The W3C appears to be shifting toward lowercase usage in the next version of HTML, and case-sensitivity will probably become more important to HTML usage as XML's impact spreads.

The BODY element is where nearly all the content appears. Information in the HEAD, apart from the title at the top of the browser window, will normally remain invisible to the user.

Information in the BODY section produces the actual look of the Web page and gets most of the attention. For example, most Microsoft Word users leave the file properties box (which acts like the HEAD element) turned off; it rarely seems worth the bother of entering search keywords for every single file. What matters to the average user is the text in the document, with all of its formatting. The BODY element in HTML is similar to the main body of a word-processing document. Within the BODY element, all text and tags are sequential, following the usual left-to-right down-the-page (but possibly another pattern if you use non-European character encodings). Most of the elements within the BODY define formatting or create things like images, Java applets, form fields, buttons, and checkboxes. HTML elements provide markup for the appearance and placement of text and other objects on a page — nothing in the body of the document specifies meta-information.

The original HTML tags defined document structures in a general way, and formatting was roughly associated with those structures. The structures were logical rather than appearance-based. H1 indicated a top-level header, not 24-point Helvetica bold underlined. EM meant emphasis, not bold, italic, or underlined. Because the Web was originally designed to run on a wide variety of equipment, from NeXT cubes to VT-100 terminals to PCs and Macs, its originators stayed away from such presentation-specific tags, leaving it to browser implementers to decide how to format each tag. Some early browsers even allowed users to specify styles for tags as part of their browser preferences.

A simple document created with an early version of HTML might look like this:

```
<HTML>
<HEAD><TITLE>Simple Document, early HTML</TITLE></HEAD>
<BODY>
<H1>Introduction to HTML</H1>
```

```
<P>This page has been created purely with logical tags.
No additional formatting has been specified by the
designers.</P>
<P>While it might be nice to specify text like we could
in Quark XPress, we'll settle for applying
<EM>emphasis</EM> where appropriate,
<CITE>citations</CITE> when necessary, and maybe
highlight a <VAR>variable</VAR> along the way. We can
also indicate code listings:</P>
<CODE>
10 PRINT "HELLO WORLD"<BR>
20 END<BR>
</CODE>
<P>Bulleted lists are easy too:</P>
<UL>
<LI>HTML Structures</LI>
<LI>CSS Structures</LI>
<LI>XML Structures</LI>
</UL>
<P>Numbered and lettered lists are also fun:</P>
<OL>
<LI>Item #1</LI>
<LI>Item #2</LI>
</OL>
</BODY></HTML>
```

Even in the latest browsers, this simple example produces varied results. In Figures 2-1 and 2-2, you can see that Netscape Navigator 3.0 rendered EM, CITE, and VAR in italics, while Internet Explorer 3.0 rendered VAR in a monospace typeface and used a different background color as well.

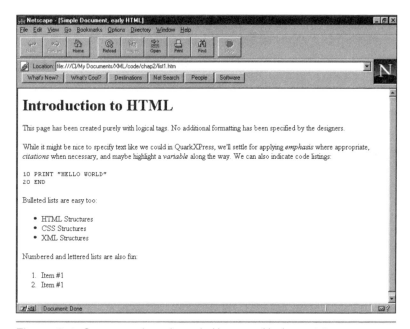

Figure 2-1 *Structure-oriented tags in Netscape Navigator 3.0*

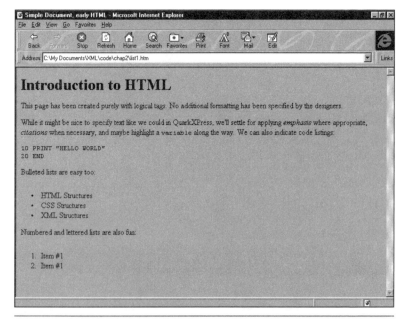

Figure 2-2 *Structure-oriented tags in Microsoft Internet Explorer 3.0*

These differences in presentation made designers extremely unhappy. Used to WYSIWYG tools, they quickly demanded stronger, more consistent formatting controls. The FONT element gave them many of the tools they wanted, whereas tables, frames, and new attributes for wrapping text around graphics made it easy to place that formatted text more precisely where they wanted it to go. Best of all (apart from some cross-platform font issues), the browsers would render the pages nearly identically. The following code uses formatting codes rather than logical codes to produce text somewhat similar to that of the previous example.

```
<HTML>
<HEAD><TITLE>Formatted Document, later
HTML</TITLE></HEAD>
<BODY BGCOLOR="#FFFFFF">
<FONT FACE="Arial, Helvetica" SIZE=7><B>Introduction to
HTML</B></FONT>
<FONT FACE="Arial, Helvetica" SIZE=3>
<P>This page has been created with specific formatting
tags instead of logical tags.</P>
<P>Since we'd like to specify text like we could in
QuarkXPress, we'll use bold for <B>emphasis</B> where
appropriate, italic for <I>citations</I> when necessary,
and maybe highlight a <FONT
FACE="Courier"><B>variable</B></FONT> with bold Courier.
We can also indicate code listings with Courier:</P>
</FONT><FONT FACE="Courier" SIZE=2>
10 PRINT "HELLO WORLD"<BR>
20 END<BR>
</FONT>
</BODY></HTML>
```

This time, the document looks nearly identical in Netscape (see Figure 2-3) and Internet Explorer (Figure 2-4). All the fonts are the same size, all the formatting is identical, and we don't need to worry about as much variation across browsers.

As convenient as this may be, it has some unfortunate side effects and doesn't completely address all aspects of page design. Our simple example didn't really abuse HTML, but pages that use tables and documents exported from traditional WYSIWYG document creators (Microsoft Word, for instance) can end up with a profusion of FONT elements that sometimes take up more space than the actual content. They also don't address all aspects of page layout, which is another giant problem they pose for designers. Netscape and Microsoft continue to address many layout issues, especially whitespace, in different and uncontrollable ways. Tag-based formatting just isn't enough.

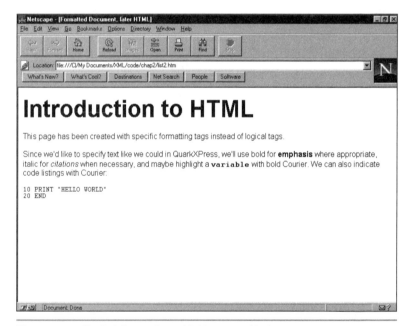

Figure 2-3 *Explicit formatting with Netscape Navigator 3.0*

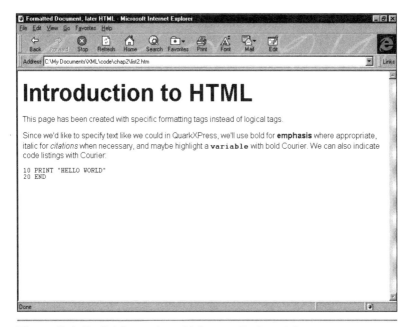

Figure 2-4 *Explicit formatting with Internet Explorer 3.0*

Structured Formatting: Cascading Style Sheets

As part of a general effort by the W3C to return HTML to its more structured past while still addressing the needs of Web designers for whom control of overall appearance is the largest roadblock to effective Web use, the W3C released the Cascading Style Sheets Level 1 specification in late 1996. Microsoft jumped on the bandwagon immediately, implementing some CSS features in Internet Explorer 3.0 and adding considerably more robust functionality in 4.0. Netscape, which originally proposed its own JavaScript Style Sheets standard, has also lined up behind CSS, implementing much of CSS in Netscape Communicator 4.0. Cascading Style Sheets Level 2, which became a recommendation in May 1998, continued the development of this technology, though CSS Level 2 has yet to be implemented in the browsers currently available.

Cascading Style Sheets can separate the formatting information from the body of documents, storing it separately in a STYLE element or a separate document, though inline styling, using a STYLE attribute to indicate formatting for particular elements, is also available. The *Cascading* refers to the ability to combine multiple style sheets and inline styling, simplifying the task of creating master templates and then making modifications as needed. Cascading Style Sheets uses the document structure as a framework, which is then annotated with formatting information and displayed (or printed, or read, or presented somehow) by an application, typically (for now) a Web browser.

For our first style sheet demonstration, we'll spruce up our earlier logical tag demonstration, providing specific formatting definitions for all the tags involved. It's the same HTML we used before, with the addition of a simple STYLE element:

```
<HTML>
<HEAD><TITLE>Formatting with CSS, modifying standard
HTML</TITLE>
<STYLE TYPE="text/css"><!-
H1 {font-family: Arial, Helvetica; font-weight: bold;
font-size: 24pt}
EM {font-weight: bold; font-style: normal}
CITE {font-style: italic}
VAR {font-family: Courier; font-weight: bold}
CODE {font-family: Courier}
LI {font-family: Arial, Helvetica}
-></STYLE>
</HEAD>
<BODY>
<H1>Introduction to HTML</H1>
```

```
<P>This page has been created purely with logical tags.
No additional formatting has been specified by the
designers.</P>
<P>While it might be nice to specify text like we could
in QuarkXPress, we'll settle for applying
<EM>emphasis</EM> where appropriate,
<CITE>citations</CITE> when necessary, and maybe
highlight a <VAR>variable</VAR> along the way. We can
also indicate code listings:</P>
<CODE>
10 PRINT "HELLO WORLD"<BR>
20 END<BR>
</CODE>
<P>Bulleted lists are easy too:</P>
<UL>
<LI>HTML Structures</LI>
<LI>CSS Structures</LI>
<LI>XML Structures</LI>
</UL>
<P>Numbered and lettered lists are also fun:</P>
<OL>
<LI>Item #1</LI>
<LI>Item #2</LI>
</OL>
</BODY></HTML>
```

 Note

The HTML comment delimiters inside the STYLE element won't affect the style-sheet processing, but will keep older browsers that don't understand style sheets from displaying the style sheet content as part of the Web page.

As you can see in Figures 2-5 and 2-6, we now have considerably more control over the appearance of this document in both Netscape Communicator 4.0 and Internet Explorer 4.0. (Earlier browsers, except Internet Explorer 3.0, will ignore the STYLE element because we placed comments around its content. Internet Explorer 3.0 will interpret the tags but won't let them override how it originally planned to format the HTML, resulting in bold italic for the EM tag, for instance.)

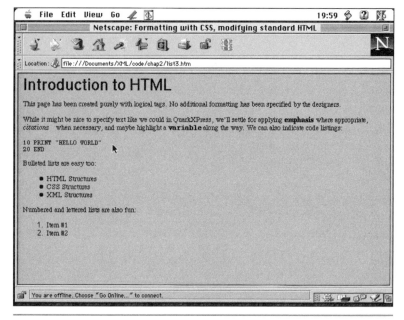

Figure 2-5 *Simple style sheet in Netscape Communicator 4.0*

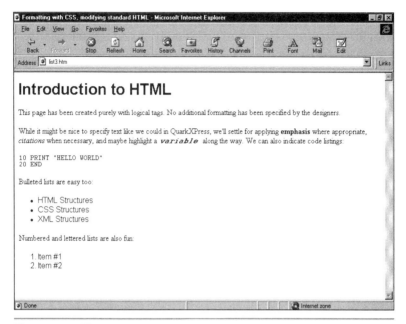

Figure 2-6 *Simple style sheet in Internet Explorer 4.0*

How does this work? CSS uses selectors — which in their simplest form correspond to element names — to identify targets for formatting. The information in curly braces following the selector is a set of properties and their values, which will be applied to all elements that meet the criteria established by the selector. The general syntax is:

```
selector {property-name: value; property-name: value;}
```

Whitespace is unimportant — style sheets may be formatted however is most convenient for readers. Many designers use one line per property value, making it easy to see the information as a list and to pick out particular properties. For the most part, reading style sheets is simple. The style sheet used above, included the line:

```
H1 {font-family: Arial, Helvetica; font-weight: bold;
font-size: 24pt}
```

In this case, the selector refers to all H1 elements. H1 elements will be displayed using the font family Arial if available, and Helvetica if not. (If neither of them is available, the browser will revert to its default. Using 'sans-serif' as the value simplifies this process.) The H1 elements will be bolded, and displayed as 24-point type.

Style sheets enable developers to specify formatting precisely, giving them exact control over fonts, colors, positioning, and white-space issues. Table 2-1 lists a small selection of CSS properties that will be especially helpful with XML, that is, when the vendors get around to implementing CSS for XML.

Table 2-1 *Some Useful CSS Properties*

Property	Notes	Acceptable Values	Level
background	Specifies all the possibilities for a background in one value.	A collection of the values for the other background properties.	1,2
background-attachment	Specifies whether the background scrolls with the content or remains fixed in one place.	Scroll, fixed, inherit.	1,2
background-color	Background color for the element.	A color name (like 'white') or hex representation (like #FFFFFF for white).	1,2
background-image	Background image of an element.	URL identifying the image.	1,2
background-repeat	Identifies whether the background should repeat.	Repeat, repeat-x, repeat-y, no-repeat, inherit.	1,2
border	Specifies all the possibilities describing the border of the element in one value.	A collection of the values for the other border properties.	1,2
border-bottom-color	Sets color value for bottom border.	Color name or hex value.	2
border-bottom-style	Sets the style for the border on bottom of the block.	None (default), dotted, dashed, solid, double, groove, ridge, inset, outset.	2

Property	Notes	Acceptable Values	Level
border-bottom-width	Sets width for the border on bottom of the block.	Thin, medium, thick, or an explicit measurement.	1,2
border-color	Sets color value for entire border.	Color name or hex value.	Color name or hex value
border-left-color	Sets color value for left border.	Color name or hex value.	2
border-left-style	Sets style of the border on left of the block.	None (default), dotted, dashed, solid, double, groove, ridge, inset, outset.	2
border-left-width	Sets width of the border on left of the block.	Thin, medium, thick, or an explicit measurement.	1,2
border-right-color	Sets color value of right border.	Color name or hex value.	2
border-right-style	Sets style for the border on right of the block.	None (default), dotted, dashed, solid, double, groove, ridge, inset, outset.	2
border-right-width	Sets width of the border on the right of the block.	Thin, medium, thick, or an explicit measurement.	1,2
border-style	Sets the style for the entire border.	None (default), dotted, dashed, solid, double, groove, ridge, inset, outset.	1,2
border-top-color	Sets color of top border.	Color name or hex value.	2
border-top-style	Sets style of the border on top of the block.	None (default), dotted, dashed, solid, double, groove, ridge, inset, outset.	2
border-top-width	Sets width for the border on top of the block.	Thin, medium, thick, or an explicit measurement.	1,2
clear	Specifies if floating blocks are allowed along the sides of an object.	None, left, right, both, or inherit.	1,2
color	Takes color value for element foreground.	Color name or hex value.	1,2

Continued

Table 2-1 *Continued*

Property	Notes	Acceptable Values	Level
direction	Identifies the direction of text flow. Important for internationalization.	ltr (left-to-right), rtl (right-to-left), or inherit.	2
display	Provides a basic description of how an element should be formatted.	Block, inline, listItem, none, run-in, compact, marker, inherit, table, inline-table, table-row-group, . itable-header-group, table-footer-group, table-row, table-column-group, table-column, table-cell, or table-caption.	1, but much enhanced in 2
float	Makes a block float.	None, left, right, or inherit.	1,2
font-family	Identifies the font or font family for an element.	Serif, sans-serif and monospace are common; may also be a particular family name ('Arial', 'Times'), though not all fonts are available on all computers.	1,2
font-size	Sets the font size for an element.	May use small, medium, or large as well as point sizes.	1,2
font-style	Sets the style of the font, where style refers to the level and type of italicizing.	Normal, italic, or oblique.	1,2
font-variant	Used to create small caps formatting.	Normal or small-caps.	1,2
font-weight	Specifies a weight for the font.	Integer values from 100 to 900 (if supported), or normal, bold, bolder, or lighter.	1,2
height	Specifies the height of the element; used for positioning elements in a space, typically a browser window.	Measurement	1,2

Property	Notes	Acceptable Values	Level
left	Specifies the position of the left edge of the element from the left edge of the window; used for positioning elements in a space, typically a browser window.	Measurement	2
letter-spacing	Provides additional spacing between letters and text.	Measurement	1,2
line-height	Specifies distance between baselines of text, allowing linespacing within blocks. May be normal, number to multiply by point size, absolute measurement, or percentage.	May be normal, number to multiply by point size, absolute measurement, or percentage.	1,2
list-style-image	Allows display of an image (rather than a standard bullet character) as bullet.	Takes a URL, none, or inherit.	1,2
list-style-position	Specifies how bullets should fit into a list of bulleted items.	Takes inside, outside, or inherit.	1,2
list-style-type	Sets the default bullet appearance. (If an image is specified, it will override this.)	Disk, circle, square, decimal, or inherit	1,2
margin	Specifies all margin properties in a single property.	A collection of the values for the other margin properties.	1,2
margin-bottom	Specifies how much empty space to leave below the bottom of the element.	Measurement	1,2
margin-left	Specifies how much empty space to leave to the left of the element.		

Continued

Table 2-1 *Continued*

Property	Notes	Acceptable Values	Level
margin-right	Specifies how much. empty space to leave to the right of the element	Measurement	1,2
margin top	Specifies how much empty space to leave above the top of the element.	Measurement	1,2
overflow	Tells the presenting application what to do if an element's contents go beyond the height and width specified.	May be visible or scroll.	2
page	Identifies pages for printing.	Takes an identifier or auto (the default).	2
page-break-after	Specifies how page breaks (in printouts) should come after the appearance of the element.	Auto, always, avoid, left, right, and inherit.	2
page-break-before	Specifies how page breaks (in printouts) should come before the appearance of the element.	Auto, always, avoid, left, right, and inherit.	2
page-break-inside	Specifies how page breaks (in printouts) should be handled within the element.	Auto, always, avoid, left, right, and inherit.	2
text-align	Specifies text alignment.	Left, right, center, or justify.	1,2
text-decoration	Specifies additional marking (typically lines) for the element text.	None, underline, overline, line-through, or blink.	1,2
text-indent	How much to indent the first line of an element.	Measurement or percentage.	1,2
text-transform	Permits the transformation of text.	None (default), capitalize, uppercase, lowercase, or inherit.	1,2

Property	Notes	Acceptable Values	Level
top	Specifies the position of the top edge relative to the top edge of the window. Used for positioning elements in a space, typically a browser window.	Usually a measurement; may also be auto or inherit.	2
vertical-align	Specifies how to align element content with respect to the baseline. Used in creating subscripts and superscripts.	Baseline (default), sub, super, top, text-top, middle, bottom, text-bottom, or a percentage or measurement above the baseline.	1,2
visibility	Whether or not to render an object transparently. Unlike display:none, doesn't prevent child elements from appearing.	Inherit, collapse, visible, and hidden.	2
whitespace	Pre-tells the browser to respect all whitespace in the element content, including line breaks, without requiring tags. Nowrap tells the browser not to break lines unless explicitly told to with a , <P>, or other line-break-forcing element.	Normal, inherit, pre, or nowrap.	1,2
width	Specifies the width of an image.	Measurement	1,2
word-spacing	Specifies additional spacing between words.	Measurement, normal, or inherit.	1,2
z-index	Identifies the z-layer of a positioned block; higher values are layered on top of lower values	An integer.	2

Note

This table is hardly complete. For complete lists of properties and values, with much lengthier descriptions of their meanings, visit the CSS Level 1 specification at `http://www.w3.org/TR/REC-CSS1` or the CSS Level 2 specification at `http://www.w3.org/TR/REC-CSS2`. The properties in these tables provide a basic set of tools for making XML pages attractive.

The rules for applying style sheets offer developers considerable flexibility, and, to a limited degree, the ability to create their own formatting-tag vocabularies. Style sheets are called cascading because you can apply multiple style sheets to the same document. The style sheets are applied in a sort of reverse precedence, where the most recent definition is applied instead of the first. Styles (and style sheets) can be applied in several ways. We have already seen a STYLE element included in the HEAD element. This technique is very useful if you're creating styles that should affect an entire document — but only one document. If you want to make styles apply to multiple documents, you should create a style-sheet document, a separate file containing style information that can be connected to HTML pages with a LINK element. You can also apply styles to individual elements, which enables you to use styles to format documents much the way the old FONT tag allowed. The STYLE attribute allows to you specify "inline" styling, setting values for CSS properties within the tags creating elements.

First, we'll apply styles to individual elements, using a few different techniques. The easiest way to format text this way is to create a surrounding SPAN or DIV element (new to HTML 4.0) that includes all the style information. DIVs create paragraph-like structures with space afterward, whereas SPANs let you format text without creating line breaks. Using SPANs and DIVs avoids all of the formatting baggage carried by other HTML elements. Neither solution applies much formatting by itself, making it easier for you to produce predictable results.

Note

Older browsers (before version 4 of Microsoft's or Netscape's browsers) don't support SPAN and DIV, making it difficult to use them for formatting with CSS in ways that fail gracefully. Even version 4 browsers implement the DIV element differently – Microsoft puts space after the DIV element that and Netscape doesn't. If you plan to use SPAN and DIV as transitional elements as you move from HTML to XML (as is done in Chapter 6), be aware that SPAN and DIV are fairly new themselves.

```
<HTML>
<HEAD><TITLE>Formatting with CSS, atomized DIVs and
SPANs</TITLE></HEAD>
<BODY BGCOLOR=#FFFFFF>
<DIV STYLE="font-size:24pt; font-weight:bold">This is a
big DIV.</DIV>
<P>This is a normal paragraph with an odd <SPAN
STYLE="font-size:14; font-weight: bold; font-style:
oblique; color: red">SPAN</SPAN> stuck in the middle of
it.</P>
</BODY></HTML>
```

This should produce the results shown in Figure 2-7.

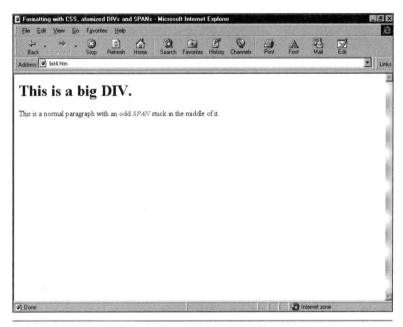

Figure 2-7 *Style attributes in Internet Explorer 4.0*

Even though you can use styles in this way to achieve formatting nirvana, you'll quickly find yourself frustrated if you need to apply the same formatting repeatedly. Using a single style to produce the same result multiple times is quick and easy, and you don't need to corrupt existing tags. The SPAN and DIV tags have two additional attributes — ID and CLASS — which let you create styles for multiple instances of the same format. The ID attribute is used to identify individual elements, so all ID values should be unique. (As we'll see later, there are ways in XML to enforce this.) The CLASS attribute is used to identify groups of multiple elements. Five different DIVs could all share the same CLASS attribute value, and therefore be formatted the same way. A tag can have both a CLASS value and an ID value; any formatting specific to the ID will have precedence over the formatting for the CLASS.

Note

All HTML elements are supposed to have ID and CLASS attributes available, and you can usually count on this with both Internet Explorer 4.0 and Netscape Communicator 4.0. For our demonstrations, we'll stick to SPANs and DIVs. XML elements may have ID attributes, but the use of the CLASS attribute is probably off-limits until and unless a new version of the CSS spec appears that takes advantage of name-spaces (see Chapter 5 for more details) to create a CLASS attribute that remains identifiable in all documents.

Our next example creates a document with a STYLE element that controls several SPAN and DIV elements in the BODY of the document. Note the way that CSS uses CLASSes and IDs differently. Although CSS will let you get away with it, you should probably avoid using the same name for a CLASS and an ID in a document.

```
<HTML>
<HEAD><TITLE>Formatting with CSS, using CLASS and
ID</TITLE>
<STYLE>
DIV.bold {font-size:24pt; font-weight:bold }
DIV.italic {font-size:24pt; font-style:italic }
SPAN.test {font-weight:bold}
SPAN#freaky {color: green; font-size:90pt; font-
style:italic}
</STYLE>
</HEAD>
<BODY BGCOLOR=#FFFFFF>
<DIV CLASS="bold">This is a big bold DIV.</DIV>
<DIV CLASS="italic">This is a big italic DIV.</DIV>
<P>This is a normal paragraph with an odd <SPAN
ID="freaky">SPAN</SPAN> stuck in the middle of it, as
well as a <SPAN CLASS="test">bold</SPAN> bump and another
<SPAN CLASS="test">bold</SPAN> bump in the middle of
it.</P>
```

```
<DIV CLASS="style1">This is another big bold DIV.</DIV>
</BODY></HTML>
```

This example is a little easier to write and produces the results shown in Figure 2-8.

Figure 2-8   *Class and ID styles in Internet Explorer 4.0*

Even though STYLE elements can help you with repeated formatting in the same document, managing the formatting of a large number of documents this way is extremely difficult. A Web site that's built according to very specific rules will need an incredible amount of fine-tuning every time a designer wants to change a typeface or a color. Style sheets are the answer to this site-level problem. They enable you to manage your styles on the grand scale. Rather than putting the style information directly in the document, style sheets use selectors and pseudo-elements to identify formatting for particular elements in particular locations in the document tree. A complete list of CSS selectors and pseudo-classes, which perform similar functions to selectors (for both HTML and XML) is shown below in Table 2-2.

Table 2-2 *Cascading Style Sheets Selectors*

Selector	Meaning	Level
elementName	Selects every element whose name is *elementName*.	1, 2
elementName1 elementName2	Selects all elements named *elementName2* that are descended from (not necessarily children of) elements named *elementName1*.	1, 2
elementName1, elementName2 [,elementName3...]	Selects any elements that match selector in the list.	1, 2
elementName1>elementName2	Selects all *elementName2* elements that are directly children of *elementName1* elements, not just descendants.	2
elementName1+elementName2	Selects *elementName2* elements that follow (and are siblings, not children, in the document tree) *elementName1* elements directly.	2
[attName]	Selects elements that specify a value (it doesn't matter what value) for the attribute *attName*.	2
[attName="attValue"]	Selects elements that have the particular value *attValue* for the attribute *attName*.	2
		2
[attName~="attValue"]	Selects elements when the value *attValue* is contained anywhere in a list (separated by white space) of tokens in the attribute *attName*.	2
[attName|="attValue"]	Selects *elementName* elements with attributes named *attName* when their value begins with *attValue* followed by a hyphen. (Used to select particular language types.)	2

Continued

Table 2-2 *Continued*

Selector	Meaning	Level
.className	Selects *elementName* elements that contain an attribute named class or CLASS whose value is *className*.	1, 2 (HTML only)
#*IDvalue*	Selects *elementName* elements that contain an attribute of type ID (in HTML, named ID) whose value is *IDvalue*.	1, 2
* (asterisk)	Selects all elements, whatever their name or content. The asterisk can be used instead of an element name anywhere within a selector.	2
:first-child	Selects elements when they are the first child element to appear inside their parent element.	2
:link	Selects elements when they represent hypertext links that have not yet been visited by the user.	2
:visited	Selects elements when they represent hypertext links that have already been visited by the user.	1,2
:active	Selects hypertext links when the user is activating them.	1,2
:hover		1,2
:focus	Selects elements when the user is interacting with them (usually in a browser) in particular situations.	2
:lang(*language*)	Selects element content of the language specified. The CSS 2 specification suggests that this will work in conjunction with the xml:lang attribute for identifying element language content.	2

Cross-Reference

The use of these selectors will be explored in greater depth in Chapter 6. CSS is easy to approach, but covering all of its possibilities would require a dedicated book. *Cascading Style Sheets: Designing for the Web*, by Hakon Lie and Bert Bos (Addison-Wesley, 1997), is a good tutorial written by some of the editors of the Cascading Style Sheets specifications.

Building style sheets is very much like building STYLE elements, except that all the style information goes into a separate file that you link to all the documents that need it. CSS files look a lot like what we've done before:

```
DIV.style1 {font-size:24pt; font-weight:bold }
DIV.style2 {font-size:24pt; font-style:italic }
SPAN.test {font-weight:bold}
SPAN#freaky {color: green; font-size:90pt; font-
style:italic}
```

After you've saved this style sheet (as demo.css, for example), you can apply it to your pages. Instead of using the STYLE element, you'll need to use the LINK element. LINK has been around since HTML 2.0, but until recently, it was used only rarely. We'll use it to connect our style sheet to our previous bit of HTML:

```
<HTML>
<HEAD><TITLE>Formatting with CSS, using DIVs, SPANs, and
LINKs</TITLE>
<LINK REL=stylesheet HREF="demo.css" TYPE="text/css">
</HEAD>
<BODY BGCOLOR=#FFFFFF>
<DIV CLASS="style1">This is a big bold DIV.</DIV>
<DIV CLASS="style2">This is a big italic DIV.</DIV>
```

```
<P>This is a normal paragraph with an odd <SPAN
ID="freaky">SPAN</SPAN> stuck in the middle of it, as
well as a <SPAN CLASS="test">bold</SPAN> bump and another
<SPAN CLASS="test">bold</SPAN> bump in the middle of
it.</P>
<DIV CLASS="style1">This is another big bold DIV.</DIV>
</BODY></HTML>
```

You need to use the REL attribute of the LINK element to specify that this is a style sheet. The HREF attribute just provides the URL at which the browser can find the style sheet file. TYPE specifies the MIME type of the document. Style sheets that use CSS are of type "text/css. " As shown in Figure 2-9, the results for this style sheet look the same as they did when we included the style information in the HEAD element.

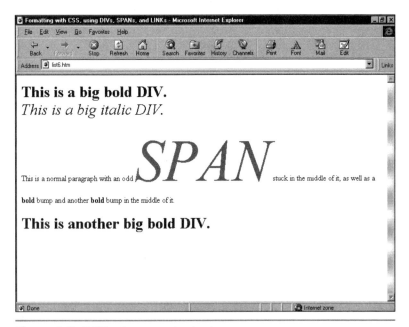

Figure 2-9 *CSS using separate sheets*

You can also provide two additional attributes. MEDIA helps the browser decide what style sheet to use for which output application. Generally, you'll provide this information when you're applying multiple style sheets to the document. Accepted values are screen, print, projection, Braille, aural, and all. MEDIA is useful, among other things, for creating styles that include or remove illustrations and other nontextual material from your documents. The TITLE attribute lets you give your style sheets user-friendly names, which make it easy for users to choose among multiple style sheets. For example, you might have style sheets titled "large-print," "normal," and "microtype."

The other important thing to remember about style sheets is that they cascade. Although this may conjure up images of waterfalls and rapids, it really just means that an HTML element will accept formatting from the style that is closest to it. The most immediate style is embedded directly in the element, as a STYLE attribute. That overrides all other styles. The next style in order of precedence is a STYLE element in the HEAD element of the document. Receiving the least precedence are any styles loaded through the LINK element, even though browsers may allow users to choose among multiple styles connected to a document. In that way, users can choose large print if they need it, or a style that hides all the graphics in a document for an unvarnished look at the text.

 Note

You can also link style sheets from within a <STYLE> tag, using the @IMPORT URL (stylesheetURL) syntax. LINK is preferred, however, because of its greater flexibility.

In practice, organizations can create style sheets for use by their entire group, but individual pages can override the look of the site. For example, a large company could create a standard style sheet for all of its documents but allow departments to create their own style sheets that override the corporate standard. Individual page designers (at the risk of getting fired, of course) could then apply the corporate and the department style sheets to their documents, while making changes through STYLE elements and attributes.

Although you can use style sheets to go wild and format your documents every which way, this is strongly discouraged. CSS can do a lot more than replace the FONT element, but it requires cooperation and coordination. Using the CLASS attribute successfully means creating standards that go across pages, making it easy for a designer (or a group of designers) to create specifications that don't need to be rebuilt from the ground up every time someone needs a new page. The ID tag can benefit from similar coordination, helping designers implement one-on-a-page models that can highlight the latest news or create a new design twist. Even though CSS is all about formatting, it emphasizes structure in an effort to place formatting into a repeatable, controlled environment. This structure may not matter very much for small sites, but it can make managing large sites infinitely easier.

At this point, you may be starting to wonder why you need anything beyond CSS to create your own vocabularies and move beyond HTML. Even though we haven't seen everything CSS can do, it does enable you to create almost any formatting you need. You can create character- and paragraph-level formats, control whitespace, specify the position of your elements in x and y pixel measurements, turn your documents whatever color you want, and even create special effects for the first character or first line of a paragraph. CSS lets you have it all, as far as recreating the wonderful world of WYSIWYG layout is concerned. Unfortunately, creating your own tags with CLASS and ID is still really about formatting, not about data. This is where the XML is necessary — XML will let us smoothly combine the power of CSS with powerful structures for managing data, helping us create documents that look good and work well at the same time.

Note

Cascading Style Sheets is still growing, and is finding much use outside of its original HTML home in W3C projects like Synchronized Multimedia Integration Language (SMIL) and Structured Vector Graphics (SVG). See `http://www.w3.org/Style/CSS` for the latest information. The www-style@w3.org W3C mailing list (subscribe by emailing www-style-request@w3.org) and `comp.infosystems.www.authoring.stylesheets` newsgroup are forums for discussing CSS issues and implementations.

XSL: A Different Approach, Coming Soon

Cascading Style Sheets work by annotating existing document structures with presentation information. Extensible Style Language (XSL) takes a much more dramatic approach, transforming the document into a new document tree that may be composed of formatting objects, which an application can then display. XSL uses XML syntax for its style sheets, and is mostly XML-focused. XSL can be used to generate HTML (which is convenient if you need to present XML information to users without XML support in their browsers), but "the HTML way" receives very little consideration from the XSL Working Group.

Caution

All of the information in this section regarding XSL is subject to (possibly drastic) change. The information you read here is based on the 16 December 1998 Working Draft, not a final W3C Recommendation. For the latest information on XSL, be sure to visit `http://www.w3.org/Style/XSL/`. A mailing list for XSL discussion is also available – see `http://www.mulberrytech.com/xsl/xsl-list/` for archives and information.

XSL is derived in large part from the Document Style Semantics and Specification Language (DSSSL), which is commonly used to provide formatting information for SGML documents. DSSSL is an enormous standard capable of providing very precise formatting for all kinds of documents. Learning and implementing DSSSL, however, is an enormous task. As XML is SGML for the Web, so XSL is DSSSL for the Web. (There is also DSSSL-O, a lightweight online profile of DSSSL, that could contend with XSL.) DSSSL and its derivatives use SGML rather than XML, and their syntax is quite incompatible with XML. XSL's developers are trying to build a style language as powerful (or close) as DSSSL, but one that uses XML syntax and is simple enough for common use over the Web. How compatible (or convertible) the two standards will be remains a mystery until the final recommendation is issued. Unlike XML, which specified compatibility with SGML as an explicit goal, XSL isn't bound by backward compatibility.

 Cross-Reference

For an excellent tutorial on DSSSL, see Paul Prescod's "Introduction to DSSSL" at `http://cito.uwaterloo. ca:80/~papresco/dsssl/tutorial.html`. For information on DSSSL-O, see `http://sunsite.unc.edu/ pub/sun-info/standards/dsssl/dssslo/dssslo.htm`.

XSL is comprised of two key tools: a transformation engine ("tree construction") that converts the original document tree into a document tree that can be presented, and a formatting vocabulary that describes the presentation of information for layout, typesetting, and so forth. So far, most implementations (including Microsoft's Internet Explorer 5 beta) have focused on XSL's transformation engine, not its formatting objects. As a result, most of the people currently working with XSL are developers transforming from one XML vocabulary to another, not designers laying out document templates. Several proposals for separating XSL into two separate standards, one for transformation and one for formatting, have emerged on the XSL mailing list. The working group's reaction to these proposals hasn't yet appeared — by the time you read this, the current XSL may well be two different pieces! The two parts will be discussed below in separate sections.

Note

If you want the details on XSL now, keep reading. If you'd rather wait until you've learned more about XML, skip to the next chapter and come back to XSL when you are ready.

Cross-Reference

For a list of tools that can be used to process XSL, `visit http://www.xmlsoftware.com/`.

Tree Construction (Transformations)

When an XSL processor is invoked by an application, it loads a style sheet. That stylesheet contains rules for transforming the original document structure into a new document structure. The rules are expressed as a set of templates that apply to various elements in the original document and produce a new document based on the original document. This approach makes it very easy to do things like reorder documents, hide and display information that may or may not be relevant, convert tables into graphs (using a vector graphics markup language like the W3C's Structured Vector Graphics, SVG), or just convert XML documents into HTML for presentation in older browsers (which is what we'll do in the examples).

XSL uses patterns to identify parts of the document tree that need processing and template rules to describe the processing that should take place. In some ways, XSL is like a programming language, with structures that test equality and perform processing based on the results of that processing, but the overall approach is very different. (And, for now at least, there isn't any support for ECMAScript, as was proposed in the initial draft from Microsoft, Inso, and ArborText.) Patterns are somewhat like CSS selectors, identifying the elements to which a particular template will apply, but with a completely different syntax. Table 2-3 contains examples of XSL pattern syntax, taken from the 16 December 1998 Working Draft.

Table 2-3 *Sample XSL Pattern Syntax*

Pattern	Meaning
elementName	Matches all elements with the name *elementName*.
elementName1 | *elementName2*	Matches all elements with the name *elementName1* or *elementName2*.
elementName1 / *elementName2*	Matches all elements with the name *elementName2* that are children of (contained directly within) *elementName1*.
elementName1 // *elementName2*	Matches all elements with the name *elementName2* that are descendants of (contained anywhere within) *elementName1*.
@attributeName	Matches all elements with a value (any value) for the attribute *attributeName*.
*	Matches all elements.
@*	Matches all attributes.
elementName1[*elementName2*]	Matches all elements named *elementName1* that contain children named *elementName2*.
elementName[*@attributeName*]	Matches all elements named *elementName* that have attributes named *attributeName*.
elementName[*@attributeName="value"*]	Matches all elements named *elementName* that have attributes named *attributeName* with the value *value*.
.	Matches the node (typically an element) currently being processed.
..	Matches the parent of the node currently being processed.
comment()	Matches all comments within the current node.

These patterns are then compared to documents, and transformations applied based on how the patterns matched and what the template rules specified. Template rules are probably best explained with examples. We'll start with a very simple initial document.

```
<?xml version="1.0"?>
<?xml-stylesheet href="test.xsl" type="text/xsl"?>
<test>this is a test</test>
```

Cross-Reference

The weird-looking construction <?xml-stylesheet href=" test.xsl" type="text/xsl"?> is an XML processing instruction, which will be covered in Chapter 5.

To convert this lucky document into a viewable HTML document, we'll apply the XSL style sheet below.

```
<?xml version="1.0"?>
<xsl:stylesheet xmlns:xsl="http://www.w3.org/TR/WD-xsl">
<xsl:template><xsl:apply-templates/></xsl:template>
<xsl:template match="textnode()"><xsl:value-
of/></xsl:template>

<xsl:template match="/">

<html>
<body>
<xsl:for-each match="test">
       <p><b>
             <xsl:apply-templates/>
       </b></p>
</xsl:for-each>
</body>
</html>
</xsl:template>
</xsl:stylesheet>
```

Note

More XML weirdness! Don't worry about the XML used here; we'll cover namespaces (which account for both the xmlns attributes and the xsl: in front of the element names) in Chapter 5 as well.

Which then produces the results:

```
<html>
<body>
       <p><b>
this is a test
       </b></p>
</body>
</html>
```

Internet Explorer 5.0 displays those results, as shown in Figure 2-10.

Figure 2-10 *Generating simple HTML using XML and XSL in Internet Explorer 5.0*

XSL includes a large set of rules that can be combined to convert attribute values to element text, recombine content in different sequences (including sorting), add numbering and other document-centered information, build macros for later reuse, respond to different conditions, and perhaps eventually provide capabilities for extending XSL itself, possibly with ECMAScript, as was noted above.

Formatting

XSL doesn't annotate the document tree; instead, the tree construction side of XSL builds a new document of formatting objects, which may have attributes that further define how they are to be presented. Effectively, XSL's formatting objects are a presentation-centered vocabulary for XML, no better than HTML for searchability and reuse, but designed purely as a front-end for presentation. A listing of formatting objects in the 16 December 1998 Working Draft is reprinted here.

Note

The list of formatting objects is *very* subject to change. It is presented here to give you an idea of what capacities XSL may have, but the final version may end up looking very different.

fo:basic-page-sequence	fo:block	fo:character	fo:display-graphic
fo:display-link	fo:display-rule	fo:display-sequence	fo:inline-graphic
fo:inline-link	fo:inline-rule	fo:inline-sequence	fo:link-end-locator
fo:list-block	fo:list-item	fo:list-item-body	fo:list-item-label
fo:page-number	fo:queue	fo:simple-page-master	

Each of these formatting objects may be further defined using formatting properties — attributes much like the properties of CSS. Formatting properties range from simple things like color, font-family, font-size, and line-height to more sophisticated properties like line-spacing-precedence, escapement-space-end, hyphenation-char, and contents-rotation.

XSL's Future

XSL may have a bright future as a transformation tool and heavyweight formatting engine. Its usefulness on the Web will depend heavily on how much support the browser vendors provide. While Microsoft has moved forward aggressively with its XSL transformation engine for Internet Explorer 5 (which can also be used on the server side through Active Server Pages), Netscape has shown much less interest, and no other contenders have (yet) appeared. Whether XSL can supplement or replace CSS in this environment is questionable. On the server side, however, the various XSL transformation tools may play a key role in easing the transition from HTML to XML, converting "alien" XML to "friendly" HTML (or even HTML+CSS) for browsers that don't understand XML. XSL may also have a role to play in a number of the server-side processing tools, from Active Server Pages to Java servlets and CGI programming, giving programmers a generic tool for creating templates and modifying document structures that doesn't require explicit coding.

Cross-Reference

For an interesting counterpoint to the XSL approach, see Håkon Wium Lie's "Formatting Objects Considered Harmful" at `http://www.operasoftware.com/people/howcome/1999/foch.html`.

Chapter 3

Simple XML:
Building Structures

Now that we know that there is a complete set of formatting tools available that we can use to make documents appear as they were intended, we can forget about how the documents will be presented for a little while. The use of XML requires a different focus, demanding that designers examine the way that their documents are built rather than the way they are formatted.

If you diagrammed sentences in English classes (it's okay if you hated it), you've been through the drill before, although on a different level. Instead of looking at structures at the sentence level, we'll be examining structures at the document and data-structures levels, identifying titles, sections, subsections, paragraphs, lists, figures, item numbers, and item descriptions rather than nouns, verbs, and prepositions. XML offers developers the opportunity to create documents with built-in frameworks that make it much easier to create consistent results time after time, capable of carrying useful, and reusable data.

Browsers and Parsers

The explosive growth of the Web was made possible by several different factors: the simplicity of HTML, the relative ease of setting up an HTTP (Web) server, and the rapid proliferation of browsers, of which Netscape and Microsoft Internet Explorer are the most prominent. Even the earliest browsers, created at CERN in 1991, were meant to give users quick access to documents, letting them move from document to document without any complex transactions getting in the way. This was one of HTML's largest breaks with SGML; it was as significant a break as using markup tags for formatting as well as structure. HTML browsers didn't worry about checking document syntax; instead, they parsed the document (the computer equivalent of reading the document) and presented their results. The results weren't, and still aren't, always pretty. Finding a missing end tag in a large, heavily formatted document is a difficult task at best, requiring designers to compare their codes with the results generated by a particular browser. HTML browsers have always been very forgiving as far as code they will accept, but the results they present can be ugly. The ugliness may not show up on the screen display, but lies in the code used to create it, information that is difficult to reuse.

Note

Outside the mainstream of browser development were a few browsers that did validate HTML to some extent. For instance, Arena, a W3C testbed browser, had an option to indicate broken tags. The direction taken by the market, however, was clearly in favor of putting something on the screen, however odd, rather than pestering readers with error messages.

SGML has always been more focused on parsing documents than on presenting them. A parsing program takes a large file, usually text, and breaks it down into its component parts. In SGML, this meant that a program would examine a file, compare it to a DTD, break the document into its component parts, and validate the document against the definition. "Broken" SGML is easy to find, although the reasons for its being broken are frequently more difficult to determine. Because SGML parsers usually validate files, and because SGML is not directly concerned with formatting, programs for managing SGML paid a lot more attention to making sure that an SGML document was properly coded rather than to presenting it attractively. Bad markup could prevent a document-management system's sophisticated tools from accepting the document at all.

Browsers combine a parsing engine with a presentation engine, though they typically use a different model for parsing. HTML browsers don't validate HTML even against their internal definitions. Instead, they parse the file and do what they can with the tags they can understand. If they can't understand a tag, they ignore it. If there's a missing closing tag, they take their best guess at where it would most likely have been. Attributes may have an effect or may be ignored, depending on whether the browser understands them. This uncontrolled model has made it much easier for amateurs to publish Web pages, increasing the number of authors dramatically. The downside is a lot of poorly written HTML. This same situation has allowed the browser developers to get away with private additions to the language, since one company's additions wouldn't "break" another company's browser. But the page might not look as good, because the tags are ignored. Although pages might look best on a particular browser, the worst that could happen to a user opening them in the "wrong" browser was missing or oddly presented information. Designers who wanted to make everything look perfect in every browser were bound to be disappointed, but at least a lowest common denominator of development was available.

XML's demands for conformance to standards may come as a shock to HTML developers. XML parsers (which may rest underneath browsers that display the parsed information) are far pickier about syntax and structure than HTML browsers. By demanding that authors get the syntax and structure right, rather than forcing the browser to figure out what's supposed to be in the document, XML makes it much easier for parsers, both in performance and in reliability. XML documents are intended to parse consistently, every time. (As we'll see, there are a few variations in output depending on the type of parser, but even these are very limited.)

Because the parsers don't have to spend time rebuilding broken documents, they should be able to perform their tasks far more efficiently than their HTML cousins. They should be able to focus on building a tree structure from the tree structure already included in a document rather than a presentation based on mixed-up structures in a stream of information. XML standards refer to processors (parsers), not to browsers, because much XML development will be intended for machine-readable data applications rather than graphically exciting Web pages. Any kind of application may be built on top of a parser, and browsers are only a small, though important, part of the XML vision. Browsers remain extremely useful, presenting XML workers with a friendly and accessible tool for reading information, but the browser is only a window to a much larger project.

Netscape and Microsoft are both integrating XML into their browsers, but browsers will only be one small part of the XML toolset. XML still allows for a good deal of HTML-style free-form development, but it enforces the rules much more strictly, as we'll see. Developers will be happiest in the long run if they use the strongest set of tools available for structure building, but not all applications will need that level of effort. It's quite possible to create documents easily in a format that both validating parsers and browsers can understand.

Building Blocks

XML uses structures that are very similar to HTML, which isn't surprising given their shared roots in SGML. Underneath those syntactical structures is a language for defining document structures that gives XML the power HTML lacks. We'll start by examining the structures on the surface of HTML and then dig down until we've uncovered enough to begin building some simple XML documents.

Note

The documents created in this chapter will work well in non-validating parsers, which don't check the overall document structure. Chapter 5 will explain the additional tools needed to work in a validating parser environment. Lightweight applications and experimental development are more likely to use non-validating parsers, while heavier-duty document-management and other standards development activities will rely heavily on validation.

Elements and Tags

Even though HTML designers have used the terms elements and tags fairly interchangeably, the difference between them is significant. A tag is a piece of markup: <P>, <B>, or <LI> for example. An element is a fully formed application of those tags. A paragraph element might look like this:

```
<P>This is a <EM>sample</EM> paragraph element. It
includes several other elements, including an emphasis
(EM) element that includes the word 'sample' and a
<B>bold</B> element that includes the word bold.</P>
```

This text includes six tags (three opening, three closing) but only three elements. The paragraph element includes two other elements. The nesting rules which have frustrated designers since HTML first appeared, rely on this distinction between tags and elements. The following code is illegal HTML, even though some browsers will render it properly anyway:

```
<B>This is bold. <I>This is bold italic.</B> This is
italic.</I>
```

In my word processor, I get away with this every day. I don't need to convert text back to normal before I'm allowed to add additional formatting; formats are understood to be additive and can layer on top of each other. If the <B> and <I> tags were simply for formatting, this code would work the same way. It doesn't work that way in HTML (or XML or SGML), however. That kind of code attempts to create elements whose beginning and end tags overlap, as shown in Figure 3-1

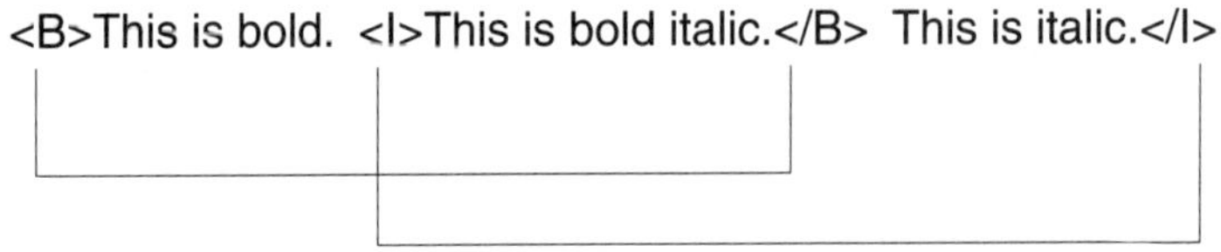

<B>This is bold. <I>This is bold italic.</B> This is italic.</I>

Figure 3-1 *Overlapping elements are prohibited.*

Overlapping elements produce all kinds of ambiguity, especially when content (and formatting) get more complicated. In HTML, the proper way to produce the result shown in Figure 3-2 is to use the following code:

```
<B>This is bold.</B> <I><B>This is bold italic.</B></I>
<I>This is italic.</I>
```
or
```
<B>This is bold.</B> <I><B>This is bold italic.</B> This
is italic.</I>
```
or
```
<B>This is bold. <I>This is bold italic.</I></B> <I>This
is italic.</I>
```

These three ways take more tags, but the beginning and end tags do not overlap. The first sample variation uses the most markup but is probably the safest way to create this text, especially if you anticipate cutting and pasting or otherwise moving it around. The other two variations use fewer markup tags and take advantage of HTML's ability to nest tags and allow elements to absorb the formatting of the element surrounding them. The only change is whether the bold italic element is an italic element nested in the bold element preceding it or a bold element nested in the italic element that follows it. Figure 3-3 shows these three variations on nesting.

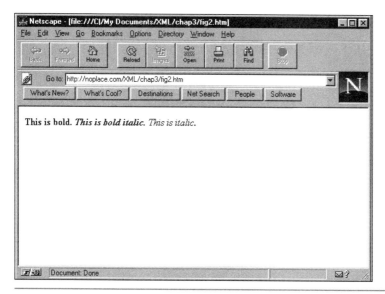

Figure 3-2 *Bold, bold italic, and italic*

```
<B>This is bold.</B> <I><B>This is bold italic.</B></I> <I>This is italic.</I>
```

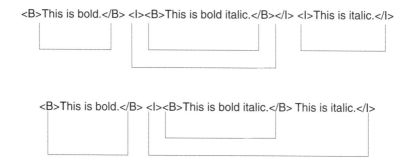

```
<B>This is bold.</B> <I><B>This is bold italic.</B> This is italic.</I>
```

Figure 3-3 *Acceptable element creations*

I always recommend creating the most containerized solution (like the first variation here), so that you can pick up elements and move them around without worrying about losing half your structures.

Note

The very fact that there are three different possible interpretations of the "correct" meaning of a set of broken HTML tags illustrates the problems that malformed syntax can cause developers who need to be able to refer to document structures in their scripting and styling. Developers who apply style sheets or try to reference elements through the document object model will get mixed and unpredictable results when they work with broken code. XML solves this problem by prohibiting broken code.

XML is more particular than HTML in a few other significant respects. HTML is very forgiving about leaving off closing tags and quotes around attributes and can even sometimes forgive stray <, >, and & symbols in the text. The browsers tend to parse HTML as well as they can but do not worry too much about where an element is supposed to end. Many HTML elements, including the commonly used IMG, HR, and BR elements, don't normally have closing tags.

XML is not this forgiving. For starters, unlike HTML (and even SGML) it's case-sensitive. Tags must match in capitalization as well as meaning. To be well formed, the minimal acceptable level of XML compliance, a document must have closing tags of some kind for all opening tags, as well as quotes around all attributes. Leaving these tags and quotes off should generate an error when the page is loaded. "Empty" elements that don't bracket any text must either be given closing tags (as in
</BR>) or have a slash at the end of their tag (
 or <BR />), which acts as an equivalent. Some HTML browsers treat the useless end tag as a second tag (adding an extra break, for instance), and don't like the mysterious slash at the end of the normal tag. Putting a space between the element name and the slash (
, for instance) seems to work in most browsers — including Netscape Navigator, Internet Explorer, and Lynx — so that is probably the best way to handle this situation until XML browsers become standard. Markup symbols in the text may not generate errors, but they will certainly cause problems and keep the document from being technically well-formed. The built-in entities for encoding <, >, and & are the same in XML as they were in HTML (<, >, and &).

 Caution

XML doesn't provide nearly as full a list of built-in entities as does HTML. Chapter 5 will examine ways to remedy that situation.

At this point, it is unclear how tightly browsers and even parsers will enforce these rules. Given their HTML heritage, browsers may remain more forgiving than the standard. Despite that likely forgiveness, I strongly recommend complying with all of XML's rules. You'll have better structured documents that are easier to debug and manipulate as a result.

Elements and Attributes

Although some elements are extremely simple (for example <B> or <BR> in HTML), others need much more information. Writing <IMG> in an HTML document produces nothing, because an IMG tag needs an SRC attribute to figure out what image it's supposed to display. Most elements, even the simplest ones, now have attributes in the latest HTML standard, 4.0. Attributes give designers much more control over elements, allowing them to specify formatting, label elements for scripting, make elements respond to user actions, and define default behaviors.

XML is much pickier about the use of quotes in code than HTML is; get used to always surrounding attribute values with quotes to avoid annoying and mysterious errors. Single quotes and double quotes are both acceptable, though both have to be one or the other. Even though double quotes are more common, single quotes are handy if an attribute must include a double quote.

It's not always clear when information belongs in an attribute or when it deserves an element of its own, especially when it comes to formatting tags. Although the W3C tends to favor putting formatting information into elements rather than creating new elements, it hasn't always been that clear. Compare for example, the following two pieces of HTML code:

```
<P><FONT FACE="Arial">This paragraph is in Arial, except
for <B><FONT FACE="Times New Roman">this
piece,</FONT></B> which is in Times New Roman
bold.</FONT></P>
```

and

```
<P STYLE="font-face:Arial">This paragraph is in Arial,
except for <SPAN STYLE="font-face:Times New Roman; font-
weight: bold">this piece,</SPAN> which is in Times New
Roman bold.</P>
```

The second style is the newer standard, applying style information rather than font tags. It requires the creation of many fewer elements, which (as we'll see later) is a tremendous aid when you begin to apply style sheets and manipulate elements dynamically through scripting. The FONT element has been officially "deprecated" in HTML 4.0: it is no longer recommended. Although it's still a part of the standard and will probably be available for many browser versions to come, the next version of the HTML standard will probably not mention it.

Note

The element/attribute distinction will be more important if you work with the Document Object Model, which promises to bring sophisticated dynamic HTML and XML to the browser (and consistently across browsers and other applications, if the vendors faithfully implement the W3C specification). The elements you create in your documents can be scripted as objects. The properties of those objects are simply the attributes of the elements, making it easy to change appearance, position, and even content interactively even after the page has loaded.

The logic behind what defines an attribute and what defines an element isn't always clear. Lists could have been defined in such a way that the list items were attributes of the main list element, but this would have created gigantic opening tags with multiple repetitive parts sprawling across pages. Because it doesn't make much sense to build pages that way, the creators of HTML opted to define certain types of elements, lists, that contain child elements, the list items. On the other hand, the INPUT element creates several different kinds of interface pieces—fields, checkboxes, radio buttons, and so on—using the same element name and a different set of attributes for each item. Defining the INPUT element is complex and messy; requiring several pages to explain the possible combinations of relevant attributes needed to create different types of input. The INPUT element is an example of overextending one element with attributes to accomplish a task that would probably be easier to manage with separate elements.

It's hard to overdose a document with attributes in simple XML, because the lack of standards makes it difficult to develop them and make them meaningful. As XML applications become more sophisticated, attributes will become more important, especially in standards created using XML. Attributes enable XML tags to pass more information to dedicated programs about the way their information should be handled, possibly about the way it should be presented, and even whether it *should* be presented.

Finding the right balance of attributes and elements is difficult for beginning document designers. HTML doesn't always provide the best examples, and there are few other widely used formatting languages. Consequently, developers should create some sample documents and then try to mark them up. When you think you've reached a decent balance, show someone else your document and see if he or she can understand the markup and describe how the document is composed. If that person can describe it back to you in familiar terms, you've probably done well.

Tip

To really refine your strategy, ask the other person to mark up a new document using the rules you've provided. Although you may feel that you need the flexibility of well-formed documents, in the long run it will keep you from using much of XML's more advanced potential. Work this way with well-formed XML for a while, then transform your impromptu standard into a written DTD. It will make your documents much easier to manage.

Professional designers team with others on a regular basis for this type of consultation, but individual designers who need to build their own document structures often don't have those resources available. Designers working with HTML are concerned about whether the document looks right when it appears on a reader's screen; designers working with XML are more concerned about whether the document is easy to create on the author's screen. Using elements and attributes inappropriately is the fastest way to snarl what might seem like a reasonable representation of document structure.

Note

For a comprehensive discussion of document structure design issues, see Rick Jelliffe's *The XML and SGML Cookbook* (Prentice-Hall, 1998) and David Megginson's *Structuring XML Documents* (Prentice-Hall, 1998). Holy wars about when to use elements and when to use attributes have snarled discussions for years, but these two books provide an enormous number of balanced examples as well as theories.

XML and HTML

The W3C refers to XML as a part of its Architecture domain, but describes HTML, Style Sheets, and Document Object Models as part of its User Interface domain. The reality is more complicated than that: XML promises to have a significant impact on the user interface as well as on HTML itself. XML itself is not an official replacement for HTML, but the W3C plans to redesign HTML as a set of XML modules in the fairly near future. The architecture designation is appropriate to a certain extent, though, because XML is more a tool for creating structures than for applying those structures to a particular interface. As we'll see throughout the book, however, these roles can blur, making it difficult to tell which parts of XML are architecture and which are more directly interface-related.

XML is larger than HTML. HTML is an application of SGML, a particular set of tags defined by a DTD written for SGML parsers. (Originally, HTML was just a set of tags that looked like SGML tags, but over time the standard has been written as an SGML application.) XML is a subset, technically, "an application profile or restricted form," of SGML, containing a subset of SGML's tools for defining instances. Most of HTML (with a few key exceptions, like the SCRIPT element) can be readily described in XML. Consequently, it's reasonably easy to integrate XML and existing HTML sites. XML allows you to extend HTML, maintaining compatibility for the most part (remember the note above about closing tags), and allowing you to move well beyond the limited set of tags available in the older markup language.

Note

Mixing HTML and XML remains somewhat controversial, and the W3C has yet to announce how to go about this project. The XML in HTML meeting note (`http://www.w3.org/TR/NOTE-xh`) provides some guidelines, though it is notable that it refers consistently to legacy HTML as "crud."

Most HTML documents can be converted to well-formed XML syntax very easily. We will do just that to our first XML document — an HTML document preceded with a processing instruction that declares this document is XML as well as HTML:

```
<?xml version="1.0"?>
<HTML><HEAD><TITLE>Our first XML Document</TITLE></HEAD>
```

```
<BODY BGCOLOR="#FFFFFF">
<H1>Welcome to XML</H1>
<P>Welcome to your first well-formed XML document. There
isn't too much exciting going on here, but there will be
soon.</P>
</BODY></HTML>
```

The first line is the XML declaration, a creature not normally seen in HTML. In this case, the declaration merely announces that this is an XML 1.0 document. Although well-formed documents should have an XML declaration to announce that they are in fact XML, this statement is not always required. The version identifies this as a document that uses version 1.0 of XML, making it easy for later versions to identify themselves to browsers and parsers. If you don't specify the version number, 1.0 is the default. Specifying version may not seem important, but it will keep your documents functioning when the rules change, which is likely to happen at some point in the future.

Cross-Reference

The XML declaration will receive considerable additional coverage in Chapter 5.

The only other modification we made to the HTML was guaranteeing that all the tags are evenly matched (all start tags have end tags). Empty elements (like <BR>) can generally be converted to work with both XML parsers and old browsers by putting a space between the element name and the /> -
, for example. For new documents, these tasks aren't too difficult, but legacy HTML will present many problems, especially hand-coded HTML. (Most of the WYSIWYG HTML tools available can apply closing tags by default.) The old HTML may still work in a browser; however, it can't be read as XML. If you have questionable HTML, either fix it or don't mark it as XML.

Note

The worst conversions won't be documents, which can be cleaned up fairly easily with utilities like Dave Raggett's TIDY (`http://www.w3.org/People/Ragget/TIDY`). Applications that output HTML are going to need considerable revision, debugging, and testing, especially if the coding logic produces 'broken' HTML.

Creating Your Own Markup: A Well-Formed Document

You can use the XML declaration we just declared as the beginning of your own XML documents. It's like working without a safety net though, because you define no structures to protect you from your own mistakes, but it does give you a reasonable place to start designing your elements. Some designs are best constructed by looking at the top levels of the problem and carefully analyzing them, whereas others are best created by working from the bottom up. Choosing sample documents and marking them up in an experimental process may help you choose your elements and attributes more carefully.

The documents in this section are well-formed — they use syntactically correct markup to produce XML that a computer can interpret, but they don't include a DTD that specifies requirements for all of these tags and makes it possible to validate the document. Well-formed documents are more of a convenience and an agreeable means for maintaining backward compatibility with most HTML documents than a recommended way of working. Even though creating your own tags can be downright liberating, it's only part of what XML intends to accomplish. The discipline that a DTD imposes can be irritating, but it makes interpreting and reusing document content much easier. (Application builders in particular will welcome the guaranteed structures that validation can provide.) Well-formed XML documents are more organized than HTML; however, you'll only realize the full potential of XML when you take advantage of its more powerful tools for creating structures that apply to a set of documents rather than just a single document.

For the examples in this section, we'll use two simple documents: a recipe and a catalog page. The recipe is fairly simple: title, ingredients, and instructions. Still, there are a few layers of structure here that must be organized if this document is to work. The ingredients and the instructions are both lists, although the instructions could be presented as a paragraph if that is more convenient. Ingredients often have alternates. Even the instructions can vary: most instructions are about preparation, but some are serving suggestions. Marking up this recipe is a little more complicated than formatting it for a browser:

```
<?xml version="1.0"?>
<RECIPE AUTHOR="Simon St.Laurent">
<RECIPENAME>Super-Duper Grilled Cheese</RECIPENAME>
<DESCRIPTION>Succulent grilled cheese sandwiches that go
beautifully with soup but are still delightful on their
own.</DESCRIPTION>
<INGREDIENTLIST>
<TITLE>Ingredients: </TITLE>
<INGREDIENT><REALINGREDIENT>2 Tablespoons
butter</REALINGREDIENT> (or <ALTERNATEINGREDIENT>non-
stick spray</ALTERNATEINGREDIENT> if preferred)
</INGREDIENT>
<INGREDIENT><REALINGREDIENT>8 slices wheat
bread</REALINGREDIENT> (or <ALTERNATEINGREDIENT>other
bread </ALTERNATEINGREDIENT>)</INGREDIENT>
<INGREDIENT><REALINGREDIENT>1/4 pound jalapeño Monterey
Jack</REALINGREDIENT> (or <ALTERNATEINGREDIENT>other
cheese</ALTERNATEINGREDIENT>)</INGREDIENT>
<INGREDIENT REQUIRED="no"><REALINGREDIENT>2 bottles
beer</REALINGREDIENT></INGREDIENT>
</INGREDIENTLIST>
```

```
<INSTRUCTIONS>
<STEP>Melt butter in frying pan over low to medium heat.
</STEP>
<STEP>Slice cheese into thin slices. </STEP>
<STEP>Place cheese slices evenly on 4 slices bread; cover
with other slices. </STEP>
<STEP>Fry sandwich carefully in butter, flipping
repeatedly to avoid burning. </STEP>
<STEP CLASS="Serving">Cut sandwiches into quarters
diagonally. </STEP>
<STEP CLASS="Serving">Serve hot with beer. </STEP>
</INSTRUCTIONS></RECIPE>
```

The markup doesn't need to be done this way precisely; you may have tag names that you prefer or an industry standard for cookbooks may appear, in which case you should probably follow the standard. The key things to notice about this markup are that all elements have opening and closing tags and that a few of the elements have attributes that mark them as optional steps or serving suggestions. A real cookbook could be considerably more detailed and would probably have more sophisticated recipes.

This document doesn't have any formatting, which will be a problem in most Web browsers. You must create style sheets to provide presentation information to make this display properly in a browser, if that is the target application. In XML, parsers are supposed to respect line breaks (even without <BR> tags), spaces, and other whitespaces. At this point, no Web browser behaves this way. For the short term at least, you must use HTML formatting elements or the CSS whitespace and display styles to produce any documents that you want humans to read. XML also has its own mechanisms for declaring whether or not to pay attention to whitespace, which will be covered in Chapter 5.

Our next example is a simple catalog entry. Catalogs are generally more than a simple price list, even though price and part lists are an important part of the document. It isn't unusual for one entry in a catalog to sell multiple items — a product and accessories for example. This catalog example can be applied to a catalog with a standard format for the sales pitch and a standard set of information for pricing and shipping information. Again, you could do the markup differently, and if an industry standard exists, you're probably better off using or even extending that standard rather than creating your own.

```
<?xml version="1.0"?>
<CATITEM CATEGORY="Clock">
<ITEMNAME>Jimbo's Super Clock</ITEMNAME>
<DESCRIPTION><STORY>Ever wake up in the morning to
discover that your alarm clock didn't go off because the
power failed? Or that your roof leaked, it rained, and
the stupid thing just plain shorted out when it got wet?
Now you don't have to worry about waking up two hours
after you were supposed to be at work.</STORY>
<FEATURES>Our latest, greatest Super Clock is a dream
come true. It plugs into the wall but has its own set of
batteries and protection from short circuits. The
batteries even warn you when they're starting to fade -
and they come with a twenty-five year guarantee! This
clock is completely watertight, a sealed sphere of time
in a stainless steel case. The clock face is large enough
to read from a distance, and lights up with a touch for
those nights when you're stumbling in the dark. The alarm
starts off quiet, but gets louder and louder when you
don't turn it off—guaranteed to wake even the soundest
sleepers. A snooze feature let you sleep just a little
bit more, but it won't let you sleep in for more than an
hour past the alarm. This clock is ready to adorn your
bedroom, and even includes connections for lamp controls
to brighten your morning, and electroshock clips for
those who can't wake up any other
way.</FEATURES></DESCRIPTION>
```

```
<PICTURE SRC="supclock.gif"/>
<ITEM><PRODNAME>Jimbo's Super Clock</PRODNAME>:
<PART>SC45-A</PART> <PRICE>$199.95</PRICE>
(<AIRF>$19.95</AIRF> freight/air,
<GROUNDF>$7.95</GROUNDF> ground) <WARRANTY>Twenty-five
year</WARRANTY> Warranty. Made in
<ORIGIN>Canada</ORIGIN></ITEM>
<ITEM><PRODNAME>Lamp Controller</PRODNAME>: <PART>LC45-
X</PART> <PRICE>$25.95</PRICE> (<AIRF>$9.95</AIRF>
freight/air, <GROUNDF>$4.95</GROUNDF> ground)
<WARRANTY>Ten year</WARRANTY> Warranty. Made in
<ORIGIN>Canada</ORIGIN></ITEM>
<ITEM><PRODNAME>Electroshock Clips</PRODNAME>:
<PART>ES45-L</PART> <PRICE>$59.95</PRICE>
(<AIRF>$9.95</AIRF> freight/air, <GROUNDF>$4.95</GROUNDF>
ground) <WARRANTY>One-year</WARRANTY> warranty. Made in
<ORIGIN>USA</ORIGIN></ITEM>
</CATITEM>
```

As you can see, this starts to get fairly complicated. With appropriate style sheets or other formatting tools, you could turn this into an attractive layout on a printed page, a Web page, a screen on a CD-ROM, or a script for an infomercial complete with the price and a picture of the item for the order information section of the screen. Although XML may seem picky, requiring you to close all your tags and pay close attention to your syntax, you'll quickly find that the document-management flexibility you gain by adhering to this discipline is considerably more useful than the document-creation flexibility you lost.

Testing Documents with Parsers and Browsers

Although it's a lot of fun to hand-code documents when you're developing the tags yourself, most XML probably will be coded using programs similar to the ones developers currently use for HTML. (Much XML will be generated directly out of databases, cutting individual coders even further out of the process.) XML has much stricter standards to meet and is considerably less forgiving of missing tags than HTML. Figuring out where you forgot a tag can be frustrating under the best of circumstances, and the tools at present are fairly primitive.

One of the best of the early tools for checking your work is Lark, a non-validating parser for XML documents. Validating parsers check the XML markup against a Document Type Definition that describes the document structure, whereas non-validating parsers only check to make sure that the document is well-formed. Lark isn't exactly beautiful, but it does a very good job of presenting the structure of documents and exposing the parts in the way that a parser or browser will interpret them. (If you want to frighten yourself, apply it to some HTML documents and see how many errors it finds.) Lark is a Java application developed by Tim Bray, one of the editors of the XML specification, and is available with much (though not all) of its source code at `http://www.textuality.com/Lark/`.

Tip

A Web-based implementation of Lark, called RUWF (Are you well-formed?) is available at `http://www.xml.com`. It accepts URLs and returns either a congratulatory message that the document is well-formed, or a list of error messages returned by the parser. Badly formed documents can sometimes return an enormous list of errors.

Lark is a command-line utility at this point (Version 1.0 final beta), with no graphical user interface. To run it, you'll need a Java virtual machine that can run outside of a browser. For this example, I'll use the jview utility that comes with Microsoft Visual J++ for Windows 95, but similar tools are available in the Sun Java Development Kit (JDK), the Macintosh Runtime for Java SDK, and OS/2 Warp version 4, among others. Most people have only seen Java through an applet window in a browser, but Java is quite capable of working in text-only command-line environments as well. The jview application takes as parameters the name of the Java application (which is the same as the name of its class file, without the .class extension) and any parameters the application may need. Running a Java application without any parameters usually produces a message outlining what parameters are available. The Java application of the Sun JDK works similarly, producing identical results in my testing. I'll use both at various times in the book.

Tip

If you don't own Visual J++, don't want to download the 8.75 MB of the Sun JDK, and don't need to develop Java applications, Sun offers a slimmer Java Runtime Environment (JRE) at http://java.sun.com/. It's still 2.2 MB, but that might be enough of a trim to make it manageable.

Lark is useful for reading document structures only. Even though it does a wonderful job of matching up tags and building document trees, Lark doesn't compare the structures in your document to the structures in a DTD. We'll examine tools that handle that in later chapters. Lark is definitely a tool worth keeping around, however, especially if you plan to be creating your own document structures or must convert legacy HTML to XML.

Note

Lark does have problems with certain parameters and XML entities. Check the Lark documentation for the full details.

Our Lark example begins with a simple XML document. This document is a weather report, with only basic information encoded.

```
<?xml version="1.0"?>
<WEATHERREPORT>
<DATE>7/14/97</DATE>
<CITY>NORTH PLACE</CITY>, <STATE>NX</STATE>
<COUNTRY>USA</COUNTRY>
```

```
High Temp:<HIGH SCALE="F">103</HIGH>
Low Temp:<LOW SCALE="F">70</LOW>
Morning:<MORNING>Partly Cloudy, Hazy</MORNING>
Afternoon:<AFTERNOON>Sunny and Hot</AFTERNOON>
Evening:<EVENING>Clear and Cooler</EVENING>
</WEATHERREPORT>
```

To have Lark parse this, we need to tell the Driver class to analyze our XML file. In Windows 95 (if you have the Sun JDK installed, and the Lark files are in C:\lark), the command and its results look like the following output. Users of Microsoft's Visual J++ environment will use the command 'jview' instead of 'java'.

```
C:\My Documents\xmlaprim2\lark>java Driver weather.xml
Hello Tim
Lark V1.0 final beta Copyright (c) 1997-98 Tim Bray.
 All rights reserved; the right to use these class files
for any purpose
 is hereby granted to everyone.
Parsing...
Done.
```

If all goes well and Lark doesn't announce errors, your code is well-formed. Fortunately, Lark provides comprehensible error messages that can help you find any errors that creep into your code. For example, leaving off the final </WEATHERREPORT> yields the following session:

```
C:\My Documents\xmlaprim2\lark>java Driver weather.xml
Hello Tim
Lark V1.0 final beta Copyright (c) 1997-98 Tim Bray.
 All rights reserved; the right to use these class files
for any purpose is hereby granted to everyone.
Parsing...
Lark:weather.xml:9:43:E:Fatal: End of document entity
before end of root element.
Done.
```

Lark presents a meaningful message (that the end of the document happened before the root element was closed), as well as the line number (9) and character number on that line (43) where the error occurred.

An easier tool for some users is Internet Explorer 5, which will check documents for well-formedness as well. Loading the Weather Report Document above (without any style information) will produce the screen shown in Figure 3-4.

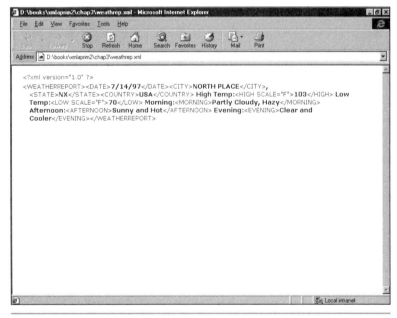

Figure 3-4 *When given an XML document with no styling, Internet Explorer 5 parses the document and displays it, including markup.*

It isn't lovely, but it's a good way to check your code. If you make a mistake, Internet Explorer 5 will notify you of that as well, as shown in Figure 3-5.

Figure 3-5 *Internet Explorer 5 will also display error messages generated by poorly formed documents.*

Internet Explorer 5's error messages aren't as comprehensive as those produced by Lark, but the two products serve different niches. Lark is really a developer's parser, designed for use in testing and processing XML documents. As a command-line tool, it reports back only the problems it finds. (The RUWF tool built on top of Lark, mentioned above, behaves similarly.) The parser built into Internet Explorer 5 is more of a production parser, optimized for speed and built into a friendly multi-purpose interface. Both models may prove useful for different projects.

Chapter 4

Plan in the Present, Save in the Future

Now that you've seen what XML looks like and the enormous power it gives the designer, it's time to look at the implications of what's been covered so far. XML allows designers to create their own tags. Cascading Style Sheets (CSS) and Extensible Style Language (XSL) can combine very nicely with XML to let you define your own formatting language. You can do almost anything you want without having to pay attention to what someone you've never met said on a committee years ago in a distant land about your particular subject area. The grammar of XML is fixed, but the vocabulary is open. XML is an extremely powerful tool, capable of amazing things. Unfortunately, XML is something like a chainsaw — incredibly powerful, capable of getting the job done without too much effort, and amazingly dangerous. Chainsaws demand regular maintenance and skilled users or they inflict tremendous damage. XML (probably) won't cause you bodily harm, but it can inflict tremendous damage as a result of poorly thought-out projects. Users who thought they could just start it up and go to work without learning about the tool and how best to apply it are in for some dark days.

XML has the potential to become the worst disaster yet to hit the Web. Sites composed of poorly written XML may look okay on the surface, but they will rapidly deteriorate into maintenance nightmares that require small armies of developers who must sort out the incompatibilities between pages on the same site. Millions of people may choose to spend their time reinventing the wheel, wasting time that could have been spent coding productively. Companies may continue to waste thousands of dollars converting information from one poorly thought-out system to another. HTML isn't always beautiful, but badly written XML can be much uglier.

XML is about much more than creating documents that look good on someone's screen. XML can be used for data transfers of any kind, including data transfers embedded in what used to be treated as "ordinary" documents. Unfortunately, that means that many more people must be involved in the process. When the Web first began creeping into businesses, it usually started in whatever group or person handled computers and networking and migrated slowly toward marketing and design. Even though different divisions of a company might all contribute to a Web site, their areas of different divisions didn't all have to look identical, and data could arrive in different formats. Web applications so far have been mostly driven by relational databases, both of which have their own format and structures. XML promises to unify all these different pieces, making the transfer of information between divisions and departments much smoother and the transfer out to the Web much easier. As these transfers increase, however, more coordination will be necessary.

 Caution

If you just want to use XML to extend your existing Web development toolset and have no interest in coordinated document management, you will see how to do so as you read the rest of this book. Keep in mind, however, that you'll be losing many of XML's advantages and you will still be spending your time building converters and hand-coding pages, much as you were with HTML. The ability to create your own tags is exciting, but it's only the beginning of what's possible. Additionally, you're exposing yourself to larger problems in the long run if you've written and used your own DTD for documents and your company develops a new, incompatible one that you are required to use.

Making this process work requires cooperation from many parts of an organization or even an industry. SGML has been mired down in committees from its very beginning, and XML will probably inspire many committee meetings of its own. This organizational quagmire doesn't have to mean endless meetings and continual reorganization or perpetually slipping release dates for the new company Web site. XML can greatly enhance collaboration, but it also takes a certain amount of collaboration to get things moving at the beginning. Developing an XML DTD doesn't have to be a company-wide initiative, however involving more people than the Web development staff is an important first step.

Who's Involved in XML?

Because XML has the potential to become a standard format for virtually all documents in an organization, many people who never thought about data formats before (and probably don't want to think about them now) are likely to be affected by XML development. Companies that have standardized on commercial document-management (mostly word-processing) tools have the opportunity to switch to a far more flexible and indeed customizable solution. Planning for a change of this magnitude will probably take years of consideration and slow conversion from the old ways to the new.

The good old days when the Web development team was a strange group of techies and designers isolated in a former storage room are coming to an end. When the Web moves inside the company, rather than just projecting data outward, the development team can no longer live at the borders of the organization. Intranets have already begun this process. Employees who might not even have computer backgrounds have become grassroots Webmasters, using personal Web servers and other small-scale tools to distribute data. Some corporations have established central Web servers for departments or divisions, giving the smaller organizations responsibility for their own content.

XML has the potential to penetrate enterprises far more deeply than even the latest wave of Intranet applications, becoming a standard format on nearly every desktop. XML is more than just a format for Web and printed documents. XML can provide a database format, a container for control instructions, a generic interchange format, and a variety of other applications that will undoubtedly come along. XML's extreme flexibility gives it incredible power to reach into nearly every data processing application, not just word processing and Web development. Even XML documents that were created for the limited worlds of word processing and Web development may end up mined for useful information, a much easier task when documents are created using well-crafted XML.

This expansive quality of XML means that developers must talk to many more people inside an organization than Web developers have had to in the past, in order to develop standards that meet the organization's needs. Organizing Web development has in the past been mostly a matter of interface design and content automation — taking content from various sources, converting them to HTML, and presenting them attractively. Organizing XML development requires close examination of content design and workflow automation. Presentation may still be important, but XML allows developers to ask that documents use XML and a standard DTD as their native format, avoiding the costs of conversion and opening up powerful new possibilities for document management. This obviously won't happen immediately; the process may take years, but it probably won't happen at all if developers lurch forward with poorly designed document structures that cause more mayhem than they fix.

Avoiding that mayhem requires considerable consultation with users. Even if your Web-development efforts have been moved from the computing department to marketing, it's time to go back to computing and talk about what can be done to ensure compatibility in the long run. Designers who have spent the past few years forcing HTML to present pages precisely the way they want them must talk with database managers whose data are organized in enormous tables, and agree on some common solutions. Companies that may have standardized on a particular desktop applications suite to avoid the headaches of constant file conflicts may find that their large investment was merely an interim solution and that the real tools for document interchange are only starting to appear. Convincing users of the need to change will be a difficult process, even if software vendors extend support (as several have promised) for the new tools XML makes available.

Focus on Structure

The most difficult demand that XML makes of developers is that they standardize their document structures. This doesn't mean that every single document must look the same; it means that developers must examine the components that go into their pages and create standards. HTML provided some tools for creating structures, like paragraphs, lists, and headings, but never demanded that developers apply structures rather than formatting. HTML tags had to work in concert at times, but a headline tag never required that a paragraph follow it, for example. XML can make such demands and (with a validating parser) enforce them. Taking full advantage of XML requires developers to examine their document and data structures closely and to restate them more explicitly.

Document Structure

This chapter is somewhat structured. It opened with a title, followed by some paragraphs. A heading followed, with some more paragraphs, and another heading appeared, followed by an introductory paragraph and a subhead. The text you are reading now is the paragraph below that subhead, so we are several layers down in the document hierarchy, as shown in Figure 4-1.

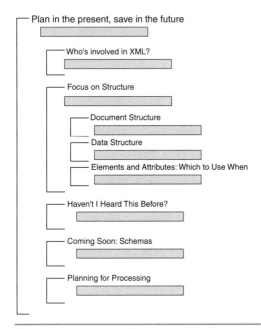

Plan in the present, save in the future

Who's involved in XML?

Focus on Structure

Document Structure

Data Structure

Elements and Attributes: Which to Use When

Haven't I Heard This Before?

Coming Soon: Schemas

Planning for Processing

Figure 4-1 *A map of this chapter*

Not every document has a structure as complex as this chapter, but most documents have some kind of structure. Memos, for example, begin with the names of the recipient(s) and the sender(s), as well as the date and other company information. The text that follows is less structured. Letters frequently provide more information, especially in a business environment, frequently including the sender and recipient's addresses as well as a statement addressing the letter (Dear John), a closing (Sincerely), a signature, and a clear copy of the name of the sender. Attachments may be noted, as may typists and others involved in the preparation of the document. Documents may be more complex than these basic examples, but they are very rarely any simpler.

Don't take this discussion to mean that your Web development team should be enforcing standards for company memos and other documents, even though that might eventually be a reasonable goal. (It's a project we'll tackle in Chapter 8, as well.) Many companies' attempts to standardize formats of commonly used documents have been met with resistance. For a wide variety of reasons, people do not like to format their memos the same way as everyone else. When developing standards for company documents, try to allow for some flexibility—at least on stylistic matters like font and size, if not on header information. Pushing standardization too hard is likely to keep the standard from ever being applied, especially in these early stages when friendly tools for applying standards have yet to appear.

HTML took a relatively simple approach to documents; identifying distinct components and creating tools for reproducing them. However, it did not link the parts in any particular way (with the significant exceptions of lists, forms, and tables). Most elements in the BODY section of an HTML document can appear anywhere, in any order. There are no rules declaring that H2 elements must appear only after H1 elements; H2 elements can appear anywhere in the document, with or without other headlines. The only limitations in HTML are those that create block elements. For example, H2 elements don't work well inside H1 elements.

```
<H1>This is the top<H2>This is the middle</H2>This is the
end</H1>
```

This line of code fails to produce a single line with two sizes of header. Figure 4-2 shows the results.

Apart from this kind of misbehavior, HTML puts very few constraints on the way its document parts are used. List elements are expected to appear in a list, but the browser will cope if they aren't; the same is true of form elements. Table elements (rows and columns) don't make sense outside the context of a table and would be ignored. HTML's lack of structural constraints makes it much easier for beginners to create pages that resemble their creators'

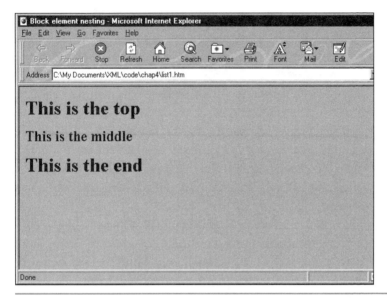

Figure 4-2 *Block-element nesting misbehavior*

expectations. Even if HTML had such structures, they wouldn't have been enforced because HTML has no requirement for document validation.

XML enables developers to create document structures many times more complex than those available in HTML. Document structures are useful because they guarantee that documents have all their required elements, and that document authors haven't run completely amok, creating their own wild formats and putting information into the "wrong" places. These XML structures enable document-management systems to check on completeness and to assist formatting engines in producing visually appealing representations of XML documents. Combined with style sheets, document structure elements make it possible to use XML to create readable, highly formatted Web pages, complete with headlines, subheads, paragraphs, citations, indented blocks, and all the structures previously available in HTML.

Document structures are fairly easy to identify by looking at a document. Their primary mission is to provide a roadmap to the information, enabling readers to find the information they need at a glance. Not surprisingly, most SGML implementations have been targeted at documentation projects, which tend to produce enormous amounts of information that need structure to help readers find their way through. Documentation usually follows strict conventions, often resorting to paragraph numbering for easy references (for example, see paragraph 1.3.2 for detailed information about widgets). Projects that already have strong structures are easy targets for markup languages; the real challenges are less structured documents that contain multiple types of information.

When developing DTDs based on document structures, developers should check to see what has already been done. Large companies and other organizations may already have their own SGML standards. Organizations of every size may need to adhere to standards to enable them to circulate information easily. Document structures are much less likely than data structures to demand their own unique DTDs (a memo is pretty much a memo, whatever organization or individual produced it).

Developers in need of some inspiration may want to examine the work of the Text Encoding Initiative (TEI) (`http://www.uic.edu/orgs/tei`). This academic organization has produced an enormous set of standards for scholarly document encoding. Written to provide standards for the conversion of printed books to electronic formats that scholars could use more readily, the TEI DTDs provide extensive frameworks for all kinds of materials from prose to poetry to plays to commentaries. TEI standards regularly cross the boundaries between document structure encoding and data encoding. In fact, they demonstrate how blurred the distinctions can be. Nevertheless, their adaptations of markup structures to a variety of document types are generally well thought-out and informed by implementation as well as prior planning.

In general, good document structure systems are usually more obvious than good data structure systems. Most organizations have already given some thought to these issues, and many have even considered their impact on document presentation, storage, and management. Desktop publishers have had to develop a sense of the structures regarding their materials, Web developers have had to build homes for a variety of different types of information, and technical writers and other documentation writers have generally had to work with preset document structure expectations. XML offers developers the chance to codify these structures and possibly make them more interoperable. XML's freedom from formatting information gives it the flexibility to deal with all these situations, making it possible for newsletter information to reappear on a CD-ROM, the Web, or even in a printed company history without too much mangling and rebuilding along the way. Building abstract document structures makes producing and managing documents much easier in the long term.

Data Structure

If the document structures provide a table of contents for documents, the data structures provide the index. Document structures organize your document to help readers understand the structure of an argument or follow an extended discussion without getting lost. Data structures reflect the content directly, with little concern for where they appear in an overall document structure. A DTD may require that they appear in a particular document structure, but they often have more freedom to "float" within a document.

The ability to create structures based on data content gives XML most of its practical advantage over HTML. Even though document structures are useful, they have little direct effect on the ways that computers can reuse the information in documents. They may enable management systems to identify the locations of information more precisely, but they do very little to help them actually retrieve the information. Document structures help humans read documents, but they do very little to help computers find the critical pieces of data they need without human assistance. A table in the middle of a document may be easily identified as a table, but without additional information, a computer cannot extract data from that table for reuse in analysis. Table headers may be useful to a certain extent, but as soon as multiple tables with similar headers appear in a document, which is a common situation, the computer is stuck once again when it tries to determine what information is relevant.

XML promises to help both computers and humans asses the data in a document and extract it for reuse or modification. Best of all, XML enables users to collect data that are scattered throughout a document as well as data that is carefully collected in a table or other formatting structure. When working on a suitably marked-up document, parsers can return information in a variety of formats, transforming textual data into more structured database and spreadsheet formats. Even though XML lacks tools for manipulating data within a document (calculated fields, for example), it provides the raw materials necessary for building applications around an independent data format.

Elements based on content provide document-structuring abilities as well. Apart from the fact that they can (in concert with style sheets) provide formatting based on content, these elements can be linked together with DTDs to provide datasets, not just individual atoms of data. In the catalog example from Chapter 3, for example, the last few lines were the actual ordering and shipping information:

```
<ITEM><PRODNAME>Jimbo's Super Clock</PRODNAME>:
<PART>SC45-A</PART>  <PRICE>$199.95</PRICE>
(<AIRF>$19.95</AIRF> freight/air,
<GROUNDF>$7.95</GROUNDF> ground) <WARRANTY>Twenty-five
year</WARRANTY> Warranty. Made in
<ORIGIN>Canada</ORIGIN></ITEM>
```

```
<ITEM><PRODNAME>Lamp Controller</PRODNAME>: <PART>LC45-
X</PART> <PRICE>$25.95</PRICE> (<AIRF>$9.95</AIRF>
freight/air, <GROUNDF>$4.95</GROUNDF> ground)
<WARRANTY>Ten-year</WARRANTY> Warranty. Made in
<ORIGIN>Canada</ORIGIN></ITEM>
<ITEM><PRODNAME>Electroshock Clips</PRODNAME>:
<PART>ES45-L</PART> <PRICE>$59.95</PRICE>
(<AIRF>$9.95</AIRF> freight/air, <GROUNDF>$4.95</GROUNDF>
ground) <WARRANTY>One-year</WARRANTY> Warranty. Made in
<ORIGIN>USA</ORIGIN></ITEM>
```

Each ITEM element includes a set of other elements, all of which can be made to be required with a DTD. These sets of elements could be treated as rows in a database, as shown in Table 4-1.

Table 4-1 *Sets of Elements Treated as Rows in a Database*

Prodname	Part	Price	AirF	GroundF	Warranty	Origin
Jimbo's Super Clock	SC45-A	$199.95	$19.95	$7.95	25 years	Canada
Lamp Controller	LC45-X	$25.95	$9.95	$4.95	10 years	Canada
Electroshock Clips	ES45-L	$59.95	$9.95	$4.95	1 year	USA

These datasets can be stored in any order within the database. The sequence in which information is presented in XML is not bound by the sequence within the database, nor is the database bound by the sequence in the XML. Use whatever sequence seems most appropriate for each media. Making datasets such as these work effectively requires more coding than the well-formed piece we originally used, but this certainly provides a much stronger starting point than what was possible with HTML. The relational model of tables of data will not always be appropriate to XML, which offers considerably more flexibility, but the groundwork for easy transfers between the two information models is easy to build.

Previously, tools for data interchange using basic text (usually ASCII) formats relied on one of two scenarios — fixed-length fields or delimiters. Fixed-length fields are designed for older technologies, like mainframes that stored all their information in tightly coded tables. For situations where information fits a tightly marked container and can be counted on never to exceed a preset maximum length, fixed fields can be handy. The receiving machine needs to know the boundary positions between the fields; then, it can chop the long string of characters it receives into usable fields. If one character slips, however, the data become useless. Delimiters use a different technique for indicating boundaries, inserting a previously agreed on character (like a comma) between each field and a different character (often a carriage return) between each record. The first line of the file containing the data is usually a list of field names, themselves delimited. Delimiters remain very popular; even one of the latest tools available for data presentation, Internet Explorer 4.0's Tabular Data Control (TDC), relies on delimited text data.

Neither of these solutions is very useful for data that need to be mixed with less structured information or data that aren't strictly text and numbers. (Given a large enough binary file, the code for the delimiter is likely to creep in at some point, disrupting the program trying to read the delimited file. This could happen with XML as well, even though XML provides an entity mechanism that should prevent it from happening with either valid or well-formed XML.) Both solutions have served well as interim techniques for managing information transfers, but XML promises a much more flexible and indeed much more reliable mechanism for information transfers.

Consider the following data table:

FirstName	LastName	ClassName
John	Nickelson	Introductory French
John	Nickelson	Introductory Geometry
Sarah	Angleton	Advanced Calculus
Carrie	Milton	Introductory French
Carrie	Milton	Advanced Calculus
Timothy	Shore	Introductory Geometry

If exported to a text file, delimited by commas, the information would look like:

```
FirstName,LastName,ClassName
John,Nickelson,Introductory French
John, Nickelson,Introductory Geometry
Sarah,Angleton,Advanced Calculus
Carrie,Milton,Introductory French
Carrie,Milton,Advanced Calculus
Timothy,Shore,Introductory Geometry
```

In an XML file, this information could appear mixed with other information that carries additional meaning to both humans and computers:

```
<?xml version="1.0" standalone="yes"?>
<HEADER><HEADLINE>Alert!</HEADLINE>
To:<TO>All teachers</TO>
From: <FROM>Registrar's Office</FROM>
Re: <SUBJECT>Students left off rosters</SUBJECT>
Date: <DATE>9/13/1997</DATE></HEADER>
<MESSAGE>The following students were inadvertently left
off the course lists previously distributed. Please add
them to your lists. If you have any questions, please
contact the Registrar's Office.</MESSAGE>
<COURSELIST>
```

```
<COURSEITEM>
<STUDENT IDNUM ="A0653B"><FIRSTNAME>John</FIRSTNAME>
<LASTNAME>Nickelson</LASTNAME></STUDENT>
<CLASSNAME>Introductory French</CLASSNAME>
</COURSEITEM>
<COURSEITEM>
<STUDENT IDNUM ="A0653B"><FIRSTNAME>John</FIRSTNAME>
<LASTNAME>Nickelson</LASTNAME></STUDENT>
<CLASSNAME>Introductory Geometry</CLASSNAME>
</COURSEITEM>
<COURSEITEM>
<STUDENT IDNUM ="A0653C"><FIRSTNAME>Sarah</FIRSTNAME>
<LASTNAME>Angleton</LASTNAME></STUDENT>
<CLASSNAME>Advanced Calculus</CLASSNAME>
</COURSEITEM>
<COURSEITEM>
<STUDENT IDNUM ="A0653D"><FIRSTNAME>Carrie</FIRSTNAME>
<LASTNAME>Milton</LASTNAME></STUDENT>
<CLASSNAME>Introductory French</CLASSNAME>
</COURSEITEM>
<COURSEITEM>
<STUDENT IDNUM ="A0653D"><FIRSTNAME>Carrie</FIRSTNAME>
<LASTNAME>Milton</LASTNAME></STUDENT> <CLASSNAME>Advanced
Calculus</CLASSNAME>
</COURSEITEM>
<COURSEITEM>
<STUDENT IDNUM ="A0653E"><FIRSTNAME>Timothy</FIRSTNAME>
<LASTNAME>Shore</LASTNAME></STUDENT>
<CLASSNAME>Introductory Geometry</CLASSNAME>
</COURSEITEM>
</COURSELIST>
```

The XML version, even the section that carries the same information as the delimited text version, is considerably more verbose; however, it is capable of serving multiple purposes. With the help of a style sheet, this document can be posted to a Web site, printed, or sent as e-mail to MIME-enabled mailreaders. Even though transmissions directly to humans are important, the automation potential of this document is even greater. It provides both document and data structures, which overlap and reinforce one another. The traditional style of the memo is preserved, and the HEADER element contains information that is normally carried at the top of a memo. However, the information is marked up to indicate smaller chunks of data, enabling a document-management system to store this memo and provide access to it in a number of ways. Readers can find it in lists sorted by recipient, sender, date, subject, or even headline. Searches can find information here on students whose first name is "Carrie" or by students taking "Introductory Geometry."

An enterprising teacher maintaining a database of students can connect the XML information provided in the COURSELIST elements and import the list directly, without retyping student names. A good parser could even grab the student's ID number from the IDNUM attribute of the STUDENT element and store it along with the name and class information, enabling the teacher to link to other information in a central database regarding that student. Perhaps most exciting of all, the school's central database can generate these files automatically, creating an easy way for administrators to "push" information out to teacher's own databases without maintaining constant connections or linking everyone to a gigantic central system. If you can imagine a cut-and-paste mechanism that reliably transferred information between dramatically different systems and applications, you can see a small bit of the promise of XML.

These systems don't exist yet; even the few places that use SGML extensively probably haven't connected their data from the central documents to distributed databases via memos. Office automation on this level promises to build many new data-driven workflow applications, as well as finally reducing the amount of repetitive data entry that remains a constant task even in today's ubiquitous computing environments. According to the September 1997 *Byte*, 90%

of business data currently lives outside of databases, as memos, spreadsheets, letters, proposals, documentation, and assorted other forms of information. Connecting those documents with a document-management system (as opposed to a database) is the real promise of XML. Making the document-management system meaningful will require considerable effort building infrastructure, a significant part of which is creating DTDs that provide information about the information in the document.

Developing DTDs that reflect data structures is frequently more difficult than developing document structures. Like relational databases, data structures are very clear in highly structured environments, but they can be extremely murky in ordinary documents. Deciding what counts as data and finding ways to mark it meaningfully are both difficult tasks. Different sectors of an organization may apply data very differently. For example, the individual parts listed on an order are critical information to a shipping department. Nevertheless, they are only of marginal interest to accounts receivable and are interesting only in the aggregate to corporate management. Different priorities can lead to different proposals for data structures and data management, much as they have in other applications of information technology.

One key element that is missing in XML is data typing. An enormous number of developers, especially database developers and programmers, have found this "missing feature" a difficult stumbling block. This issue appears on XML development mailing lists on a regular basis, and is probably the heaviest burden XML bears as a result of coming from document-processing origins rather than data processing. Because the SGML world was tightly focused on documents, document management, and making document presentation easier, data typing was never really an issue. XML 1.0's position as a subset of SGML made it difficult to add features like this, and they are only now arriving in the schema proposals discussed at the end of this chapter. The early rush to XML by programmers (rather than Web developers and other document creators) has created new demands that XML was not originally well-equipped to handle; the retrofit is in progress.

Note

XML does provide some support for describing data types through notations, described in the next chapter. Notations are fairly controversial and widely held to be underspecified, and better at describing the type of large chunks of information (like file formats), rather than small chunks (like integers). Notations may be a useful stopgap until schemas actually arrive.

Despite the potential for chaos, some basic rules for data design remain useful in deciding which pieces of data rate their own elements and how they should be broken down. Data should always be broken down to the smallest parts that will ever be needed, like what is done in creating a normalized relational database. The preceding example could have provided the first name and last name as one element, NAME, instead of two elements, FIRSTNAME and LASTNAME. This would certainly be easier for the document creators, who must mark up each element separately, but would cause problems for anyone else who needed to sort the class lists by last name. More complex structures can be built by nesting these smaller pieces in container elements (the STUDENT element, in this case). If the information was actually coming from a database, this structure would be easy to automate, both for exporting the data to XML and for importing it from XML. Hand-coders and document authors forced to deal with the complexity of nested tags may disagree, requiring compromise in many cases. To accommodate the varied uses of different users, compromise on the nesting of sub-elements within larger container elements may also be necessary.

Making these data structures work requires more than just creating a DTD; it requires continuous negotiation between developers and their user communities. Developers who are lucky enough to build standards only for themselves will be a distinct minority in the

XML community. Making XML's promise of content-based documents come to pass will require considerable political as well as technical skill and will often require a team that can handle both sides of the equation.

Elements and Attributes: Which to Use When

A constant problem in developing DTDs involves elements and attributes. HTML requires many attributes to make its formatting precise, and HTML developers are comfortable manipulating attributes. Despite that comfort level, it is probably better to refrain from using attributes in XML except when they contribute to a specific goal. Developers creating well-formed XML aren't likely to use many attributes except perhaps the STYLE attribute from HTML, but developers creating DTDs will need to address the issue constantly.

Attributes are an excellent tool for passing along extra information about your element to an automated processor—a parser, a browser, or a conversion tool. They are not a good place to actually store data. Using attributes when you need to store data (for example, <STUDENT FIRSTNAME="John" LASTNAME= "Nickelson"> </STUDENT>) could work only in a situation in which XML was transferring data between two computers; it would produce only blank space on the screen if a user were to open it in a browser. In addition, you would lose the opportunity to nest more information inside the attributes. Elements can contain other elements, but attributes can contain only one value. The IDNUM attribute used previously is an appropriate use of an attribute. IDNUM is a hexadecimal identifier for the student that only has relevance to a central database someplace. It shouldn't be part of the memo's visible content, but it may be useful to a database, enabling it to connect to the original data source and collect more information. Generally, you should use attributes to store information that may not be useful to humans directly but may help computers process the element properly. If you don't, you'll be walking into a maintenance nightmare.

Tip

Remember that you don't need to use attributes to hide information from the user. The CSS display property can be set to "none" to keep elements from appearing in a browser window. XSL has similar mechanisms.

Haven't I Heard This Before? XML and SGML's Promises

The promise of a universal file format is hardly new. SGML has been promising similar breakthroughs for the last 15 years, and has very little to show for it except for significant use in mammoth organizations like the IRS, Department of Defense, and IBM. SGML is capable of everything that XML can do and considerably more. Despite its power, though, the only variety of SGML that has caught the wider public's interest is HTML, which has very little of SGML's power. Why should XML be any different?

XML has several advantages over SGML. Its largest advantage is that HTML has paved the way for it. The syntax of nested elements and attributes is now familiar to a very large number of people who had not heard of it five years ago. But HTML developers are frequently frustrated by the limitations of the blunt tools they have had to use and are looking for significant improvements in their toolsets. XML and CSS seem to offer possible improvements over HTML, by enabling Web developers to create documents to their own specifications rather than those of browser developers. Although XML is much more than a tool for Web development, developers' previous experiences with the Web opens a doorway by which XML can enter into many organizations.

XML's second advantage is that it is considerably simpler than SGML. Even though it will probably sprout extensions and eventually come to resemble its overgrown parent, XML provides developers with much less to learn initially and fewer odd subtleties to master. Although XML has been developed by a W3C working group that grew out of an SGML group, the XML developers seem determined not to replay SGML's reputation for mind-boggling complexity. XML promises to remain a markup language standard that ordinary users can comprehend, requiring XML gurus only occasionally.

The last significant advantage XML offers is the support of the SGML community, which seems interested in promoting this new descendant. The SGML community is adjusting a few of the SGML standards to help ease XML's way to full compliance. Although many SGML books remain high-level textbooks, costing upwards of $50, SGML knowledge has filtered down to a broader base, including several trade computer books. SGML consultants who know the document-management side of the product can offer their services to companies in need of a makeover. It remains to be seen whether the significantly different SGML and HTML communities can work together at this intersection, but the expertise is available.

Cross-Reference

If you want to learn about prior SGML implementations, see *$GML: The Billion Dollar Secret,* by Chet Ensign (Prentice-Hall, 1997).

Coming Soon: Schemas

DTDs do a good job of describing document structures, but they have come under attack for a number of reasons and may eventually become a "legacy" technology. DTDs are perceived by their detractors as doing both too much and too little, in a quirky syntax familiar to SGML gurus but odd to the rest of the world. DTDs do too much because they provide tools for providing document content (entities) as well as describing document structure. DTDs do too little because they provide few facilities for describing document content, like the data types noted above. DTD syntax in XML 1.0 was definitely constrained by the requirement that XML be compatible with SGML, pretty much requiring the use of a subset of SGML DTD syntax.

Numerous proposals have emerged to replace or supplement DTDs, and the W3C XML Working Group has set up a schema working group. XML-Data (http://www.w3.org/TR/1998/ NOTE-XML-data/), a schema proposal from Microsoft, ArborText, and DataChannel, arrived even before XML 1.0 was complete. Document Content Description (DCD — http://www.w3. org/TR/NOTE-dcd) is a more recent successor, submitted by Microsoft and IBM. XML-Data and DCD both provide a "complete" solution for replacing DTDs, including support for entity declarations and datatyping. Over the summer of 1998, the members of the XML-Dev mailing list (including this author) created their own schema language, then known as XSchema but submitted to the W3C as Document Description Markup Language (DDML — http://purl.oclc.org/net/ddml). Unlike XML-Data and DCD, DDML expects that entity declaration will receive it own standard, and plans to build on other datatyping standards, taking a more modular approach. Another proposal, Schema for Object-oriented XML (SOX — http://www.w3.org/TR/ NOTE-SOX/) takes an object-oriented programming approach to schema development. None of these proposals is in general use or has been fully implemented, but all provide tools for describing XML documents using other XML documents. Another tool in development at the W3C, Resource Description Framework (RDF), could be used for describing document structures but aims at the larger world of metadata.

Cross-Reference

For more about the XML-Dev mailing list, see the archives at http://www.lists.ic.ac.uk/hypermail/xml-dev/.

At present, it's definitely worth the trouble of learning DTDs, despite their odd combination of features and unusual syntax. You'll be better able to understand the schema proposals when they arrive, and tools for converting DTDs to schemas should closely follow the arrival of the schema recommendation. Whether or not you like DTDs, they remain the foundation for XML and will undoubtedly be a key part of the vocabulary used to describe their successor or complementary technologies.

Planning for Processing

XML is "bigger" than HTML and SGML in a number of ways, capable of reaching into more areas of computing, from Web browsers to word processors to resource files to databases to control systems. As a result, developers need to be more aware of the possibility that structures designed for one purpose will end up being processed for another purpose entirely. XML removes the moorings that had attached data permanently to particular applications. Its simple unambiguous document structures enable applications to reach into any XML document and explore and process it. XML makes the creation of powerful generic frameworks capable of storing information of wildly different types possible. While this may not be the goal of everyone creating XML document structures — after all, short term goals remain vividly important — it's something that needs to be remembered at all times in the XML document structure and application development processes.

Web developers, document authors and managers, and application programming developers have so far been hampered by a lack of tools. XML creation is still a pioneering effort; developers have little to work with because programs that support XML have just started appearing. Nonetheless, one of the most magical features of XML is that today's documents can work with tomorrow's applications; the basic element and attribute structures are strongly fixed, but flexible enough to keep up with a wide variety of needs. XML developers also have a rich heritage of examples to draw on from the SGML world and the promise of ever-increasing XML support from major vendors.

Cross-Reference

Developers who need a heavy-duty introduction to the processing of building large-scale document standards in XML may want to explore *Developing SGML DTDs: From Text to Model to Markup*, by Eve Maler and Jeanne El Andaloussi (Prentice-Hall, 1996). Although the book is about SGML (it came out before XML existed), it provides a useful and readable guide to information modeling and to the processes – political and technical – that go into building standards and applications with SGML.

Chapter 5

Mortar and Bricks: Document Type Definitions

Now that we've explored some of the theoretical aspects of XML document creation, it's time to open the toolbox. Although the tools for creating validated XML may look a little strange, the logic behind them is not really that complicated. Creating a Document Type Definition is not an easy process, but a well-written DTD is well worth the effort. DTDs provide a useful set of strictures that can ease application development and authoring, and provide many useful features for reducing the size of your XML documents as well. Even if you don't plan to write your own DTDs, knowing how to read DTDs may be useful during a late night of work on documents created with a poorly documented DTD.

 Caution

Many of the features described here work in several different places. A few work only in external DTDs, some work only in DTDs (internal or external), and some work in documents only. SGML developers need to be especially careful because many tools that worked in a variety of places in SGML have been restricted to provide only a subset of their previous functionality in XML.

Parsing: An Introduction

Basically, parsing is just the interpretation of text. Computers can't really read, but they can interpret text files. Markup languages simply aid this interpretation, specifying explicitly to computers (or occasionally to humans) the nature of chunks of text. In HTML this is fairly straightforward: putting text between a start tag and an end tag means that the text is to be formatted in a particular way. <I>This is italic.</I> should produce: *This is italic.* HTML browsers understand that all characters placed between the sequence <I> and the sequence </I> should be displayed in italic.

SGML and XML take a more sophisticated approach to interpreting text. HTML browsers interpret the text according to a hard-wired set of rules, created by the browser developer based on their interpretation of HTML and the various standards surrounding it. HTML browsers do the best they can parsing text, in the sense already described. XML and SGML parsers, on the other hand, check the document's markup to make sure it fits a set of rules. XML parsers check at least for well-formedness, a minimal set of rules. Both SGML and XML can require documents to conform to a complex set of specifications outlined in document type declarations. Documents that conform to a DTD are said to be valid; parsers that can interpret DTDs and check document structures against their strictures are called validating parsers.

The XML 1.0 Recommendation refers to two components of a larger system for reading and interpreting XML. The first is the XML processor, which (outside of the XML 1.0 specification itself) is typically called a parser. The job of the XML processor is to load XML files and any supporting files they use, check to make sure that they follow the necessary rules, and build document tree structures that can be passed on to the application. The rules for XML processors are slightly different depending on whether they are validating or non-validating. Essentially, validating parsers check document structure as well as syntax. The application is the part of the system that acts upon that tree structure, processing the data it contains. The application could be a browser that displays the information in the tree structure on the screen, a browser that uses style sheets to render a more pleasing view, or a printing application that formats the information for a printer. It also could be a reader application that turns the computerized text into audio for blind users. The application doesn't necessarily produce output that humans can read. Instead, it could treat the XML as control information for machine tools or a set of orders that need immediate shipping. The XML application can implement just about any data-dependent process.

This separation of markup syntax (which parsers handle) from formatting (which applications handle) can make interpreting XML more complex than interpreting HTML. The <I> tag means the same thing on any HTML browser — start italics here — but it's not that simple with XML. <I> could mean start italics, or it could indicate an ice cream flavor, or it could signal comments about IBM. In fact, it could signal just about anything, depending on how the application interprets it. In HTML, the browser combines the parser and the application and follows a somewhat strict set of rules for how it interprets particular tags. XML is quite flexible about the final interpretation of the marked-up data, although it is far stricter than HTML about the markup itself.

Creating DTDs is a necessary step in building robust applications. DTDs provide critical information that enables XML processors to parse the code and make certain that it contains all the information the application needs, in a form the application will accept. The DTD provides a critical link between the data files given to the XML processor and the data that are transmitted from the XML processor to the application. DTDs help computers understand structures that may seem obvious to humans. In this chapter and throughout the book, the focus is on creating DTDs and valid documents. Because XML is so new, there aren't very many applications for it. Developing complete applications that apply XML is beyond the scope of this primer, although several road maps will be presented. In this chapter, Microsoft Internet Explorer 5.0, which contains a parser, will be used to render XML code.

 Tip

XML can be processed with a wide variety of parsers. In Chapter 3, we saw the Lark parser, a nonvalidating parser that can check a document for well-formedness but doesn't validate against DTDs. An additional module that adds validation to Lark, Larval, comes in the Lark distribution. Other parsers are available. SP (http://www.jclark.com), a validating SGML parser can parse XML documents as well. SP's author, James Clark, has also produced Expat, a C parser at the heart of Perl's XML support and Netscape's Mozilla browser project. Aelfred, a small nonvalidating parser from Microstar (http://www.microstar.com), is designed for use in applets. XML4J, from IBM (http://www.ibm.com/xml), is a validating parser that can be used with many supporting tools from IBM. For a more complete list, visit http://www.xmlsoftware.com/parsers/. If you're an author or just a reader, you're more likely to work with a friendlier browser or another application, but to programmers, these free parsers are valuable tools.

Starting Simple

The details involved in building DTDs can be daunting, even to experienced HTML coders, SQL developers, and C++ and Java programmers. XML has toned down SGML's reputation of complexity, but XML still has some strange detours and odd passageways. The various parts of the XML standard refer to each other constantly, requiring page flipping on an enormous scale. To avoid marching forward into quicksand, we'll start with lightweight documents that demonstrate some of XML's tools. The examples in this first section will use many parts of XML without explaining them in depth; the detailed explanations are in the following sections.

Unfortunately, the explanations aren't likely to make too much sense until you've seen some XML in action. This brief section is here to present a general idea of the appearance of a valid XML document, not to explain the details. These examples move quickly, so remember, it's just a quick tour so that you can see what valid documents look like.

Note

Although you can work with these examples and try to validate them, this first section is here mostly to give you a picture of what XML documents and DTDs look like in their raw form. All of the examples in this chapter are available for download at http://www.simonstl.com/xmlprim2/.

Initially, our examples use an internal DTD. DTDs can appear in the document they describe or in separate files. Most large-scale projects will use external DTDs stored in centralized file structures, but this simple document probably won't be managed in any large-scale system. The document begins with the XML declaration, followed by a document type declaration that includes a few elements, attributes, and entities:

```
<?xml version="1.0" encoding="UTF-8"?>
<!DOCTYPE DOCUMENT [
<!ELEMENT DOCUMENT (#PCDATA)>
<!ENTITY Description "This is entity content.">
]>
<DOCUMENT>This is element text and an entity
follows:&Description; </DOCUMENT>
```

Internet Explorer 5.0 will let us validate this document, though it takes a little work to make it happen. By default, Internet Explorer 5.0 only checks for well-formedness, and an obscure JavaScript switch has to be set to turn on validation. As a result, if you want to validate your documents against a DTD, there are a few steps you have to take. (Generally, validation in IE 5.0 is still easier than validation on the command line with a raw validating parser.)

First, you need to get the code that performs the validation. If your XML pages are on an HTTP server, you can do your validation directly from Microsoft's Web page. If not, you'll need to save a copy of the page to your system, open it as a file in Internet Explorer 5.0, and then validate them. The "validator" is available from Microsoft at `http://msdn.microsoft.com/downloads/samples/internet/xml/xml_validator/default.asp`.

Tip

Put a copy of the validation page into the same directory as your XML files. That way, you'll only need to open the validation page there and use the relative paths to the files – just the file name.

The validator, shown in Figure 5-1, allows you to enter a URL or paste in some raw XML code for validation. Results will appear at the bottom of the page.

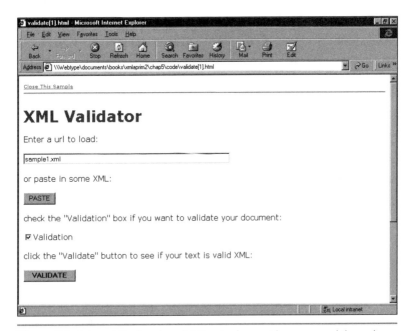

Figure 5-1 *Internet Explorer's validation tools must be accessed through a Web page.*

Loading the code shown above into the validator will produce the results shown in Figure 5-2 at the bottom of the Web page.

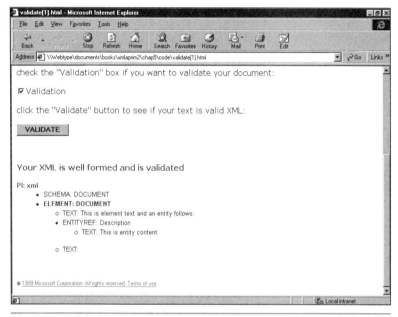

Figure 5-2 *Internet Explorer will expand entities as it validates documents.*

Internet Explorer (technically, the parser inside Internet Explorer) interpreted the declarations, allowing the creation of the DOCUMENT elements and expanding the &Description; entity. This code doesn't do much yet, but it provides a basic framework upon which a structure can grow. The XML declaration on the first line of the document tells the parser the version number of the XML used and that the document is encoded in a manner compatible with the UTF-8 standard, which includes the standard Latin-1 set of characters for most European languages. The document type declaration on the next line (<!DOCTYPE name [...]>) creates a DOCUMENT definition, which includes two key pieces — an element and an entity. (You need to choose Source from the View menu to see the full DTD, which is hidden by the browser so it can display more content.) The element declaration on the third line (<!ELEMENT name data) announces a DOCUMENT element that can contain parsed character data (#PCDATA), and the entity declaration on the fourth line (<!ENTITY name EntityDefinition>) provides a particular value to go with the name "Description." The actual markup includes only a single DOCUMENT element. This element contains some text and an entity reference, which is the entity name (from the declaration) preceded by an ampersand and followed by a semicolon. By the time IE 5 displays the document, it has expanded the entity. From these humble beginnings, we can create more complex types that begin to define a sample document.

Our next example will add several attributes to the DOCUMENT element, providing some information that a document management system could use for tracking. The <!ATTLIST name data...> declaration will enable the DOCUMENT element to carry a tracking number and a security level.

```
<?xml version="1.0" encoding="UTF-8"?>
<!DOCTYPE DOCUMENT [
<!ELEMENT DOCUMENT (#PCDATA)>
<!ATTLIST DOCUMENT
     trackNum CDATA #REQUIRED
     secLevel (unclassified|classified) "unclassified">
<!ENTITY Description "This is a very simple sample
document.">
]>
<DOCUMENT trackNum="1234">This is element text and an
entity follows:&Description; </DOCUMENT>
```

The attribute list declaration (<!ATTLIST name values>) should go under the element to which it refers, although it technically doesn't have to because it names the element. The two attributes are of different types. The trackNum attribute can have any value of type CDATA. CDATA (as we'll see in much more detail later) is character data. Most attributes will be of type CDATA. The attribute declaration also announces that it is required (#REQUIRED). Attributes may also be optional (indicated by #IMPLIED, or a default value) or have fixed values assigned to them by default (#FIXED followed by the default value). The second attribute, secLevel, can accept only one of two values-unclassified or classified. (The | symbol always indicates an OR statement in XML markup.) The default value, which is specified after the listing, is unclassified. The actual document element contains the required trackNum but not the secLevel attribute, so the default value of unclassified will apply.

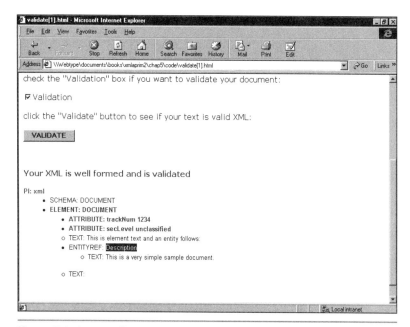

Figure 5-3 *Internet Explorer will apply default values for attributes to documents.*

Internet Explorer 5.0 has hidden the DTD, but its impact was clear — the secLevel attribute is shown with a value of "unclassified," the default value declared in the DTD, even though it wasn't in the document. If you add a secLevel attribute with a value of "NONE" to the DOCUMENT element, Internet Explorer will report the errors shown in Figure 5-4.

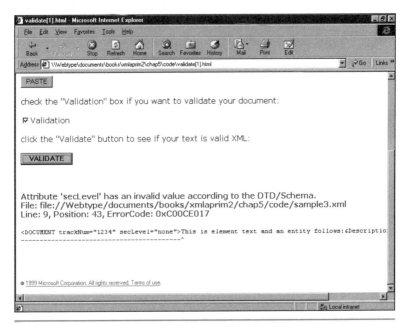

Figure 5-4 *Internet Explorer reports the first validation error in a file.*

Now that the example element has attributes, let's give it some additional elements to oversee. XML enables developers to identify what content elements may hold, of what type, and in what order and frequency. Our example will acquire a title, an author, and a description of the document. The title must appear one time only, the author field must appear at least once, summary elements are optional, and a special note element may appear only once or not at all. All of these elements must appear in the order listed.

```
<?xml version="1.0" encoding="UTF-8"?>
<!DOCTYPE DOCUMENT [
<!ELEMENT DOCUMENT (TITLE,AUTHOR+,SUMMARY*,NOTE?)>
<!ATTLIST DOCUMENT
    trackNum CDATA #REQUIRED
    secLevel (unclassified|classified) "unclassified">
<!ELEMENT TITLE (#PCDATA)>
<!ELEMENT AUTHOR (#PCDATA)>
<!ELEMENT SUMMARY (#PCDATA)>
<!ENTITY Description "This is a very simple sample
document.">
]>
<DOCUMENT trackNum="1234">
<TITLE>Sample Document</TITLE>
<AUTHOR>Simon St.Laurent</AUTHOR>
<SUMMARY>This is element text and an entity
follows:&Description; </SUMMARY></DOCUMENT>
```

This produces a fairly rigid document structure, built by the (TITLE,AUTHOR+,SUMMARY*,NOTE?) part of the DOCU-MENT element declaration. Because all the entries are separated by commas, they must appear in the order listed. TITLE, because it has no suffix, must appear once and only once. The plus following AUTHOR requires it to appear at least one time, and possibly many more. The asterisk following SUMMARY enables any num-ber (including zero) of SUMMARY elements to appear at this point. The question mark after NOTE makes it an optional ele-ment, but it can only appear once. Internet Explorer 5.0 returns the document structure shown in Figure 5-5.

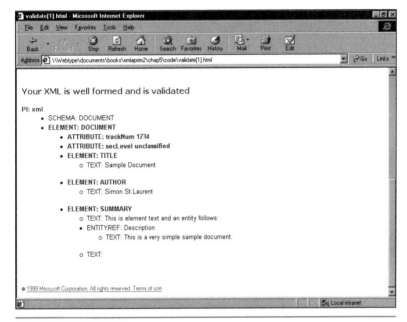

Figure 5-5 *Internet Explorer will validate nested structures.*

Changing the sequence of the elements in this document will make the parser fail because the document will no longer conform to the structure specified in the DTD—it will no longer be valid. For example, moving the SUMMARY element above the TITLE element produces the error shown in Figure 5-6.

Our next example will expand the DTD one level deeper, providing more information under the AUTHOR element. In this case, the author can identify both an organization (company or university) and a name.

```
<?xml version="1.0" encoding="UTF-8"?>
<!DOCTYPE DOCUMENT [
<!ELEMENT DOCUMENT (TITLE,AUTHOR+,SUMMARY*,NOTE?)>
<!ATTLIST DOCUMENT
     trackNum CDATA #REQUIRED
     secLevel (unclassified|classified) "unclassified">
<!ELEMENT TITLE (#PCDATA)>
```

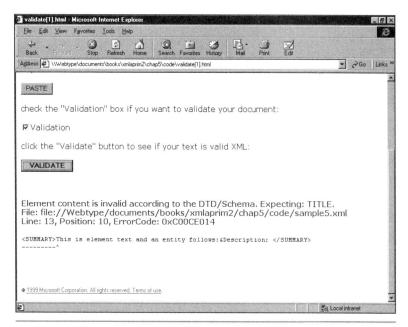

Figure 5-6 *Internet Explorer 5.0 will report document structure errors in documents it validates.*

```
<!ELEMENT AUTHOR (FIRSTNAME, LASTNAME, (UNIVERSITY |
COMPANY)?)>
<!ELEMENT FIRSTNAME (#PCDATA)>
<!ELEMENT LASTNAME (#PCDATA)>
<!ELEMENT UNIVERSITY (#PCDATA)>
<!ELEMENT COMPANY (#PCDATA)>
<!ELEMENT SUMMARY (#PCDATA)>
<!ENTITY Description "This is a very simple sample
document.">
]>
<DOCUMENT trackNum="1234">
<TITLE>Sample Document</TITLE>
<AUTHOR><FIRSTNAME>Simon</FIRSTNAME>
<LASTNAME>St.Laurent</LASTNAME>
```

```
<COMPANY>XML Mania</COMPANY></AUTHOR>
<SUMMARY>This is element text and an entity
follows:&Description; </SUMMARY></DOCUMENT>
```

The main change, apart from the addition of a few elements, is in the AUTHOR element declaration: <!ELEMENT AUTHOR (FIRSTNAME, LASTNAME, (UNIVERSITY | COMPANY)?)>. This declaration enables developers to create somewhat more flexible structures. In this case, the AUTHOR element must include (in this order) a FIRSTNAME element, a LASTNAME element, and either a UNIVERSITY element or a COMPANY element. (Using both elements will produce a parsing error.) Internet Explorer 5.0 seems happy enough about this arrangement.

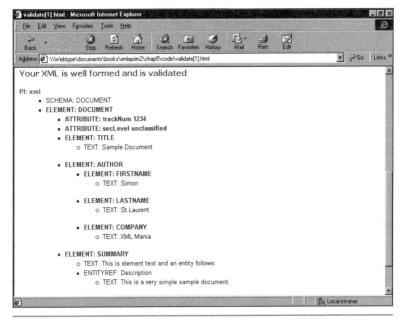

Figure 5-7 *Internet Explorer can parse structures that are many layers deep.*

At this point, the document is getting somewhat long, and most of it is just defining the document type. For our last example, we'll separate the DTD file from the actual document. The document becomes considerably shorter:

```
<?xml version="1.0" encoding="UTF-8"?>
<!DOCTYPE DOCUMENT SYSTEM " simple.dtd">
<DOCUMENT trackNum="1234">
<TITLE>Sample Document</TITLE>
<AUTHOR><FIRSTNAME>Simon</FIRSTNAME>
<LASTNAME>St.Laurent</LASTNAME>
<COMPANY>XML Mania</COMPANY></AUTHOR>
<SUMMARY>This is element text and an entity
follows:&Description;
</SUMMARY></DOCUMENT>
```

The <!DOCTYPE> declaration now points to a relative URL: simple.dtd, which must be in the same directory as the file. The simple.dtd file contains all the declarations that used to be in the document itself:

```
<!ELEMENT DOCUMENT (TITLE,AUTHOR+,SUMMARY*,NOTE?)>
<!ATTLIST DOCUMENT
     trackNum CDATA #REQUIRED
     secLevel (unclassified|classified) "unclassified">
<!ELEMENT TITLE (#PCDATA)>
<!ELEMENT AUTHOR (FIRSTNAME,LASTNAME, (UNIVERSITY |
COMPANY)?)>
<!ELEMENT FIRSTNAME (#PCDATA)>
<!ELEMENT LASTNAME (#PCDATA)>
<!ELEMENT UNIVERSITY (#PCDATA)>
<!ELEMENT COMPANY (#PCDATA)>
<!ELEMENT SUMMARY (#PCDATA)>
<!ENTITY Description "This is a very simple sample
document.">
```

To see the results, load the document into Internet Explorer 5.0 as usual. As you can see by the expanded entity and default value for the secLevel attribute, it did find the DTD.

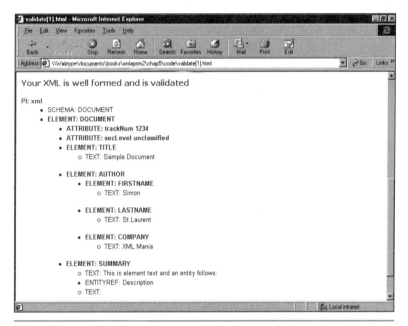

Figure 5-8 *Internet Explorer can load and validate documents that use external document type definitions.*

Now that we've created a workable DTD, let's examine the parts that go into defining an XML document. The following sections discuss the techniques needed to connect an XML document to a DTD and then explore XML data and document structures in greater depth.

How Documents Get Their Bearings: The Prolog

Although not technically a part of a DTD, the opening prolog, which contains the <?xml?> declaration and the following document type declarations are the glue that bind DTDs to the code that applies them. These strange-looking new declarations perform some of the functions that the HTML and HEAD elements offer in HTML, but they answer somewhat different questions. They hold only a few pieces of information, all of which are key to telling the browser how to interpret the code that follows. Although the HEAD element could contain interesting information, that information affects only a few specific parts of the presentation, like the title and possibly some scripting information. Specifying what version of HTML was used in a document could be useful for designers or automated HTML editors, but the browser doesn't really care — it will interpret the code to its own specifications, not those of a committee far away. In XML, the prolog tells the parser (though not the application) in fairly specific terms how to interpret the document.

<?xml?>: A Very Special Declaration

Valid XML documents should always begin with the XML declaration. The XML declaration contains version information, encoding information, and information about which if any DTDs the document will use. Even though the contents of the XML declaration give only a very broad idea of the kind of XML document that follows, they provide critical basic information to the parsers that interpret the document. The XML declaration looks like a processing instruction, covered below, but it isn't one. The XML declaration includes several parts: the opening <?xml, version information, the standalone declaration, the encoding declaration, and the closing ?>. None of this information is technically required. XML declarations can have missing parts, and documents can be well-formed without having an XML declaration. The version information and the declarations have default values that parsers can use.

Caution

Unlike the HTML element, the XML declaration has no closing tag. </?xml> should *never* appear in a document. The XML declaration is an opening statement and nothing more.

The version information in this first version of XML is quite simple: version="1.0." Version 1.0 will be the default, providing a base for all future implementations of XML. Whatever happens to the standard, leaving out the version completely or specifying version 1.0 should mean that the documents and document type declarations written for version 1.0 will be interpreted as originally intended even when XML reaches version 7.3 or even 20.0.

Note

Unlike HTML, which arrived as version 0.9 when it became publicly available, XML has been at version 1.0 since the working drafts first appeared.

The standalone declaration announces whether a document contains references to external document type declarations. The value may be either "yes" or "no". If no standalone declaration appears, the default is "no". Valid documents are required to provide an honest answer for this declaration. Documents may make references to external entities, and still claim "yes", but may not refer to external DTDs. The W3C Recommendation suggests that any XML document can be converted into a standalone document for processing if necessary, and some simple applications may well choose to reject all documents that are not standalone documents. In general, however, document developers who are building sets of valid documents will most likely anwswer "no" or leave out this declaration entirely.

Caution

The standalone declaration is better at creating confusion than solving problems for most people. It should only be used when you are completely certain that a document doesn't rely on any external sources of DTD or entity information, but the declaration actually doesn't need to be present in those cases. The W3C is considering work on canonical XML documents which must be standalone, and which may give this feature some use; until then, don't use the standalone declaration. See the section at the end of this chapter on parser behavior for more information.

The encoding declaration addresses complex issues related to internationalization. XML enables developers to specify which of several different character encoding schemes should be applied to a document. The default scheme is UTF-8, which includes direct representations of most of the characters used in English using values of 0-127 for the ASCII set of characters, and provides multibyte encodings for Unicode characters with higher values. UCS-2, which XML parsers are required to support, applies the Unicode/ISO/IEC 10646 standards, which extend the character space to 16 bits, enabling values from 0 to 65,535, a very significant expansion that includes most modern languages. (There are still significant problems with Chinese characters and several other character and glyph sets that remain under negotiation.) XML parsers can (although they aren't required to) support several other encodings, including ISO 8859-1 through ISO 8859-9, which represent most European languages, and EUC-JP, Shift_JIS, and ISO-2022-JP, which represent Japanese. The encoding scheme's name must always be enclosed in single or double quotes and described using the Latin character set. For example, to declare that a document uses XML version 1.0 and the UTF-8 encoding, the XML declaration below is appropriate:

```
<?xml version="1.0" encoding="UTF-8"?>
```

Unicode and Other Encodings

While most English-speaking developers have grown used to the standard character sets available for that language, developers elsewhere have strained to use their languages in computers that weren't really designed to accommodate them. After several years of development, the Unicode standard is finally gaining some use, chipping away at the 8-bit character sets that have dominated computing since the arrival of the (later extended) 7-bit ASCII character set. Unicode offers 16 bits, for 65,536 possible characters.

Although ASCII is adequate for most documents in English, the limitations of a 128-member character set rapidly became clear (even when expanded to 256 members) as computers began to spread to areas using other languages. Even Latin-based European alphabets have enough accented and other special characters to fill up the 256 spaces rapidly. Adding Cyrillic, Greek, Turkish, Hebrew, or Arabic characters to that moves well beyond the available space. Character and glyph sets for Asian languages have tens of thousands of ideographs. Creating standards that will work for all of these languages is a complex task, demanding political and technical compromise.

XML requires that parsers support UTF-8, UCS-2, and UTF-16. The encodings required or recommended for support in the standard are those in Table 5-1.

Table 5-1 *Common XML Encoding Schemes*

Encoding Scheme	# of Bits	Notes
UCS-2	16	Canonical Unicode character set
UCS-4	32	Canonical Unicode character set, using 32 bits
UTF-8	8	Unicode Transformation – 8 bit
UTF-7	7	Unicode Transformation – 7 bit (for mail and news)
UTF-16	16, 32	Unicode format that escapes 32-bit characters
ISO-8859-1	8	Latin alphabet No. 1 (Western Europe, Latin America)
ISO-8859-2	8	Latin alphabet No. 2 (Central/Eastern European)
ISO-8859-3	8	Latin alphabet No. 3 (SE Europe/miscellaneous)
ISO-8859-4	8	Latin alphabet No. 4 (Scandinavia/Baltic)
ISO-8859-5	8	Latin/Cyrillic
ISO-8859-6	8	Latin/Arabic
ISO-8859-7	8	Latin/Greek
ISO-8859-8	8	Latin/Hebrew
ISO-8859-9	8	Latin/Turkish
ISO-8859-10	8	Latin/Lappish/Nordic/Eskimo
ISO 10646	32	32-bit extended set; includes Unicode as subset
EUC-JP	8	Japanese (uses multibyte encoding)
Shift_JIS	8	Japanese (uses multibyte encoding)
ISO-2022-JP	7	Japanese (uses multibyte encoding; for mail and news)

Developers used to working with the ASCII set of characters shouldn't have too much difficulty because most of the standards include that set as a base. Because the default set for XML is explicitly declared to be UTF-8, developers can expect most pages in English to display without difficulty. The Unicode UCS-2 standard begins with a code sequence that identifies it, and parsers should be able to auto-detect it. A well-written parser will be able to protect users to some extent from the seemingly random characters that currently fill screens when users visit pages written in different encodings than the default.

Unfortunately, displaying all these character sets still requires additional operating system support. Windows NT and Solaris 2.6 and 7 both offer native Unicode support, but developers on other platforms will need additional language kits that enable the conversion between formats. Collecting an adequate set of fonts to represent multiple languages remains a problem, but support to do so is rapidly increasing. Programming languages have similar problems; most use an 8-bit space for character data. Java already uses Unicode as its default format for character information, giving developers a ready-made language for Unicode text processing. Unicode support is growing, and XML's use of it as a standard should widen its acceptance.

 Cross-Reference

See the section on xml:lang, below in the Attributes section, for another tool that makes XML more useful in multilingual situations.

Document Type Declarations

After the opening prolog has announced that this is an XML document, the document type declarations announce what kind of XML document it is to be. Document type declarations glue the DTDs to the actual document or may even provide their own declarations about the structure of the document. Although internal DTDs (which are declared in the document they apply to) can be used and may be appropriate for certain situations, using external DTDs is often preferable. Keeping DTDs separate makes them considerably more reusable across multiple documents and assures document managers that developers and authors aren't taking liberties with the DTD to suit their own purposes which can create incompatible document types. There are drawbacks to using external DTDs that will be explored at the end of the chapter as well, but most large document systems (and even Web sites) will want to refer to a single library of DTDs that applies to multiple documents in the system.

Note

Whenever the acronym DTD appears in this book or in other XML document, always assume that it stands for document type definition, *not* document type declaration.

A document type declaration always begins with <!DOCTYPE, followed by the name of the DTD, followed by a declaration of the DTD or a link that points to where the DTD can be found, and finally a > to close the declaration. The name of the DTD doesn't need to correspond to the file name of the DTD file specified, but it should convey some sort of intelligible description of what the DTD is for and (most importantly) match the name of the root element used by the document. After the name, the declaration can either provide a DTD within the declaration itself, enclosed in braces ([ ]), which we'll demonstrate in some of the following examples, or provide a link to a file containing the DTD. The reference to the DTD file is an external entity; external entities will receive additional coverage later in the entities section. For now, we'll just discuss how to apply them in this situation.

Some DTDs are public standards, available in standardized format to a large number of users. Others are locally developed, useful for a Web site, a business, or perhaps a small industry. For the first type, the PUBLIC keyword is more appropriate; for the second, only the SYSTEM keyword should be used. The PUBLIC keyword first provides a public identifier (in quotes) that the parser can use to locate the standard if it is connected to a library of standards. Following that is a URL (also in quotes) that can lead the parser to a copy of the DTD. (Unless you know that your users will be accessing this document through an application that can understand public identifiers and locate documents based on them, *always* provide a URL.) The SYSTEM keyword is followed only by the URL. Large document management systems may well have libraries of DTDs available to parsers, but developers of other types of projects may not have such resources. The following two document type declarations link the document to the same DTD, but the first also provides a public identifier for the DTD.

```
<!DOCTYPE manual PUBLIC "-//loopbackInc//DTD manual//EN"
"http://www.simonstl.com/dtds/manual.dtd">
<!DOCTYPE manual SYSTEM
"http://www.simonstl.com/dtds/manual.dtd">
```

DTDs can also be nested—one DTD file may call another through parameter entities. DTDs are cumulative, although an internal DTD will always have precedence over an external DTD.

The public identifier structure uses the same format as SGML public identifiers. If the entity or DTD described is an ISO standard, the identifier starts with "ISO". Otherwise, the first character is a plus (+) if the standard is officially approved by a standards body, or a minus (-) if it is not, followed by two forward slashes (//), after which an identifier of the owner of the DTD appears. After two more slashes the type of the document (DTD, for example, or TEXT) appears followed by whitespace and the name of the document. After yet another two slashes, the language identifier appears, using the codes specified in ISO 639 (EN, for example, is English).

Comments

Comments are another critical part of XML. They appear in both documents and DTDs. Comments in XML behave much like comments in HTML. Comments begin with <!— and end with —>, and processors ignore their content, enabling humans to put anything they want inside. XML comments can not have two consecutive dashes (—) in their content because it may confuse parsers that interpret that as the end of an SGML comment. XML comments can appear in both documents and DTDs. XML comments can't appear inside of tags or in declarations and will not work in CDATA. (In CDATA sections, the comment symbols are treated as regular characters and will appear as part of the document.) The parser will always ignore the contents of comments, though it may pass them on to the application. The following is a sample comment:

```
<!-This is a comment. Please ignore me if you are
parsing.->
```

Comments in XML may be used in both DTDs and documents, but they are critically important in DTDs. Comments are the signposts future editors will need to understand the structures you have created. Comments can explain otherwise mysterious entity references and are useful for labeling declarations, especially if element names are abbreviated. Comments may seem like wasted space to developers with perfect memories, but a DTD without comments is truly wasted space to the next developer who must work with it.

Processing Instructions

Technically, processing instructions, which begin with <? and end with ?>, don't directly affect the document structure, except that the application receives notice of their existence. (XML processing instructions must end with ?>, instead of the SGML standard of >.) The first word of the processing instruction (the "target") must be composed of letters, digits, periods, dashes, underscores, or colons, and begin with a letter or an underscore. (The use of colons is discouraged because of Namespaces, described below.) The remainder of the processing instruction may be composed of any characters, including equals signs and quotes. Processing instruction provide information to outside programs, like formatters, that are less concerned with the syntactical structure of a document than they are with making it look as its designers intended. Most processing instructions intended for outside formatters have their own syntax;

they needn't follow typical SGML syntax. Although it would be unusual, the following:

```
<?Jimmy - use the burnt umber crayon for this. ?>
```

could be an acceptable processing instruction if the processing application was a child named Jimmy. A more typical processing instruction might be

```
<?FormatWhiz azure-embossed-type?>
```

FormatWhiz would probably (although not necessarily) be the name of the processing application, whereas the remainder of the instructions specify unusual formatting, possibly for a business card or wedding invitation. Processing instructions have an important role to play in connecting styles to documents. Though they can't be standardized through the use of DTDs, standards for processing instructions(or PIs, as they're known) are key to creating functionality that works across multiple document types.

Processing instructions have been condemned as a diabolical means of creating unnecessarily complicated SGML that doesn't transfer well between different parsers, but the XML working group appears to have settled on it as the most appropriate syntax for telling the parser how to handle the document.

Caution

Always avoid processing instructions that begin with <?XML, <?xml, or any combination of upper- and lowercase versions of <?XML. They are expressly reserved for future use by the XML specifications.

Logical Structures

Element and attribute declarations are the core of XML. Well-formed documents can be useful for certain situations, but the element structures they use exist only in the document and in the mind of the designer. DTDs are an opportunity for developers to make their vision concrete, creating specifications for groups of documents and not just single documents. A well-written set of elements and attributes will make it easy for programs to extract useful information as well as to present it beautifully. Even though the other parts of the XML 1.0 Recommendation may assist in this task, the main work of XML consists of creating document structures using elements and attributes.

Elements

Before we discuss elements any further, we need to look at two related concepts: parent and child elements. HTML developers are accustomed to using elements without much concern for context, with the significant exceptions of list and table elements. Understanding context is a critical prerequisite to building a DTD that works efficiently. In XML, the context provider is the parent element, and the child element may provide context to elements nested inside of it. For example, in the structure:

```
<SECTION >
    <PARAGRAPH>
        <SENTENCE>
        </SENTENCE>
    </PARAGRAPH>
</SECTION >
```

the SECTION element is the parent element of the PARA-GRAPH element, which in turn is the parent element of the SEN-TENCE element. Similarly, the SENTENCE element is the child element of the PARAGRAPH element, which itself is the child of the SECTION element. XML also includes a document entity, which provides a root from which the markup tree structures can grow. If SECTION was the first element in a document, it would be a child of the document entity. (There isn't any special way to define a document entity — it just provides parsers with a place to start.)

As we saw earlier in the chapter, creating elements is very simple. The element declaration syntax is:

```
<!ELEMENT name content>
```

The name of an element must follow the same rules as the name of an entity: it must be composed only of letters, digits, periods, dashes, underscores, or colons. Colons should be reserved for use with namespace, a new aspect of XML that arrived after the completion of the XML 1.0 Recommendation, described below. The name may be defined using a parameter entity, as may the content. (Remember, if the declaration is in the internal DTD subset, the parameter entity must include the entire declaration, not just parts.) The content of an element can be of four types: a mixed-content declaration, a list of elements, the keyword EMPTY, or the keyword ANY. ANY is the simplest declaration, announcing that this element can contain all kinds of data and markup:

```
<!ELEMENT BOXOSTUFF ANY>
```

Using this declaration, all BOXOSTUFF elements will allow any kind of element or data to be included in their content. A document that used the BOXOSTUFF element declared previously could look like the following:

```
<BOXOSTUFF><DARKSPACE>emptiness</DARKSPACE>more
junk</BOXOSTUFF>
```

The DARKSPACE element would need to be declared elsewhere; otherwise, BOXOSTUFF would impose no rules on its contents.

Although using ANY is perfectly acceptable XML, I strongly recommend that developers try to be more specific about document structure. Because HTML and some other forms of markup were primarily used for formatting, tags that effectively used ANY were necessary. Forbidding the use of bold text in a paragraph would undoubtedly have caused an uproar. XML changes all that. By providing developers an opportunity to create document structures, XML promises to help create more intelligent documents. A large part of that intelligence is the kind of error-checking XML can provide when given a fully developed DTD, complete with rules that define which elements can go where. Try to restrict the use of ANY to the early stages of DTD development, replacing it with a more complete content specification as quickly as possible.

The EMPTY keyword is ANY's polar opposite. Instead of allowing *any* content, it allows no content. Elements defined with EMPTY content may have attributes but do not permit information to be stored between their beginning and end tags. The element declaration for an empty element is concise:

```
<!ELEMENT EMPTYSPACE EMPTY>
```

Using this empty tag in a document requires even less room:

```
<EMPTYSPACE />
```

Most of the time EMPTY elements will be written as only an empty element tag ending with a /> (
, for example). Typical beginning and end tags are permitted, but no elements or data may come between the tags.

Most element declarations will contain lists of elements, setting rules for which elements are required, the sequence in which they appear, and how many times they can appear. (Remember that all elements in the list must always be defined separately in their own declarations.) Parameter entities may also appear in the list, making it easier for developers to create multiple similar structures. Table 5-2 lists a few symbols to provide rules for using elements (and attributes, as we'll see later).

Table 5-2 *Symbols for Specifying Element Structure*

Symbol	Symbol Type	Description	Example	Example Notes
|	Vertical bar	Any element named may appear.	thisone | thatone	Either thisone or thatone must appear.
,	Comma	Requires appearance in specified sequence.	thisone, thatone	thisone must appear, followed by thatone.
?	Question mark	Makes optional, but only one may appear.	thisone?	thisone may appear.
	No symbol	One, and only one, must appear.	thisone	thisone must appear.
*	Asterisk	Allows any number to appear in sequence, even zero.	thisone*	thisone may be present; multiple appearances (or zero appearances) of thisone are acceptable.
+	Plus sign	Requires at least one to appear; more may appear in sequence.	thisone+	thisone must be present; multiple thisone elements may appear.
( )	Parentheses	Groups elements.	(thisone | thatone), whichone	Either thisone or thatone may appear, followed by whichone.

> **Note**
>
> SGML developers may wonder what happened to the amper-
> sand (&). XML, at least in version 1.0, does not support that
> content model group. Mixed declarations and creative use of
> OR statements can provide similar capabilities in XML.

These options create a tremendous number of possibilities, as
well as a dangerous temptation to create complex structures that
attempt to cover every possible use of child elements that seems
sensible. The following examples provide some simple examples and
explanations of acceptable declarations.

The simplest element content is the rare circumstance in which
an element may contain only one other element. This might happen
in cases where a frustrated developer needs to create a "wrapper"
element for an element in an outside DTD that can't be modified.
The declaration for WRAPPER would read:

```
<!ELEMENT WRAPPER (UNTOUCHABLE)>
```

In this case, the only acceptable use of the WRAPPER element
would be as follows:

```
<WRAPPER><UNTOUCHABLE>untouchable
content</UNTOUCHABLE></WRAPPER>
```

A more likely declaration would include two elements in
sequence. A briefing, for example, might include a title and some
content. The declarations would be

```
<!ELEMENT TITLE (#PCDATA)>
<!ELEMENT CONTENT (#PCDATA)>
<!ELEMENT BRIEFING (TITLE, CONTENT)>
```

This enables more sophisticated markup:

```
<BRIEFING>
<TITLE>Another dull briefing</TITLE>
<CONTENT>Today, too much happened for me to adequately
discuss it.</CONTENT>
</BRIEFING>
```

If the boss grew weary of such despondent headlines, the DTD could be modified to make the TITLE optional:

```
<!ELEMENT BRIEFING (TITLE?, CONTENT)>
```

In extreme cases, the CONTENT could also be made optional with the addition of a question mark. If briefings grew longer, the developer could allow writers to include multiple CONTENT elements under a single briefing element by adding a plus sign:

```
<!ELEMENT BRIEFING (TITLE?, CONTENT+)>
```

Substituting an asterisk for the plus sign would enable briefings to be shorter as well as longer, which would enable writers to create briefings with no CONTENT elements or thousands of CONTENT elements.

Although most simple documents, and some larger documents, contain single elements in reasonably obvious sequences, more complex documents need more combinations to enable greater flexibility. Paragraphs and lists can often substitute for each other. A recipe, for instance, might include a list of ingredients or a story of a trip to the grocery store. The following declarations would make either approach valid:

```
<!ELEMENT STORY (#PCDATA)>
<!ELEMENT ITEM (#PCDATA)>
<!ELEMENT INGREDIENTLIST (ITEM+)>
<!ELEMENT INGREDIENTS (STORY | INGREDIENTLIST)>
```

The XML code for an ingredient section could then look like this for a more traditional recipe:

```
<INGREDIENTS><INGREDIENTLIST>
<ITEM>Butter, enough to coat frying pan</ITEM>
<ITEM>Hot dogs, as many as needed</ITEM>
</INGREDIENTLIST></INGREDIENTS>
```

Authors who preferred to tell tales of their ingredients could use this format instead, and XML parsers would accept it:

```
<INGREDIENTS><STORY>
No one wants to talk about where hot dogs come from, but
I know their origin. They come from trucks that unload
them regularly into the backs of grocery stores. Clerks
open the boxes and put the hot dogs on the shelf. It's
really not that complicated, and at least it's plastic
wrapped. Butter works the same way, but it comes in boxes
and wax paper.
</STORY></INGREDIENTS>
```

The OR structure also makes it possible to create spaces where a limited number of elements may be used freely in combination. A discussion of poetry, for instance, might consists of quotes interspersed with commentary. The sequence wouldn't be especially predictable, but it would clearly fit within the structure of a chapter. The following declaration creates a CHAPTER element that comes complete with a title and allows multiple quotes and comments.

```
<!ELEMENT TITLE (#PCDATA)>
<!ELEMENT QUOTE (#PCDATA)>
<!ELEMENT COMMENT (#PCDATA)>
<!ELEMENT CHAPTER (TITLE, (QUOTE | COMMENT)*)>
```

The following XML document would parse properly, interpreting the (QUOTE | COMMENT)* as an invitation to use multiple QUOTE and COMMENT elements in any sequence.

```
<CHAPTER><TITLE>Bad Poetry Rocks</TITLE>
<QUOTE>I'm a poet and I didn't know it</QUOTE>
<COMMENT>This is the classic bad poem. Some might claim
that its natural rhythm makes it a fine found poem, but I
must disagree.</COMMENT>
```

```
<QUOTE>Jack and Jill went up the hill</QUOTE>
<COMMENT>Who let the nursery rhymes in?</COMMENT>
</CHAPTER>
```

QUOTE elements and COMMENT elements could appear in any sequence. Two quotes followed by a comment would be acceptable, as would ten comments with no quotes at all.

XML enables developers to create very elaborate sets of rules using the parentheses and the |, *, and + operators. It is possible to define entire documents so that all the child elements appear in the root parent element; it just takes an extremely twisted declaration, and results in markup that frequently isn't useful for very much. If a markup declaration becomes too complicated, it's usually a sign that it's time to break up the declaration and create some subelements. For example,

```
<!ELEMENT CRAZY((TITLE | ART)+, (HEADLINE | PARAGRAPH |
SUBHEAD | PICTURE | TABLE | POP-UP)*, CONCLUSION)>
```

The CRAZY element is perfectly legal. It begins with at least one of a TITLE element or an ART element. The next section, which is probably the body of the article, can include HEADLINE, PARAGRAPH, SUBHEAD, PICTURE, TABLE, and POP-UP elements in any sequence and any order. After that mess is complete, a CONCLUSION element must appear to finish the article. This declaration might be better broken up into multiple elements with more structure:

```
<!ELEMENT CRAZY (HEADER, ARTICLE+,CONCLUSION)>
<!ELEMENT HEADER (TITLE?, ART?)>
<!ELEMENT ARTICLE (HEADLINE, CONTENT)>
<!ELEMENT CONTENT (PARAGRAPH | SUBHEAD | PICTURE | TABLE
| POP-UP)*>
<!ELEMENT CONCLUSION (#PCDATA)>
```

The CONTENT element can stay mixed up because every article is bound to vary, but the rest of the document receives considerably more structure.

Mixed-content declarations are the final option. Technically, the (#PCDATA) content used in most of the examples in this chapter is a mixed-content declaration all by itself. Mixed-content declarations can enable multiple elements to appear as child elements without requiring them to appear or making any specific demands on the sequence in which they appear. The simplest mixed-content declaration is one of the most frequent: declaring content to be PCDATA so that text and entities (but no other elements) may appear:

```
<!ELEMENT ORDINARY (#PCDATA)>
```

The ORDINARY element can now contain text or entity markup in any combination. XML offers only PCDATA for elements that need to contain text (and not only other elements). Consequently, this basic declaration will be used for nearly any leaf element. (Leaf elements have parent elements but no child elements; figuratively, they're the branches farthest out on the tree, where the action actually takes place.) In some situations, however, developers may want to allow other elements to appear in a leaf element. Not all leaf data are appropriate to every element. An ingredient, for instance, shouldn't contain a table of contents, but it might contain a note. The declaration creating an element that could hold an ingredient description and/or a note would look like:

```
<!ELEMENT INGREDIENT (#PCDATA | NOTE)*>
```

This declaration would permit INGREDIENT elements to contain the textual information they need to present ingredients, as well as NOTE elements to explain ingredients that are strange or difficult to find.

DTDs that include a significant set of child elements that can be used in multiple parent elements can be simplified with parameter entities listing the elements. The parser should parse the parameter entity and add its markup to the element content declaration.

```
<!ENTITY % parts "prologue | detail | moral | punchline |
joke">
<!ELEMENT STORY (#PCDATA | %parts;)*>
<!ELEMENT TALE (#PCDATA | %parts;)*>
<!ELEMENT FABLE (#PCDATA | %parts;)*>
```

In this case, STORY, TALE, and FABLE elements can contain text and any of the PROLOGUE, DETAIL, MORAL, PUNCH-LINE, or JOKE elements. These subelements may appear in any order and any number may appear. All other elements are prohibited from appearing in a STORY, TALE, or FABLE element.

The parameter entity could also include the parentheses and the #PCDATA declaration. Each approach has its advantages in different situations.

Attributes

Attributes have provided much of HTML's power, but they will probably be used somewhat more sparingly in XML. Attributes are most useful for storing information holding more interest to computers than to humans. Even in HTML, attributes held critical formatting information for the browser, not information about the contents of the element. Attributes remain a key part of XML, however, offering flexibility beyond that of elements, and solidifying underlying structures. Attribute declarations use some syntax similar to element declarations but tend to offer more precise definitions of the content they allow.

Attributes are defined using the following syntax:

```
<!ATTLIST ElementName
    AttributeName Type Default
    (AttributeName Type Default...)>
```

The first value in an attribute declaration is the name of the element to which the attributes apply. Although it makes a DTD more readable to include the attribute declaration right after the element declaration, this is not required. In fact, there can be multiple attribute declarations for the same element; all declarations for that element will be combined into one large set. If the same attribute is declared multiple times in that set, only the first appearance will be used. This makes it easy to extend existing DTDs without having to change them drastically.

After the element is named, an attribute definition or a list of attribute definitions may follow. A definition consists of the name of an attribute, its type, and its default value (or a specification for that value). Names of attributes must obey the same rules as names for entities and elements: they must contain only letters, digits, periods, dashes, underscores, and colons. Again, colons should be reserved for use with namespaces, a new aspect of XML that is described in its own section below. Attribute types are quite unlike the structures explored so far and define the kinds of data permitted in an attribute when used in an element instance. (An element instance is just a use of the element in the document.) Table 5-3 lists all the acceptable values for attribute types.

Table 5-3 *Attribute Types*

Type	Explanation
CDATA	The attribute may contain only character data.
ID	The value of the attribute must be unique, identifying the element. If two attributes within a document of type ID have the same value, the parser should return an error. (Note that attributes of type ID may not have default values or fixed values.)
IDREF	The value of the attribute must refer to an ID value declared elsewhere in the document. If the value of the attribute doesn't match an ID value within the document, the parser should return an error.
ENTITY, ENTITIES	The value of an ENTITY attribute must correspond to the name of an external unparsed entity declared in a DTD. An ENTITIES attribute is similar but allows multiple entity names separated by whitespace.
NMTOKEN, NMTOKENS	The value of the attribute must be a name token much like CDATA, but the characters used in the value must be letters, digits, periods, dashes, underscores, or colons. NMTOKENS is similar but allows multiple values separated by whitespace.
NOTATION	The value of the attribute must refer to the name of a notation declared elsewhere in the DTD.
Enumerated, e.g. (thisone | thatone)	The value of the attribute must match one of the values listed. Values must appear in parentheses and separated by OR (|) symbols.
NOTATION (enumerated)	The value of the attribute must match the name of one of the NOTATION names listed. For example, an attribute with type NOTATION (picture | slide) would need to have a value of "picture" or "slide," and NOTATION declarations would need to exist for both picture and slide.

Most of the time, developers will need to use CDATA, ID, and enumerated types, although the other possibilities are available. The last necessary part of an attribute declaration is the default. The default may take one of the four values listed in Table 5.4.

Table 5-4 *Attribute Defaults*

Value	Explanation
#REQUIRED	Indicates to the parser that this attribute must have a value in all instances of the element. Failure to include the attribute will result in parsing errors.
#IMPLIED	Allows the parser to ignore this attribute if no value is specified. The XML working draft states: "The XML processor must inform the application that no value was specified; no constraint is placed on the behavior of the application."
#FIXED *value*	Announces that element instances that specify that a value for this attribute must specify the listed *value*. If an element instance doesn't include this attribute, its value will be presumed to be the value specified.
defaultvalue	Provides a default value for the attribute. If the attribute is not declared explicitly in an element instance, the attribute will be assumed to have a value of *defaultvalue*.

Now that we have explanations of all these parts, it's time to see what they do. Attributes of type ID are becoming more and more common as scripting tools and other processors have scrambled to find a way to address elements individually in documents. Making these systems work effectively, however, usually requires that all elements (or at least the elements to be manipulated) have an ID value, usually listed in the id attribute. Declaring a required ID value for an element takes little effort:

```
<!ELEMENT DATABRICK (#PCDATA)>
<!ATTLIST DATABRICK
       id   ID   #REQUIRED>
```

All DATABRICK elements created in documents resulting from this DTD will be required to have unique values for their id attribute. Other attributes might enable a processing application to treat DATABRICK elements differently, based on their type.

Defining a list of possible types will make it much easier for a processing application to run smoothly.

```
<!ELEMENT DATABRICK (#PCDATA)>
<!ATTLIST DATABRICK
     id   ID   #REQUIRED
     status   (proceeding | accepted | rejected
|deferred) "proceeding">
```

DATABRICK elements now have a status attribute that informs the processing application of their status. If an element is created that doesn't specify a value for this attribute, the DATABRICK is assumed to be "proceeding" along a path of eventual acceptance, rejection, or deferral to a later date. A document management system or a database could use this attribute to limit their activities to DATABRICK elements whose status is appropriate to their work.

In cases where an attribute's presence isn't critical to proper processing, implied default values are acceptable. An application that translates documents from one DTD to another might use a comments field of some kind to keep track of the activities it has performed on the document. Only documents that had been through this process would need such a comment; documents that had been created directly in the target DTD might have no such need. To create this comment attribute, you could use the following declaration:

```
<!ELEMENT MASTERPIECE (#PCDATA)>
<!ATTLIST MASTERPIECE
     TranslationNote   CDATA   #IMPLIED>
```

This might be adequate for many situations. It might be better, however, to supply a default value instead of leaving the parser to report no value.

```
<!ELEMENT MASTERPIECE (#PCDATA)>
<!ATTLIST MASTERPIECE
     TranslationNote   CDATA   "None">
```

"None" is a slightly stronger affirmation that no translation was done, than is a notice that the attribute contained no value. It is easier to check for in a program and relieves the programmer of wondering whether the parser had a problem or there really was no value.

Fixed attribute types are somewhat unusual. They might be useful in situations where documents are fed into processors that use attributes for formatting to ensure that the results of processing all the documents created with this DTD will look similar. By specifying a fixed attribute value, a particular DTD can make certain to preserve its identity in collections of documents that use similar DTDs.

```
<!ELEMENT ARTICLE (#PCDATA)>
<!ATTLIST ARTICLE
    FormatModel    CDATA    #FIXED "Contemporary">
```

Another DTD file uses a similar declaration, but with a different fixed value:

```
<!ELEMENT ARTICLE (#PCDATA)>
<!ATTLIST ARTICLE
    FormatModel    CDATA    #FIXED "Country">
```

A processing application could take note of the FormatModel attribute and choose a set of styles appropriate to that model. It could also use the information to sort the documents in a library, enabling browsers to choose only articles that fit their design mood of the moment.

Attribute values that refer to external data sources can also be useful for processing. Although the parser itself will do nothing with the information (except pass it along), a processing application can combine that information with the markup material to create, for example, a document with pictures:

```
<!NOTATION ourFormat1SYSTEM
"http://www.simonstl.com/ourViewer.exe">
<!NOTATION ourFormat2 SYSTEM
"http://www.simonstl.com/pictures/ourPlayer.exe">
<!ELEMENT DOCUMENT (#PCDATA | PICTURE)*>
<!ELEMENT PICTURE empty>
<!ATTLIST PICTURE
     TYPE     NOTATION (ourFormat1 | ourFormat2)
"ourFormat1"
     IMAGE CDATA #IMPLIED>
```

In this case, the editor of a set of documents has decreed that all pictures must be in one of two formats. The XML document that used this DTD might look like the following:

```
<DOCUMENT>I hate my boss. He makes me use this picture
all the time:
<PICTURE TYPE="ourFormat2" IMAGE="FROGS.fm2"/>
Sometimes he lets me use this image:
<PICTURE TYPE="ourFormat1" IMAGE="BIRDS.fm1"/>
But I hate it more, so I usually stick with the frogs.
</DOCUMENT>
```

The XML Recommendation also provides two predefined attributes that assist with XML processing and help solve some of the ambiguities that remain in XML processing. The first, xml:space, helps applications determine whether or not they should pay attention to whitespace. The second, xml:lang, is designed to make it easier to present documents with content in multiple languages, supplementing Unicode's ability to present documents in different character sets. It will help significantly with presentation (some languages use different glyphs for the same character), and potentially with translation.

xml:space

Section 2.10 of the XML Recommendation defines a new attribute that allows elements to declare to an application whether their whitespace is "significant". This will probably receive extensive use in combination with XSL or perhaps the CSS whitespace property to display documents correctly, and may also have an impact in processing documents that aren't necessarily meant for display. Validating processors already must pass all non-markup characters to the application, and inform them of the element in which they appeared. This attribute acts as a flag, telling the application whether or not it should pay attention to whitespace characters.

Note

It remains up to the application whether it actually does anything with the whitespace characters. While I expect that browsers and some other XML display applications will take heed of xml:space, many other applications will find it irrelevant.

The xml:space attribute is declared as follows: (Note that this attribute still must be declared if used in documents that will be validated.)

```
<!ATTLIST element xml:space (default|preserve) 'default'>
```

The xml:space behavior is inherited from parent elements; if an element containing an xml:space value contains other elements, they too will handle whitespace as specified by the parent element. This can be overridden by a new xml:space atrribute in the child elements.

Because a default can be set in the DTD, it's simple to create documents that pay attention to whitespace by default; just set the default value of the xml:space for the root element to "preserve". For more consistent results (remember, parts of your XML document may be returned through XML-Link), assign this as the default value to all of your element types.

xml:lang

The xml:lang attribute gives XML authors a consistent way to identify the language contained within a particular element. Combined
with XML's support for Unicode, this should make it easier to present internationalized versions of information. Developers can create documents with built-in translations, or make it easier for
applications to know when to provide a translation. For example,
suppose someone was trying to present quotes in Latin, with an
English description:

```
<SECTION>
<DESCRIPTION xml:lang="en">
Caesar begins by describing the geography of Gaul.
</DESCRIPTION>
<QUOTE xml:lang="la">
Gallia est omnis divisa in partes tres, quarum unam
incolunt Belgae, aliam Aquitani, tertiam qui ipsorum
lingua Celtae, nostra Galli appellantur.
</QUOTE>
<EXPLANATION xml:lang="en">
It isn't the most thrilling opening to a great work on
war, but it does explain some key issues to Romans who
probably have never been anywhere near Rome.
</EXPLANATION></SECTION>
```

In this case, I used "en" to indicate English and "la" to indicate
Latin. An application equipped with a Latin translator might be
able to convert the Latin section, when prompted (or not), into
something resembling:

```
All of Gaul is divided into three parts, one of which is
inhabited by the Belgae, another by the Aquitani, and the
third by those who are called Celts in their own
language, and Gauls in ours.
```

A translation program would probably produce something more literal, but you get the idea. The xml:lang attribute works much like the xml:space attribute, applying to the content of child elements as well as the element in which it is actually used. If xml:lang is used in a valid document, it must be declared. (This declaration is useful for declaring default languages as well.) The following declaration syntax will create an attribute without a default value:

```
<!ATTLIST element xml:lang NMTOKEN #IMPLIED>
```

To create a QUOTE element, with a default language of English, the following declaration would be appropriate:

```
<!ATTLIST QUOTE xml:lang NMTOKEN 'en'>
```

This could still be overridden for use with Latin, French, German, or quotes in any other language with a code defined in ISO 639 or registered with the Internet Assigned Numbers Authority (IANA). ISO 639 codes can be used directly, and may be followed with a country code to more precisely define the language: "en-GB", for instance, as opposed to "en-US". IANA codes must be prefixed with i- or I-; other codes may also be used, but must be prefixed with x- or X-. Unlike most of the rest of XML, all of these codes are not case-sensitive. (This is explained in greater detail in IETF RFC 1766.)

The xml:lang attribute provides more information than the bare Unicode data, and may save applications a lot of time determining which language is used for a particular element. It isn't a cure-all, though; effective use of this element will require consistent application support and probably some fairly complex style usage. The browser developers will hopefully seize on this opportunity to sort out some of the language confusions currently pervading the web. Combined with Unicode, this attribute makes it possible to deliver on many of XML's key promises for easier internationalization.

Namespaces

Namespaces arrived after the XML 1.0 Recommendation was finalized, and have caused enormous uproar in a variety of forums.
Intended to avoid conflicts between identical tag names used in different organizations, namespaces have created new layers of potential complexity. Indeed, namespaces, which in practice look quite
simple, have generated enormous debate over the responsibilities of
parsers and applications, the weaknesses of DTDs, the importance
of XML's compatibility with SGML, and distinctions between
markup and semantics. After over a year of discussion inside and
outside the W3C, a recommendation (`http://www.w3.org/TR/`
`REC-xml-names`) has emerged. Although namespaces aren't quite
here yet (and won't be used in the examples in the rest of this book),
developers setting out to build (or sometimes read) XML DTDs
need to be aware of what they do.

Namespaces preserve the uniqueness of names by using prefixes,
separated from the element name with a colon. (The simplest, or
default, namespace, has no prefix and uses no colon.) These prefixes
can then be resolved to Uniform Resource Identifiers (URIs), which
take advantage of the naming infrastructures (notably domain
names) already available on the Web. This resolution avoids the
need to set up a new registry for XML namespaces prefixes, and also
enables the default namespace to resolve to a meaningful value,
avoiding the need to type many prefixes into documents that use (or
are dominated by) a single namespace. Before we take a look at how
namespaces are declared, let's examine some elements in a document that uses namespaces. The URI for the ssl namespace is
`http://www.simonstl.com/default;` the URI for the default
namespace is `http://www.w3.org/TR/REC-html40`. (There
doesn't actually need to be anything at the URI location; what matters is that the URI uniquely identifies the namespace.)

```
<HTML>
<BODY>
```

```
<P>This is a paragraph in a document that uses the HTML
namespace as a default, but which contains
<ssl:hedge>some</ssl:hedge> elements from
<ssl:adjective>another</ssl:adjective>
<ssl:noun>namespace</ssl:noun> as well.</P>
</BODY>
</HTML>
```

The application should be told (or capable of figuring out — it's not clear yet) that the HTML, BODY, and P elements belong to the namespace identified as `http://www.w3.org/ TR/REC-html40,` while the ssl:hedge, ssl:adjective, and ssl:noun elements belong to the namespace identified as `http://www.simonstl. com/default.` The application should receive qualified names from the processor, in which the prefix is removed and the element (or attribute) name is delivered as a pair — the namespace identifier and the element name. In the event that two organizations chose to use the same prefix, the prefix could be changed — only the URI behind the prefix should matter to the application. At this point, in a perfect world, only the declaration for the namespace would need to be changed.

Namespaces are declared using attributes that begin with xmlns'. (Remember, attributes and elements that aren't originally created by the W3C can't start with xml, so this is a safe name to use.) These attributes may be declared in the DTD, and use default values to ease things along, or they may be declared explicitly in the document. (See the last paragraph of this section for warnings about namespaces and validation, however.) The declarations behave a little bit strangely, somewhat like the inheritance effect exhibited by xml:lang and xml:whitespace, but because the name of the declaration can vary, it's a bit more complex. The mechanism is fairly simple. If an element contains an attribute that begins with xmlns, that attribute defines a namespace for both the element itself and any child elements, unless overridden by a new definition in one of the child elements. In this case, the new definition holds for that elements and all of its child elements. If the attribute name is simply xmlns', it defines the default namespace, which applies to all elements that don't have a colon in their name. If the attribute name is xmlns:*prefix*, then the attribute defines a namespace for all elements that begin with *prefix:*. The namespace URI is defined in either case as the value of the attribute. For example:

```
<DOCUMENT xmlns="http://www.simonstl.com/"
xmlns:HTML="http:// www.w3.org/TR/REC-html40">
<HEADER>This is <HTML:I>my</HTML:I> header.</HEADER>
<CONTENT>
<P xmlns="http://www.w3.org/TR/REC-html40">This is a
paragraph filled with <B>HTML</B> elements, so I figured
it was <I>better</I> to set the default namespace to
<EM>HTML.</EM></P>
<PAR>This is a paragraph in the http://www.simonstl.com
namespace, again.</PAR>
</CONTENT></DOCUMENT>
```

The elements in this document set are in the namespaces listed in Table 5-5.

Table 5-5 *Namespace Results, Listed in Sequence*

Prefix	Element Name	Element is in Namespace	Sets Namespace
Default	DOCUMENT	http://www.simonstl.com HTML: http://www.w3.org/TR/REC-html40	default: http://www.simonstl.com
Default	HEADER	http://www.simonstl.com	
HTML	I	http://www.w3.org/TR/REC-html40	
Default	CONTENT	http://www.simonstl.com	
Default	P	http://www.w3.org/TR/REC-html40	default: http://www.w3.org/TR/REC-html40
default	B	http://www.w3.org/TR/REC-html40	
default	I	http://www.w3.org/TR/REC-html40	
default	EM	http://www.w3.org/TR/REC-html40	
default	PAR	http://www.simonstl.com	doesn't set, but reverts to parent element (CONTENT)'s default namespace.

This mechanism provides a lot of flexibility, and can accommodate many different namespaces. In well-formed documents, adding a namespace is as easy as adding an attribute; in valid documents, it requires creating an attribute with a name appropriate to the prefix to be used. This mechanism makes it easy to mix and match namespaces within a document, and can support unlimited (until your parser or application breaks) numbers of namespaces without conflict.

The problems with namespaces arise primarily from the fact that the parsing software already developed for XML 1.0 (and SGML) doesn't provide support for changing prefixes or reporting namespaces. In a namespace-enabled world, prefixes are only abbreviations for the namespace, changeable and ephemeral creatures. In the current world of validation with DTD's, changing prefixes means changing the element name, which means that the document isn't valid — period. The impact of namespaces on validation hasn't yet been explored completely, but their use will probably mean a serious break with the installed base of SGML software and a significant break with software built for XML 1.0. Some parsers are already being updated to handle this situation, but addressing these issues directly may require significant revisions to the XML Recommendation itself, probably in another version. But for now, namespaces hold a lot of promise.

Data Structures and Types

Now that we have document structures, we must look at the data contained in those structures. As HTML developers discovered when they tried to convert old files to HTML, the use of characters like <, >, and & for markup creates significant problems. A site I once converted from a Macintosh HyperCard stack, for example, worked very well except for the page on AT&T, which had missing characters throughout. XML applies a few SGML solutions to HTML's problems, adding some apparent complexity but solving the problems much more thoroughly.

Although XML has simplified SGML's data types considerably, we need to consider a number of issues that never cropped up in HTML. XML can have two types of data in documents: #PCDATA, or parsed character data, which is ordinary marked-up character data, and CDATA, which is character data without any markup. CDATA is useful for situations in which a document contains no markup and many <, >, and & symbols. By default, XML assumes that all information is PCDATA. CDATA can also appear in documents, in sections marked as pure character data. To declare a section as CDATA, mark its beginning with <![CDATA[and its end with]]>. (This will fail if the data includes any]]> sequences, which would be a highly unusual occurrence.) For example, the CDATA section in:

```
<?xml version="1.0" encoding="UTF-8"?>
<DOCUMENT><![CDATA[@#X! <<<<  >> & <<<<<
>>>]]></DOCUMENT>
```

will be interpreted as the characters "@#X! <<<< >> & <<<<< >>>" and will not generate a parsing error. When queried for the text in this document, a parser will return the information contained in the CDATA section:

```
@#X! <<<<  >> & <<<<< >>>
```

If this text wasn't "escaped" with the CDATA declaration, parsers would stop at the first < sign because it appears to open a tag with no proper closing. Even though using CDATA prohibits developers from using markup in a section of text, the tradeoff may be worth it if the section doesn't require markup anyway. If it needs markup, replace the offending characters with their entity equivalents, as discussed later in the chapter.

Note

The use of CDATA to escape text is actually a specific example of a more general SGML technique – marked sections. Marked sections follow a <![*keyword*[*data*...]]> syntax. Even though developers may use this syntax for CDATA, the SGML RCDATA, TEMP, IGNORE, and INCLUDE keywords are not available in XML documents. IGNORE and INCLUDE marked sections, are, however, available within DTDs and will be covered later in this chapter.

One missing feature, which many developers have complained about, is that XML doesn't have any way to require that elements contain more specific types of data, like text or numbers or currency. Several proposals for this "stronger typing" are under development.

The W3C is currently examining this issue in the context of schemas (described further in Chapter 13), which may provide considerably more functionality than DTDs. In the meantime, any such enforcement of data types will be the responsibility of the processing application, not the XML parser.

Entities

XML offers two kinds of entities — general entities and parameter entities. HTML developers will be familiar with using predefined general entities for encoding unusual characters and characters used for markup (the infamous <, >, and &). Although defined in DTDs, general entities are used to add information to documents, substituting their value for the entity reference, which takes the form &name;. Parameter entities are defined and used only in external DTDs. They can save developers typing, as do general entities, but they can also give developers tremendous power to include other DTDs and other information in their DTD. Parameter entities enable developers to reuse and subset older DTDs, avoiding the perpetual reinvention of the wheel and making the expansion of previously existing DTDs easier.

General Entities

General entities are used throughout HTML to provide representations of characters that are either outside the basic ASCII character set or interfere with markup. XML has fewer problems with this for several reasons. The character encodings already described will enable developers to include characters from other languages and writing systems more directly, easing the need for those kinds of character-representation entities. The option to "escape" characters with CDATA sections also makes it easier to include the characters that interfere with markup, especially for large chunks. Still, CDATA is somewhat clunky for regular use. XML includes a few built-in entities, although not nearly as many as HTML. XML's five built-in entities are listed in Table 5-6.

Table 5-6 *Entities Built into the XML Standard*

Entity	Character Represented
&amp;	ampersand (&)
&lt;	less-than sign (<)
&gt;	greater-than sign (>)
&apos;	apostrophe (')
&quote	quote (")

Even though these entities are certainly useful and help developers keep their content out of the way of markup, they offer only the tiniest taste of the powerful things XML can do with general entities. Developers can define entities just as they can define elements. General entities are simple and make many complex and annoying tasks very simple, especially when it comes to filling in boilerplate text. The syntax for defining a general entity is fairly simple:

```
<!ENTITY Name EntityDefinition>
```

The name of the entity must be composed of letters, digits, periods, dashes, underscores, or colons, and begin with a letter or an underscore. (The use of colons is discouraged because of namespace, described previously.) The entity definition may contain any valid markup and must be enclosed in quotes. The syntax for using an entity in the markup is also simple:

```
&Name;
```

The ampersand must appear at the start, and the semicolon must be at the end. No additional whitespace is permitted around or inside the entity.

Creating entities this way is useful for repetitive information that is prone to change during the lifetime of the document. For example, during the development of a manual for the first version of a product, the developers may not even know the name of the product. Rather than introducing possible errors by doing a search-and-replace when the product is finalized, the developers can use an entity reference to make sure that the product is referred to correctly. For example, the code name of a project might be "Crystal". In the prerelease version of the documentation, developers could create the following entity reference:

```
<!ENTITY ProdName "Crystal">
```

Whenever the product was referred to, they would then use an entity reference rather than the actual name of the product;

```
&ProdName; is a remarkable advance, guaranteeing users
happier days.
```

would be interpreted as

```
Crystal is a remarkable advance, guaranteeing users
happier days.
```

When the final product name was finalized, transforming Crystal into RF-2000-QJ-46, the developer could just change the entity reference:

```
<!ENTITY ProdName="RF-2000-QJ-46">
```

This text would then be interpreted as

```
RF-2000-QJ-46 is a remarkable advance, guaranteeing users
happier days.
```

It sounds a bit stilted, but determined developers could even create entities that address different grammatical positions (possessive, for example), if they needed to go that far. Entities are extremely useful for legal contracts and other such documents that are mostly boilerplate text. A simple contract where the only parts that change are the name of one of the parties and the amount of money involved could be written as

```
<CONTRACT>&boilerplate1; <PAYMENT>$100,000.00
(US)</PAYMENT>&boilerplate2;<RECIPIENT>Lucky
Author</RECIPIENT></CONTRACT>
```

Most contracts are open to more change than this form would allow, but many contracts can be broken down into standard clauses, enabling the regular use of entities.

Nevertheless, the main use of general entities is still for presenting characters that aren't in the usual (normally ASCII) set. Character references enable developers to include characters that aren't easily inputted or that might not be understood consistently. For example,

```
<!ENTITY THORN "&#222;" >
```

when used on systems using Latin-1 or Unicode encoding, will produce an Icelandic Thorn, a character not frequently seen on American keyboards. The built-in ampersand entity is declared as

```
<!ENTITY amp "&#38;">
```

Although developers could use these codes directly in XML without going to the trouble of creating an entity declaration, naming these characters tends to produce a much cleaner document. ISO 8879 (SGML) includes a full set of standard named entities used in SGML. The SGML markup uses codes, however, which most early XML parsers probably won't be able to process. A large set of entity DTDs written for XML is available at `http://www.schema.net/entities/` and includes a wide variety of different characters and marks. You can either examine the code and add the parts you need to your own DTD or use parameter entities (described later in this chapter) to include the entire entity DTD in your own DTD.

Note

Entities have their own quirks. It is permissible to use markup inside of an entity, but using entities inside of entities takes some extra effort. The parser will examine the entity for markup when it is added to the document text, and errors in entity coding can produce mysterious parsing errors. Always test your entities before using them, and always make sure that the content of an entity is appropriate to its destination in the document.

One quirk in particular is worth additional mention. XML parsers interpret entities according to a strict set of rules, which tend to result in entities being parsed more than once. This can make it difficult to include entities within entities in certain situations. This situation comes about because some entities — all the parameter entities and character references — are parsed when the computer parses the DTD. When the entity is placed in the document, all entities are parsed. This situation is highly unusual (happening mostly when developers use the character reference equivalents for ampersands and less-than signs), but developers whose entities mysteriously wreak havoc on their documents should parse their entities separately and inspect their results.

Not all entities refer to XML data. "Unparsed" entities must refer to information in files stored outside of the XML document itself. In the SGML world, unparsed entities are used to connect images and other files to SGML documents in a more formal way than HTML's <IMG SRC="*filename*"> approach. Entities that refer to binary (nontextual) data are required to be external (i.e., they must use SYSTEM or PUBLIC identifiers), and to use the NDATA keyword after the entity definition to specify the entity's data type with a notation identifier. An external binary entity referring to a GIF file, for example, should conclude with NDATA gif. External unparsed entities may not appear directly in XML documents using the &name; syntax. Instead, the name of the entity should appear in an attribute that has been declared to be of type ENTITY or ENTITIES. The application can then decide what to do with the information in the external unparsed entity.

Note

External unparsed entities were left in the specification to accommodate legacy SGML documents. The "SGML way" of including binary data requires many more steps than the "HTML way;'" which relies on the server (and file extensions) to identify content types. Many XML users will never need to declare these entities or support this kind of processing – it depends on what style the applications they use demand.

Parameter Entities

The parameter entity, the other kind of entity, is for use only within DTDs. Parameter entities carry information for use in the markup declaration, often a set of common attributes shared by several elements or a link to an outside DTD. Parameter entities whose references are purely within the DTD are known as internal entities, whereas references that draw information from outside files are external entities. Even though parameter entities may considerably simplify the creation of a DTD, they should be used with caution. Entities by their nature require a lookup to determine their contents. This isn't too difficult for computers, but it can become extremely complex for unfortunate humans who have to sort out obfuscated XML.

Parameter entries use a percent sign (%) both in their references and in their declaration. The percent sign differentiates a general entity from a parameter entity. The syntax for a parameter entity declaration is:

```
<!ENTITY % Name EntityDefinition>
```

The space between the percent sign and the name of the entity is mandatory. As was true for general entities, the name of the entity must be composed of letters, digits, periods, dashes, underscores, or colons and begin with a letter or an underscore. The entity definition may contain any valid markup and must be enclosed in quotes. The value of the entity definition must resolve to something that makes sense in the context in which the entity will be used; otherwise, the parser will fail to understand the DTD and will return errors.

Internal parameter entities behave much like general entities, but operate in the DTD rather than the document content. For example, a DTD for a document set that contained a variety of quoted materials might use a common set of attributes for all the different kinds of materials — letters, diaries, novels, poems, and quotations.

To make the documents more readily searchable, all of these elements need to have attributes that identify the language in which they are written and a copyright date to determine whether or not they remain in copyright. An entity declaration that provides these attributes might look like the following:

```
<!ENTITY % sourceinfo
"LANGUAGE CDATA #REQUIRED
COPYRIGHTDATE CDATA #REQUIRED">
```

Using that entity in a declaration only requires calling it with the %*name*; syntax:

```
<!ELEMENT LETTER (#PCDATA)>
<!ATTLIST LETTER %sourceinfo;>
<!ELEMENT QUOTATION (#PCDATA)>
<!ATTLIST QUOTATION %sourceinfo;>
```

(There is no space between the percent sign and the entity name when the entity is used; the space is used only when the entity name is declared.) The language and copyright date information will flow right into the QUOTATION and LETTER attribute declarations. When the parser encounters the %sourceinfo; notation, it will expand the entity to include the full value announced elsewhere in the DTD. QUOTATION and LETTER and any other elements that use the contents of the sourceinfo entity will require attributes indicating language and copyright date. This becomes more useful as the number of repetitive elements and the length of the attributes list grow.

Caution

The XML 1.0 Recommendation places a somewhat tricky restriction on the use of parameter entities in the internal subset (that is, the DTD information declared directly in a document). Parameter entities that are used in the internal subset may only contain complete declarations, not the partial declarations used above. This places severe restrictions on the flexibility of parameter entities in the internal subset, and is yet another good reason to keep your DTDs in external files.

External entities let developers link to materials entirely outside of their documents or their DTD and use the same syntax as the document type declaration described previously for linking to outside files. Entity values must use SYSTEM identifiers and may also use PUBLIC identifiers when appropriate. Most XML developers will probably find themselves linking to external documents using SYSTEM identifiers unless document management systems become used enough for most document users to have access.

The contents of the files linked to by external entities are required only to make sense in the context in which they are used. Generally, they will consist of declarations or parts of declarations, although under certain circumstances they may also contain binary data, like GIF files. Parameter entities are frequently used to combine several DTD subsets or to include large lists of general entities. The files referred to by external entities may also include other external entities. Parsers will return an error if these references are circular — if document A refers to document B, which refers to document C, which refers to document A again, the parser will stop. External entities may resemble trees with many branches, but those branches are not allowed to grow back into the trunk. Too many branches, of course, will produce incredibly unwieldy DTDs, which are nearly impossible to understand.

Our example for external entities will simply combine two lists of general entities for use in a single DTD. (The use of parameter entities to nest more complex DTDs will be covered in later chapters.)

It is always a good idea to include comments with external entity declarations — the URLs in SYSTEM identifiers and even the more complete information in PUBLIC identifiers are often cryptic. Our first entity file, companies.dtd, includes the following:

```
<!ENTITY GLW "Corning Incorporated">
<!ENTITY IBM "International Business Machines">
<!ENTITY T "American Telephone and Telegraph">
```

Our second file, states.dtd, includes the following:

```
<!ENTITY NC "North Carolina">
<!ENTITY ND "North Dakota">
<!ENTITY NJ "New Jersey">
<!ENTITY NM "New Mexico">
<!ENTITY NY "New York">
```

Our DTD, although simple, is also stored in an external file:

```
<!-The following entity connects to a list of companies
using stock ticker symbols as entity references. ->
<!ENTITY % companies SYSTEM "companies.dtd">
<!-The following entity connects to a list of states
using postal abbreviations as entity references. ->
<!ENTITY % states SYSTEM "states.dtd">
<!ELEMENT DOCUMENT (#PCDATA)>
%companies;
%states;
```

The sample XML file that uses these references reads as:

```
<?xml version="1.0" encoding="UTF-8"?>
<!DOCTYPE DOCUMENT SYSTEM "penex.dtd">
<DOCUMENT>The company &GLW; is headquartered in &NY;, as
is &IBM;. &T; is headquartered in &NJ;.</DOCUMENT>
```

Parsing this should yield the results shown in Figure 5-9:

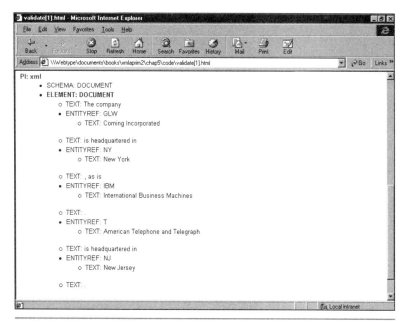

Figure 5-9 *Internet Explorer 5.0 will resolve general entities referenced by parameter entities.*

As we'll see in later chapters, parameter entities can be a very useful tool for simplifying complex markup and managing multiple DTDs.

Notation Declarations

Notation declarations are an announcement that data from an outside (nonXML) source is needed in the document and notifies the application that nonXML data may need to be processed. Notation declarations must be used with external unparsed entities to identify the type of information represented by the entity, are sometimes used as an attribute value, and are sometimes used in combination with processing instructions to provide a means of handling nontextual information within a document. The notation declaration tells the processor what kind of information there is; the processing instruction announces what process should be used to handle it. Notation names can also be used as attribute values.

The syntax for notation declarations is similar to the document type declaration:

```
<!NOTATION Name ExternalID>
```

The name of the notation must be composed of letters, digits, periods, dashes, underscores, or colon, and begin with a letter or an underscore. (The use of colons is discouraged because of namespaces, described previously.) A typical notation declaration might read:

```
<!NOTATION gif SYSTEM "image/gif">
```

The parser does nothing to check the information at the External ID; it just passes the information on to the processing application. If the processing application can handle the information, that's wonderful. If it can't, it doesn't matter to the parser. The SYSTEM keyword may be followed by a reference to an application that can present the data, but the processing application is definitely not required to use that application. (If a Macintosh or UNIX user was reading this file, a Windows executable wouldn't help them much anyway). More typically on the Web, notation declarations will specify MIME content types. PUBLIC identifiers may also be used to identify notations, as they commonly are in the SGML world. Notations that the processing application cannot understand may be errors, but they aren't XML errors. The parser will continue its work without announcing an error. The application, of course, may announce its own errors.

Marked Sections in DTDs: IGNORE and INCLUDE

Developers who need to test different structures while keeping track of alternatives may want to use the IGNORE and INCLUDE marked sections in DTDs. IGNORE and INCLUDE let developers turn portions of a DTD on and off. IGNORE and INCLUDE are particularly useful for developers who are combining several DTDs and need to limit the side effects of multiple files colliding, or for developers who need to create a single core DTD with optional subsets. IGNORE and INCLUDE sections may be nested inside other IGNORE and INCLUDE sections, but like elements, their beginnings and ends may not overlap.

The syntax for IGNORE and INCLUDE resembles that of CDATA:

```
<![IGNORE[ declarations ]]>
<![INCLUDE[ declarations ]]>
```

Neither IGNORE nor INCLUDE may appear in the middle of a declaration; both must address a single declaration or a set of declarations. For example,

```
<![IGNORE[<!ELEMENT YUCK (#PCDATA)>]]>
<![INCLUDE[<!ELEMENT HOORAY (#PCDATA)>]]>
```

would keep the YUCK element from being parsed and would allow the HOORAY element to be parsed normally. Applied in this way, IGNORE seems like a handy way to edit out useless parts of a DTD, and INCLUDE seems to be just plain useless. Parameter entities give INCLUDE and IGNORE the power they need to be meaningful additions to the XML vocabulary. Instead of using INCLUDE and IGNORE directly to change code throughout a DTD, developers can use parameter entities to make all those changes in one place. This makes INCLUDE and IGNORE far more convenient and occasionally even necessary. The following example provides a simple demonstration:

```
<!ENTITY % invoice "IGNORE">
<!ENTITY % receipt "INCLUDE">
<![%invoice; [
<!ENTITY notice "Please remit the following payment
within thirty days.">]]>
<![%receipt; [
<!ENTITY notice "Thank you for your prompt payment. The
sums below have been collected and recorded.">]]>
<!ENTITY address "555 Twelvetwelve Lane">
```

Depending on the values assigned to invoice and receipt, the general entity notice will provide either the voice of a bill collector or a grateful vendor. To change the output, just switch the values of the two entities. The value of the address entity (probably that of the company), on the other hand, will be the same in either case. Similar markup could continue throughout the DTD, with parts inappropriate for receipts being deleted. Switching the DTD over to receipts would require editing only two lines of the file rather than demanding a search-and-replace of the entire document. In the next chapters, we'll explore more uses of this limited but powerful tool.

Note

In SGML, IGNORE, and INCLUDE also work in documents, but XML has banished them to the DTD.

Putting It All Together: Documents, Parsers, and Various Quirks

Although the syntax may seem a little strange, and a few pieces (like data types) are missing, XML DTD syntax isn't really that hard to understand. Unfortunately, there are a few complications lurking under the surface of XML, some of which have potential to cause serious aggravation. The distinctions between well-formedness and validity are one of the largest danger zones, made even uglier by the provision of a few exemptions for non-validating parsers. Although simple well-formed documents, in the sense described in Chapter 3, will work in most situations, many well-formed documents take advantage of some of the tools described in this chapter as well. Not all of those tools are required to be available in parsers that only check well-formedness, making it possible for variations to creep into the way an XML document is interpreted.

The basic problem comes from a separation between documents and the parsers (processors in the spec) interpreting them. Parsers may be validating or non-validating. Validating parsers check to make certain that documents are valid, while non-validating parsers only check that they are well-formed. Non-validating parsers do, however, read the DTD information, and assign default values for attributes and expand entities based on the information in the DTD. For this reason alone, it's often useful to create a DTD even for documents you don't plan to validate. It's also a good idea to make sure that any DTDs you use for documents actually provide the full structure needed for validation, even if you're just trying to get default values for attributes.

Documents may conform to sets of rules that make them valid, well-formed, or none of the above. While it would have been nice for validation to be a simple superset of well-formedness, thereby enabling all valid documents to be well-formed, it doesn't quite work out that way. All valid documents are technically well-formed, but non-validating parsers (i.e., parsers that check only for well-formedness) aren't required to load pieces (typically DTDs or entities) external to the document. As a result, a document that works under a validating parser may *not* work under a non-validating parser that doesn't load information referenced by a document. It may parse, but it may come up with missing information and errors that the parser is not required to report.

This opens up the potential for some fairly disastrous situations. Non-validating parsers vary in their behavior. Microstar's Aelfred will read external DTDs and apply the default values, while James Clark's Expat does not (it may optionally read external general entities). Since Expat is used in both Netscape's Mozilla open-source browser project, and the XML::Parser module for Perl, this is a likely possibility. Applications that depend heavily on default values for attributes might find those values missing when one of these non-validating parsers is used in place of a validating parser. This could happen for a number of reasons, including:

- A user changed the settings in their browser to a fast load mode

- A developer decided to change the parser used in an application (thanks to the SAX and DOM standards, it isn't that hard)

- Documents that were designed for use in one application now need to be reused in a different application

If you open your XML documents and find unexpanded entities ("What's this &sunset; in the middle of the paragraph?") or some functionality disappears (probably because of lost default values for attributes), you've encountered this problem. The means for avoiding it are reasonably clear, though not always workable. One way to avoid this issue is to include all DTD information in the internal subset. Putting every declaration into every file will ensure that even parsers that won't fetch external resources have a complete set of declarations on which to operate. This may require the creation of gateways that gather all declarations and pile them into the main file at key interfaces between applications that will use external resources and those that won't. (Developing tools that do this efficiently will probably take a fairly long time.) The W3C's XML Document Syntax Working Group is pondering a canonical XML format, in which all declarations are already expanded, as a means around this issue. An alternative, only available to those with total control over an environment (typically application developers that won't be using browsers as an interface), is to use external resources and simply accept that other tools will be incapable of using those files.

Cross-Reference

For an excellent summary of what non-validating parsers are required to do, see John Cowan's "Non-Validating XML Parsers: Requirements" list at `http://www.lists.ic. ac.uk/hypermail/xml-dev/9808/0019.html`. For more on Expat's behavior, see `http://www.jclark.com/xml/ expat.html`.

One last warning about XML parsers is in order: some parsers are more conformant to the W3C Recommendation than others. Some parsers, like Aelfred, have been built for maximum efficiency and minimum file size. As a result, it deliberately omitted some relatively obscure well-formedness checks. (This is subject to change — see the latest readme files at `http://www.microstar. com/aelfred` for details.) Aelfred may therefore accept some documents that stricter parsers will ignore. The situation also remains a bit murky for parsers that claim to be 100 percent compliant with the specification, as no complete or official test suite is yet available to verify conformance. OASIS (`http://www.oasis-open.org`), an SGML consortium, is at work on a test suite, but has not yet released it. So far, mixing parsers seems to be okay in most situations. The specification, though difficult to read, is fairly precise. If, however, you find an odd glitch or two, be sure to check your work using multiple parsers (or multiple applications that use different parsers) and notify the parser or application developers.

Now that we have the tools, it's time to start making them work. The next chapter will take all these strange parts and start applying them to real documents and practical situations.

Chapter 6

Re-creating Web and Paper Documents with XML

Now that we've covered all the parts involved, it's time to create some valid XML documents with reasonably complex DTDs. Despite the many parts involved, creating a DTD doesn't need to be painful. Developers converting documents from HTML or a word-processor style sheet often find that their document structures are actually simplified. This chapter will examine the production and implementation of two sample DTDs for document production, including DTD development, document coding, and style-sheet creation for browser viewing of the documents, as well as a wrapper DTD for working with legacy text content.

 Note

None of the examples in this chapter include links to other documents. Links in XML are considerably more sophisticated than those in HTML and will receive separate coverage in Chapters 10 and 11. For now, familiarize yourself with the syntax of XML DTDs and learn the structures that exist within a document rather than throughout a site.

To XML from HTML

Many organizations already store huge quantities of information in HTML. After spending hours to convert it to HTML from some other format, many of these information keepers probably aren't thrilled to heari about this great new development that promises to sweep away HTML (not to mention the rest of their document formats). However, most of the HTML information already created will probably never be formally converted to XML, and if it is, that conversion is likely to be automated. Because HTML files have often been developed to look a certain way, the appearance of finished HTML on the screen has taken precedence over the structure underlying the code. Developers on a deadline must have something to show the client; if broken code doesn't bother the browsers in which it's viewed, it isn't likely to bother the client. Add to that the fact that much HTML is coded by hand (or by tools that litter the page with extra markup), and the odds of HTML pages being close to well-formed XML drop precipitously.

HTML provides a set of structures that represent generic structures for documents, plus a set of tools for formatting these structures. HTML doesn't provide vocabulary for features specific to particular kinds of documents or data. For a time it seemed that HTML was losing its status as a vocabulary for describing structures and becoming a vocabulary for describing formatting. With the rise of style sheets and the W3C's return to prominence as the keeper of HTML specifications, HTML has returned to its roots describing structures, leaving (much) formatting to style sheets. Recent HTML standards have used SGML as their formal vocabulary, creating a description of "valid" HTML in SGML. The next revision of HTML, called XHTML, discussed in greater depth in Chapter 13, is converting HTML to a set of XML modules. If all that is needed are technically valid XML documents, it might be appropriate simply to convert from current forms to this XML-ized version of valid HTML. But remember that valid XML is not necessarily easily managed. Targeted vocabulary that reflects specific content rather than generic structure (or worse, presentation) is the main advantage of using XML as a file format, and using the HTML DTDs will not provide that.

Note

If you want to use some of the HTML elements in your documents, John Cowan's Itsy-Bitsy Teeny-Weeny Simple Hypertext (IBTWSH) DTD may be useful. It's available at `http://www.ccil.org/~cowan/XML/ibtwsh.dtd`. It, describes only a subset of HTML and keeps element names in uppercase.

For many Web documents, the conversion process will probably take place by hand, as it would with paper documents. Tools can "learn" the format of a set of pages and extract the needed content, but sets of HTML pages that aren't generated by machines rarely follow a format consistently. The text on one page may include five paragraphs, whereas another page may have no text at all. For example,

```
<HTML>
<HEAD><TITLE>Joe's Catalog - Money
Counters</TITLE></HEAD>
<BODY BGCOLOR="#FFFFFF">
<H1>Money Counting Equipment</H1>
<H2>Basic Money Counter</H2>
<H4>Count your cash without spending all of it!</H4>
Joe's is pleased to announce this NEW addition to our
line. People with piles of change can sort their money
easily, and wrap it for the bank. Makes the change box a
lot more useful!<BR>
Price:<B>$14.95</B>, <FONT SIZE=1>plus $4.95 shipping and
handling. </FONT><P>
```

```
Also available: Paper Coin Wrappers, bag of 100:
<B>$2.95</B><P>
<H2>Standard Money Counter</H2>
<H3>Count and collect your cash automatically!</H3>
This money counter wraps your change automatically—just
feed it the plastic change rolls. You'll feel just like
the bank when you read its LED display announcing how
much change you've gathered.<P>
Special guarantee: 100% accuracy on wrapping or your
money back!<BR>
Price:<B>$64.95</B>, <FONT SIZE=1>plus $7.95 shipping and
handling. </FONT><P>
Also available: Plastic Coin Wrappers, box of 400:
<B>$10.95</B><P>
<H2>Super-Duper Money Counter</H2>
Tired of change? This machine counts bills as well. Feed
it the take from a cash register and watch it count away.
Spits out old bills in a separate tray for easy counting.
Saves hours of effort spent counting pennies—and
twenties!<BR>
Price:<B>$649.95</B>, <FONT SIZE=1>plus $29.95 shipping
and handling.</FONT><P>
Uses plastic coin wrappers above, and Paper Bill
Wrappers, box of 1000: <B>$10.95</B><P>
</BODY></HTML>
```

This document, viewed in a browser, presents a simple catalog page of money counters, as shown below in Figure 6-1.

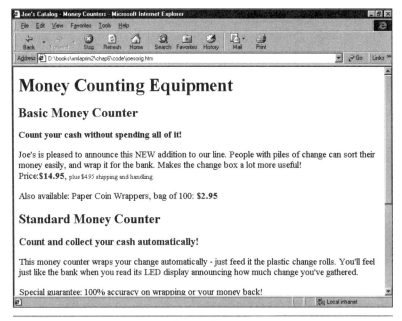

Figure 6-1 *The HTML version of Joe's Catalog*

Even though this document has some clear parts that could easily
be converted to a DTD, the style of coding isn't exactly conducive to
automatic conversion to XML. The text is littered with "extra guar-
antees" and "also availables" that neither appear consistently nor use
the same format. This looks like an old hand-coded HTML document, which uses the <P> tag at the end of a paragraph rather than
enclosing paragraphs in <P>...</P>. Although it might be possible
to write a program that converts this, Joe will probably be better off
either developing a DTD and having someone convert it by hand or
making it well-formed by adding closing tags.

A DTD for Joe's catalog that is based on its content rather than its presentation could read like the following:

```
<!ELEMENT CATALOGPAGE (HEADER,CATALOGITEM+)>
<!ELEMENT HEADER (#PCDATA)>
<!ELEMENT CATALOGITEM (ITEMNAME, ITEMSUBHEAD?,
ITEMDESCRIPTION*,ITEMPRICING,SUBITEM*)>
<!ELEMENT ITEMNAME (#PCDATA)>
<!ELEMENT ITEMSUBHEAD (#PCDATA)>
<!ELEMENT ITEMDESCRIPTION (#PCDATA)>
<!ELEMENT ITEMPRICING (#PCDATA|ITEMNOTE|PRICE|SHIPPING)*>
<!ELEMENT PRICE (#PCDATA)>
<!ELEMENT SHIPPING (#PCDATA)>
<!ELEMENT ITEMNOTE (#PCDATA)>
<!ELEMENT SUBNAME (#PCDATA)>
<!ELEMENT SUBITEM (#PCDATA|SUBNAME|PRICE|SHIPPING)*>
```

Joe's catalog page would need to undergo some extensive modification. For example, the DTD adds a SHIPPING element that wasn't formally represented before. Additional layers of elements must be added where there wasn't any markup before. For those reasons, Joe's catalog probably needs to be recreated by a human rather than a machine. The new page looks like the following:

```
<?xml version="1.0" encoding="UTF-8"?>
<!DOCTYPE CATALOGPAGE SYSTEM "joes.dtd">
<CATALOGPAGE>
<HEADER>Money Counting Equipment</HEADER>
<CATALOGITEM>
<ITEMNAME>Basic Money Counter</ITEMNAME>
<ITEMSUBHEAD>Count your cash without spending all of
it!</ITEMSUBHEAD>
<ITEMDESCRIPTION>Joe's is pleased to announce this NEW
addition to our line. People with piles of change can
sort their money easily, and wrap it for the bank. Makes
the change box a lot more useful!</ITEMDESCRIPTION>
```

```
<ITEMPRICING>Price:<PRICE>$14.95</PRICE>, plus
<SHIPPING>$4.95</SHIPPING> shipping and
handling.</ITEMPRICING>
<SUBITEM>Also available: <SUBNAME>Paper Coin Wrappers,
bag of 100</SUBNAME>: <PRICE>$2.95</PRICE></SUBITEM>
</CATALOGITEM>
<CATALOGITEM>
<ITEMNAME>Standard Money Counter</ITEMNAME>
<ITEMSUBHEAD>Count and collect your cash
automatically!</ITEMSUBHEAD>
<ITEMDESCRIPTION>This money counter wraps your change
automatically—just feed it the plastic change rolls.
You'll feel just like the bank when you read its LED
display announcing how much change you've
gathered.</ITEMDESCRIPTION>
<ITEMPRICING><ITEMNOTE>Special guarantee: 100% accuracy
on wrapping or your money back!</ITEMNOTE>
Price:<PRICE>$64.95</PRICE>, plus
<SHIPPING>$7.95</SHIPPING> shipping and
handling.</ITEMPRICING>
<SUBITEM>Also available: <SUBNAME>Plastic Coin Wrappers,
box of 400</SUBNAME>: <PRICE>$10.95</PRICE></SUBITEM>
</CATALOGITEM>
<CATALOGITEM>
<ITEMNAME>Super-Duper Money Counter</ITEMNAME>
<ITEMDESCRIPTION>Tired of change? This machine counts
bills as well. Feed it the take from a cash register and
watch it count away. Spits out old bills in a separate
tray for easy counting. Saves hours of effort spent
counting pennies—and twenties!</ITEMDESCRIPTION>
<ITEMPRICING>Price:<PRICE>$649.95</PRICE>, plus
<SHIPPING>$29.95</SHIPPING> shipping and
handling.</ITEMPRICING>
```

```
<SUBITEM>Uses plastic coin wrappers above, and
<SUBNAME>Paper Bill Wrappers, box of 1000</SUBNAME>:
<PRICE>$10.95</PRICE></SUBITEM>
</CATALOGITEM>
</CATALOGPAGE>
```

The structure of this document makes Joe's catalog much more machine-readable, as shown in Figure 6-2. The many different components are logically separated, making it easier for an application to access and process the information.

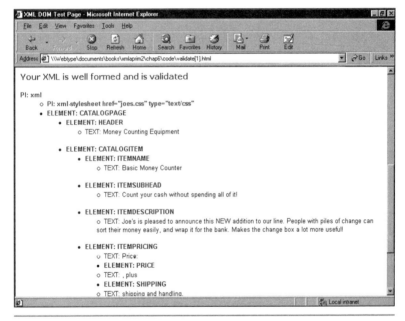

Figure 6-2 *Joe's Catalog represented with a content-focused notation*

This is still not a complete solution, although it may be all the solution Joe's Catalog wants. A more thorough DTD design might change the kinds of information presented and the order in which they appear, making the code look more like the Jimbo's Super Clock catalog example in Chapter 3 with its part numbers and freight information. The catalog as it stands now is reasonably useful for people to read, but it is still not very effective for use in an inventory system or catalog-management tool.

 Tip

Pages that are already generated by a computer will be fairly easy to convert, at least if the code or markup is written intelligibly. Search-and-replace mechanisms may be able to convert static machine-generated pages if all the material uses precisely the same markup. Better yet, if the data are still available in the original structure (database form, most likely) and are used to create pages on the fly, the scripts that create HTML can be easily modified to produce XML. Instead of placing certain formatting tags around a price, the script can place it within a <PRICE> element.

A few HTML documents are probably ready for XML now, and HTML developers can plan ahead by designing pages that will convert easily. In Chapter 2, we discussed how Cascading Style Sheets provided a CLASS attribute that HTML developers could use to create their own tags effectively. CSS has been available for over a year, and some sites created take advantage of its capacities. Developers who used CSS classes to reflect categories of content and not just formatting will be in good shape. The main difference between the structure created by CSS CLASS attributes and that of XML is in enforcement: CSS can't require classes to nest in a particular order. Still, because CSS provides formatting inheritance between elements (child elements will by default receive many of the style properties of their parents), many pages that were created with CSS reflect good XML structure and are in a good position to be converted. They work well in the newer (since version 4) versions of the Netscape and Microsoft browsers, but have problems in older versions. The following example uses a small segment of a catalog to show how CSS CLASS attributes could have worked for Joe:

```
<HTML>
<HEAD><TITLE>Joe's Catalog - Money Counters</TITLE>
<STYLE TYPE="text/css">
```

```
DIV.HEADER {font-size:24pt;font-weight:bold}
DIV.ITEMNAME {font-size:18pt;font-weight:bold}
DIV.ITEMSUBHEAD {font-size:14pt;font-weight:bold}
DIV.ITEMDESCRIPTION {font-size:12pt}
DIV.ITEMPRICING {font-size:10pt}
SPAN.PRICE {font-weight:bold}
SPAN.SHIPPING {font-weight:normal}
DIV.SUBITEM {font-size:11pt}
SPAN.SUBNAME {font-weight:bold}
</STYLE></HEAD>
<BODY BGCOLOR="#FFFFF">
<DIV CLASS="HEADER">Money Counting Equipment</DIV>
<DIV CLASS="ITEMNAME">Basic Money Counter</DIV>
<DIV CLASS="SUBHEAD">Count your cash without spending all
of it!</DIV>
<DIV CLASS="ITEMDESCRIPTION">Joe's is pleased to announce
this NEW addition to our line. People with piles of
change can sort their money easily, and wrap it for the
bank. Makes the change box a lot more useful!</DIV>
<DIV CLASS="ITEMPRICING">Price:<SPAN
CLASS="PRICE">$14.95</SPAN>, plus <SPAN
CLASS="SHIPPING">$4.95</SPAN> shipping and
handling.</DIV>
<DIV CLASS="SUBITEM">Also available: <SPAN
CLASS="SUBNAME">Paper Coin Wrappers, bag of 100</SPAN>:
<SPAN CLASS="PRICE">$2.95</SPAN></DIV>
</BODY></HTML>
```

If the catalog was organized like this, converting over to XML might require custom code that could take the DIV and SPAN elements, replace them with the appropriate elements (in this case, their CLASS attributes), and group them under appropriate parent elements. Most developers, however, won't be this lucky, unless they've just begun building their HTML documents. The page

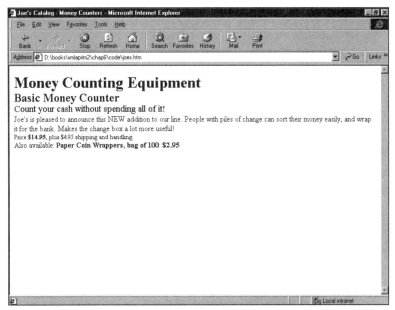

Figure 6-3 *Using DIV and SPAN elements with CSS allows developers to identify both formatting and content within HTML.*

Cross-Reference

A much more complete analysis of the needs of a catalog document will appear in the next chapter. Joe's Catalog has crossed over from HTML, but still faces a much more dramatic restructuring.

Building a style sheet for Joe's catalog using CSS won't be too difficult. The parts are easily identified, and the formatting already exists in the HTML version. Linking a style sheet to an XML document requires some extra markup. Every document that uses style sheets needs to include the line below before the appearance of the root element:

```
<?xml-stylesheet href="joes.css" type="text/css"?>
```

The big question now is whether or not Joe wants to change the look of his catalog. If not, it's pretty easy to create an appropriate style. CSS display properties, shown below in Table 6-1, make it possible for browsers to figure out a basic structure for rendering the XML elements in the document.

Table 6-1 *Display Property Values for Building Document Presentation Structures*

Display Value	Meaning	Notes
Block	Identifies the element as a separate block, which will start its text on a new line and end with a break at the end of the element. Usually, the root element is formatted using block, as are many paragraph-like sub-elements.	Appeared in Level 1, but not supported until recently. Similar to HTML DIV element in behavior.
Inline	Formats the element as part of the current block, without a break before or after. Typically used with elements that apply formatting to parts of sentences or paragraphs. (The default value.)	Appeared in Level 1, but not supported until recently. Similar to HTML SPAN element in behavior.
ListItem	Makes the element behave like an HTML list-item (LI) element, indenting it and possibly bulleting it depending on other CSS properties.	Appeared in Level 1, but not supported until recently. Similar to HTML LI element in behavior.
None	The element isn't displayed. No child elements will be displayed, either. (To hide elements but allow their children to appear, use the visible property.)	Appeared in Level 1, commonly used in Dynamic HTML.
run-in	If the element is followed by a block element, this element joins that element as if it were declared inline. If it isn't, this element is formatted as if it were declared as block.	New to Level 2.
compact	Makes lists fit in a tight space.	New to Level 2.
marker	Identifies an element with CSS content generation.	New to Level 2.

Table 6-1 *Continued*

Display Value	Meaning	Notes
inherit	Makes the element use the display properties of its parent element (which may also be inherited).	Appeared in Level 1.
table, inline-table, table-row-group, table-header-group, table-footer-group, table-row, table-column-group, table-column, table-cell, table-caption	Used to make elements into components of tables. See the chapter example below.	New to Level 2.

By combining these display properties with other formatting properties, we can build a simple style sheet for Joe's Catalog.

```
HEADER {
     display:block;
     font-size:24;
     font-family:serif;
     font-weight:bold
}
CATALOGITEM {
     display:block;
     font-family:serif
}
ITEMNAME {
     display:block;
     font-size: 18;
     font-weight:bold
}
ITEMSUBHEAD {
     display:block;
     font-size:14
```

```
}
ITEMDESCRIPTION {
    display:block;
    font-size:12
}
ITEMPRICING {
    display:block
}
PRICE {
    display:inline;
    font-family:bold
}
SHIPPING {
    display:inline
}
SUBITEM {
    display:block
}
```

The main tool used here is the style display attribute, which enables us to declare whether elements should be their own paragraph or flow with the text. If the element rates its own paragraph or line, it's styled as block. If it doesn't, it is styled as inline. The list-item option provides yet another option: separate lines, with less spacing than a block. Using the none option suppresses display of an element and all of its content. Other options (discussed in greater detail in Chapter 2) provide table structures and other features. Although it might take a little tweaking, the styles shown above produce a reasonable first draft of the catalog, as shown below in Figures 6-4 and 6-5.

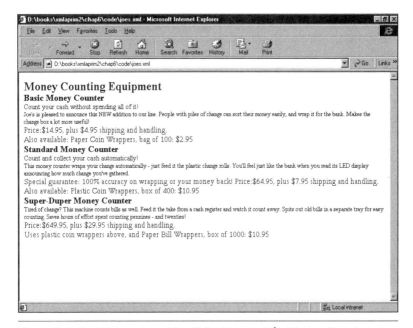

Figure 6-4 *A styled version of the XML document (in Microsoft's Internet Explorer 5) presents a prettier version of the same information, without losing the underlying structure.*

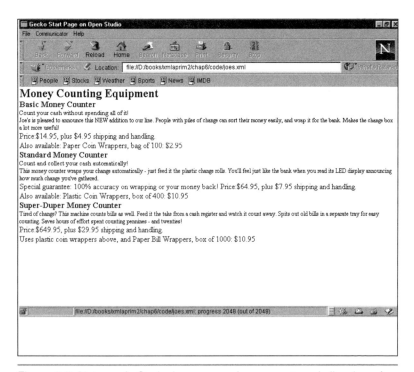

Figure 6-5 *Netscape's Gecko browser preview presents a similar view of the document.*

Caution

Although CSS and XML seem like a natural fit, CSS Level 1 has been implemented only partially (and incompatibly at times) in the current (4.0) release versions of the Netscape and Microsoft browsers. How much support for CSS Level 2 will be available in the final releases of the next versions of these two browsers is still undecided. Check with the browser vendor (or with sites like http://www.webreview.com and http://www.webstandards.org) for more details on how much of CSS is implemented in a given browser.

After you have built a style sheet, making changes is easy — just make the change at the style sheet, and all changes will flow through to the documents that call the style sheet. Extending the style sheet isn't as easy. Suppose that the PRICE element had to be displayed in red, but only for markdowns. CSS2 provides support for selectors that can respond to attribute values. (With XML, however, the CLASS attribute has no special privileges, as it did in HTML.)

```
PRICE.[status="markdown"] {
    display: inline;
    font-weight:bold;
    color:red
}
```

Remember that to use the attribute, you have to declare it in the DTD if you're using validation. With this style declared, the browser or other formattng application will turn the following price red, indicating a great bargain:

```
<PRICE status="markdown">$1.25</PRICE>
```

This will work for a while-until someone decides that the price color should also change if it's eligible for a bulk discount. Prices need to be either "fixed" or "byquantity." Even though the following style might work for a little while, it can hardly be called elegant:

```
PRICE{
    display:inline;
    font-weight:bold;
}
PRICE.[status="set"]{
    color:blue;
}
PRICE.[status="byquantity"] {
    color:green;
}
PRICE.[status="markdownset"] {
    color:red;
}
```

```
PRICE.[status="markdownbyquantity"] {
    color:brown;
}
```

Building This Book

In writing the first edition of this book, I used two kinds of style notation. Most of the styling was done using Microsoft Word's built-in style tools and a style sheet provided by MIS:Press. Some of the information — like notes, output, warnings, and sidebars — used markup notation very similar to XML. Notes, for instance, started with <NOTE> and ended with </NOTE>. Although these solutions tools work reasonably well, there are many ways they could improve. XML addresses most of those needs, simplifying the style-sheet structure and opening up new media to this document at the same time.

The styles defined in Word are a combination of structural information and formatting information, as shown in Table 6-2.

Table 6-2 *A Sample Style Sheet For a Book Chapter*

Style	Usage
TOC0 CT	Chapter number and title. This text will be used in table of contents when generated.
TOC1 A	A-head – the top level of headings in a chapter. This text will be used in table of contents when generated.
TOC2 B	B-head – the level of headings under A heads. This text also appears in table of contents.
C	C-head – level below B. Not in table of contents.
D	D-head – level below C. Not in table of contents.
E	E-head – level below D. Not in table of contents.
BT	Body text – first paragraph of text after a header, icon, list, figure caption, or other free-standing graphic. Not indented.
BT INDENT	Body text following a BT element. Indented.

Style	Usage
BL/NL1 TOP	Bulleted or numbered list – top line. (Formatted with extra space above.)
BL/NL2 MID	Bulleted or numbered list – middle lines. (Formatted with no extra space above or below.)
BL/NL3 BOT	Bulleted or numbered list – bottom line. (Formatted with extra space below.)
GL	Glossary text – word defined should be in bold, definition in normal text.
CC1 TOP	First line of multiline code listing. Formatted with extra space above.
CC2 MID	Middle lines of multiline code listing. No extra space above or below.
CC3 BOT	Last line of multiline code listing. Formatted with extra space below.
CC4 SINGLE	Single line of multiline code listing. Formatted with extra space above and below.
ICON	Icon text – used in combination with markup (<NOTE>, <WARNING>, and so on) to identify text that needs to be called out from body text.
FG	Figure caption – Figure chapterNum.FigureNum should be in bold, rest of text plain.
LC	Listing caption – goes above code listing.
TBC	Table caption – goes above table.
TBH	Table heads – use above each column.
TB	Table body.
UL	Unnumbered list.
SN	Source notes – footnotes or notes at bottom of table.

The structures defined with markup are mostly icons and bullets. Bullets are entered as <b> on PCs to avoid collisions between operating systems. Note icons are indicated as <NOTE>. A few structures are indicated with simple formatting. Keystrokes and menu items are supposed to be in bold, and titles are in italic.

Even though the current model has worked well for MIS:Press, we may be able to indicate document structures more easily and more clearly in XML. Unless MIS: Press begins to use XML-enabled publishing tools, this effort won't do much for them, but it may shed some light on how to restructure formatting styles into structural styles. Structural styles can escape from some of the redundancy that is required to make formatting styles work and make converting these documents from format to format easier.

Pass 1: A DTD That Looks Like the Old Styles

We'll start by setting up a chapter structure. Chapters will eventually become part of the larger book structure. The Chapter will include a title, a brief introduction, and a series of sections marked by A-heads. In the interest of ensuring a smooth transition, the original style names are used where possible, although spaces must be stripped out:

```
<!ELEMENT CHAPTER (HEAD?,TOC0CT, INTRODUCTORY, ALEAF*)>
```

The HEAD element uses the DTD described previously to enable style-sheet linking. The TOC0CT element performs the same duty as the TOC0 CT style: it identifies the chapter title. It contains only text:

```
<!ELEMENT TOC0CT (#PCDATA)>
```

The INTRODUCTORY element is new, introducing a chapter feature that wasn't included in the previous definition. All chapters start with text after the chapter headline. The INTRODUCTORY element is required and must consist of at least one body text (BT) paragraph. (No code listings or other subelements should appear in the introduction for now.)

```
<!ELEMENT INTRODUCTORY (BT+)>
```

The BT element is a bit more complicated because the text in it can include italic items (like citations) and bold items (like keystrokes and menu clicks—user actions). To address these needs, we'll create a few elements and a parameter entity that includes them, making it easier for us to include them in other elements.

```
<!ELEMENT CITATION (#PCDATA)>
<!ELEMENT USERACTION (#PCDATA)>
```

```
<!ENTITY % textual-elements
"(#PCDATA|CITATION|USERACTION)*">
<!ELEMENT BT %textual-elements;>
```

Note

Because the textual-elements entity describes a mixed-content model, it cannot be used in combination with other content models or appear in parentheses.

The next target is the ALEAF element. To avoid confusion with the HTML tags A and B, I've added the word LEAF to the letters for all of these sections. Because the leaves may contain a variety of content types, it's time to plan ahead and create a parameter entity. The content-elements entity will contain a list of all types of content available to a LEAF element, which includes only the PARAGRAPH element at present.

```
<!ENTITY % content-elements "BT">
```

All the LEAF elements will contain a header and paragraphs or sublevels.

```
<!ELEMENT ALEAF (TOC1A,BT,(%content-elements;|BLEAF)*)>
<!ELEMENT BLEAF (TOC2B,BT,(%content-elements;|CLEAF)*)>
<!ELEMENT CLEAF (C,BT,(%content-elements;|DLEAF)*)>
<!ELEMENT DLEAF (D,BT,(%content-elements;|ELEAF)*)>
<!ELEMENT ELEAF (E,BT,(%content-elements;)*)>
<!ELEMENT TOC1A (#PCDATA)>
<!ELEMENT TOC2B (#PCDATA)>
<!ELEMENT C (#PCDATA)>
<!ELEMENT D (#PCDATA)>
<!ELEMENT E (#PCDATA)>
```

Note that we didn't include the LEAF elements as part of the content-elements entity. This would have allowed authors to put ELEAF elements directly below ALEAF elements, violating the desired hierarchy. Instead, they remain separate, making it easier for the designer to see the structure. Using the (%content-elements |

XLEAF)* structure allows zero or more layers of content: ALEAFs aren't required to have BLEAF elements, but you can't have a CLEAF element unless it's included in a BLEAF element. (Later in this chapter, we'll change this, simplifying the structure considerably.) We have just provided the basic structure for a chapter, building a basic outline form that can go five levels deep. (If a chapter moves beyond five levels, it will be time to either reconsider the chapter's organization or add another level to the DTD.)

Now it's time to go back and add content beyond basic text paragraphs. The easiest type of information to manage in this context is code. The current style sheet uses four different styles for code, depending on the position of the line of code. In XML, what matters most is not the position of the code, but that the information is code. Style sheets clean up the presentation and apply the extra space before and after the code element. Our code element, to match the style sheet, will be named CC. By default, our CC element's TYPE attribute will be "CODE" because very few books still have textual output. For those books that do, we provide an "OUTPUT" value option for the TYPE, enabling the designer to format these two similar types slightly differently. A CC element may contain a listing caption (LC) and must include at least one CLINE (code line) element, with multiple lines available to store code as necessary.

```
<!ELEMENT CC (LC?,CLINE+)>
<!ATTLIST CC TYPE (CODE|OUTPUT) "CODE">
<!ELEMENT LC (#PCDATA)>
<!ELEMENT CLINE (#PCDATA)>
```

The next set of styles that needs an interpretation is the list styles. Currently, this style sheet includes a combined set of entries for bulleted and numbered lists, along with a separate style for unnumbered lists. This presents several options. We could maintain the style sheet as it exists now, creating one element to handle numbered and bulleted lists and another for unnumbered lists. We could break up the numbered and bulleted lists, keeping all the list styles separate. Finally, we could combine all the elements under one large umbrella.

Even though the large umbrella idea produces cleaner code (and we'll use it in the next pass); for now compatibility is important. Given the latest developments in style sheets (especially XSL), however, it seems likely that we'll want to separate bulleted and numbered lists for separate style processing. That way the style mechanism can apply numbers and bullets as appropriate, making it easier for writers to move items around without renumbering. Unnumbered lists will remain their own category.

```
<!ELEMENT BL (BLINE+)>
<!ELEMENT NL (NLINE+)>
<!ELEMENT UL (ULINE+)>
<!ELEMENT BLINE (#PCDATA)>
<!ELEMENT NLINE (#PCDATA)>
<!ELEMENT ULINE (#PCDATA)>
```

The next style we'll implement is GL, which is for glossary text. GL by itself doesn't do very much and the author has to make the glossary entry bold. Because glossaries are one of the best types of documents for manipulation, it seems reasonable to improve on this approach. The new GL element will contain a GLITEM and a GLDEFINITION, which explains the word contained in GLITEM.

```
<!ELEMENT GL (GLITEM,GLDEFINITION)>
<!ELEMENT GLITEM (#PCDATA)>
<!ELEMENT GLDEFINITION %textual-elements;>
```

ICON text is a somewhat difficult case. The ICON text by definition has a graphic floating to the left of it, but the graphic is not specified in the style sheet. Although it might be possible to create separate NOTE, SHORTCUT, WARNING, and TIP elements for each type of text instead of an ICON element, this doesn't correspond well to current practice. For now, we'll create an ICON element that contains an attribute identifying its type, allowing the application to add the graphic later, identify it, and use BT information for the content.

```
<!ELEMENT ICON (BT+)>
<!ATTLIST ICON
        TYPE    (NOTE|SHORTCUT|WARNING|TIP) "NOTE">
```

Tables are the next challenge; a challenge XML is not exactly prepared to face. Tables are often as much about formatting as about content, and they are necessary for the presentation of many types of content. The style sheet offers TBC for the table caption (which should go above the table), TH to hold the column headings, TBH for the column headings, TB for the table body text, and SN for source notes at the bottom. Ideally authors would be able to create their own mini-DTD for every table, identifying cell contents with their own element. Unfortunately, a publishing style sheet doesn't offer much room for that kind of extension. For now, we'll improvise, using the HTML-style TR and the style sheet's TB (treated much like TD in HTML). Unlike HTML, we'll require that TB elements always fit inside of TR elements.

```
<!ELEMENT TABLE (TBC*,TH?,TR+,SN*)>
<!ELEMENT TBC (#PCDATA)>
<!ELEMENT TH (TBH+)>
<!ELEMENT TBH (#PCDATA)>
<!ELEMENT TR (TB+)>
<!ELEMENT TB %textual-elements;>
<!ELEMENT SN %textual-elements;>
```

 Note

Creating table elements in XML is a tricky business. Declaring these elements is not nearly the end of this process. Making tables work requires connecting these elements to styles that reflect their nature.

The last major element that needs to be dealt with is figures. Figure images are not embedded directly in the file. Only a limited number of formats are acceptable. Figures include three parts: the picture, the figure number, and the caption describing the figure. The picture will be an empty element with attributes that explain to the processing application where to find the figure and what kind of figure file it is. The kind of file is defined using an attribute that matches a previously defined NOTATION declaration. The figure number will be part of the caption.

```
<!NOTATION tiff SYSTEM "image/tiff">
<!NOTATION bmp SYSTEM "image/bmp">
<!NOTATION eps SYSTEM "image/eps">
<!ELEMENT FIGURE (FIGREF, FG)>
<!ELEMENT FIGREF EMPTY>
<!ATTLIST FIGREF
     SRC    CDATA      #REQUIRED
     TYPE   NOTATION (tiff | bmp | eps) "tiff">
<!ELEMENT FG (FIGNUM, FDESC)>
<!ELEMENT FDESC %textual-elements;>
<!ELEMENT FIGNUM (#PCDATA)>
```

Now that we've created all of these content elements, it's time to update the content-elements parameter entity to include them.

```
<!ENTITY % content-elements "(BT | CC | BL | NL | UL | GL
| ICON | TABLE | FIGURE)*">
```

Combining all this into one gigantic DTD file gives us something we can work with.

```
<!—Chapter DTD, version 1 —>
<!—Mandatory starting elements —>
<!ELEMENT CHAPTER (HEAD?,TOCOCT, INTRODUCTORY, ALEAF*)>
<!— Chapter Title —>
<!ELEMENT TOCOCT (#PCDATA)>
```

```
<!—Chapter Introduction —>
<!ELEMENT INTRODUCTORY (BT+)>
<!—Common text elements. —>
<!ELEMENT CITATION (#PCDATA)>
<!ELEMENT USERACTION (#PCDATA)>
<!—Textual elements allows mixing w/ regular data —>
<!ENTITY % textual-elements
"( #PCDATA| CITATION| USERACTION )*">
<!—BT - Body text. Used for each paragraph —>
<!ELEMENT BT %textual-elements;>
<!—Content elements allows multiple content types in
section contents—>
<!ENTITY % content-elements "(BT | CC | BL | NL | UL | GL
| ICON | TABLE | FIGURE)*">
<!—XLEAF elements behave like X-heads in previous—>
<!—Note the structure for XLEAF elements - BLEAF
elements can only appear in ALEAF elements, CLEAF
elements can only appear in BLEAF elements, etc. —>
<!ELEMENT ALEAF (TOC1A,BT,(%content-elements;|BLEAF)*)>
<!ELEMENT BLEAF (TOC2B,BT,(%content-elements;|CLEAF)*)>
<!ELEMENT CLEAF (C,BT,(%content-elements;|DLEAF)*)>
<!ELEMENT DLEAF (D,BT,(%content-elements;|ELEAF)*)>
<!ELEMENT ELEAF (E,BT,(%content-elements;)*)>
<!—Headers for leaf sections —>
<!—A Head - appears in Table of Contents —>
<!ELEMENT TOC1A (#PCDATA)>
<!—B Head - appears in Table of Contents —>
<!ELEMENT TOC2B (#PCDATA)>
<!—C, D, E heads do not appear in Table of Contents—>
<!ELEMENT C (#PCDATA)>
<!ELEMENT D (#PCDATA)>
<!ELEMENT E (#PCDATA)>
<!—Declarations for marking code listings —>
<!ELEMENT CC (LC?,CLINE+)>
<!—TYPE attribute differentiates code listings from text
```

```
output—>
<!ATTLIST CC TYPE (CODE|OUTPUT) "CODE">
<!—LC is list caption —>
<!ELEMENT LC (#PCDATA)>
<!—CLINE represents a single line of code—>
<!ELEMENT CLINE (#PCDATA)>
<!—Declarations for lists (bulleted, numbered, unordered
lists) —>
<!ELEMENT BL (BLINE+)>
<!ELEMENT NL (NLINE+)>
<!ELEMENT UL (ULINE+)>
<!—List contents (bulleted, numbered, unordered lists)—>
<!ELEMENT BLINE %textual-elements;>
<!ELEMENT NLINE %textual-elements;>
<!ELEMENT ULINE %textual-elements;>
<!—Glossary Declarations —>
<!ELEMENT GL (GLITEM,GLDEFINITION)>
<!—Word being defined—>
<!ELEMENT GLITEM (#PCDATA)>
<!—Definition—>
<!ELEMENT GLDEFINITION %textual-elements;>
<!—Icon/Note Declarations —>
<!ELEMENT ICON (BT+)>
<!ATTLIST ICON
       TYPE   (NOTE|SHORTCUT|WARNING|TIP) "NOTE">
<!—Table Declarations —>
<!ELEMENT TABLE (TBC*,TH?,TR+,SN*)>
<!—Table Caption —>
<!ELEMENT TBC (#PCDATA)>
<!—Table Headers —>
<!ELEMENT TH (TBH+)>
<!ELEMENT TBH (#PCDATA)>
<!—Table Rows —>
<!ELEMENT TR (TB+)>
```

```
<!-Table Body (sim to HTML TD) ->
<!ELEMENT TB %textual-elements;>
<!-Table Source Note ->
<!ELEMENT SN %textual-elements;>
<!-Graphic Type Declarations ->
<!NOTATION tiff SYSTEM "viewer.exe">
<!NOTATION bmp SYSTEM "viewer.exe">
<!NOTATION eps SYSTEM "viewer.exe">
<!-Figure Declarations ->
<!ELEMENT FIGURE (FIGREF, FG)>
<!ELEMENT FIGREF EMPTY>
<!ATTLIST FIGREF
     SRC   CDATA      #REQUIRED
     TYPE  NOTATION (tiff | bmp | eps) "tiff">
<!-FG is figure description ->
<!ELEMENT FG (FIGNUM, FDESC)>
<!ELEMENT FDESC %textual-elements;>
<!ELEMENT FIGNUM (#PCDATA)>
```

Unfortunately, a gargantuan DTD requires a gargantuan document to test it out. The following code is clearly only test code, not a real chapter (although I could increase the thickness of this book dramatically by including one). Nevertheless, this code should test out most of these elements in their natural habitats.

```
<?xml version="1.0" encoding="UTF-8"?>
<!DOCTYPE CHAPTER SYSTEM "chapter.dtd">
<CHAPTER>
<TOCOCT>How to code XML</TOCOCT>
<INTRODUCTORY>
<BT>This is a chapter on how to code XML.</BT>
<BT>This is another bit of intro info.</BT>
</INTRODUCTORY>
<ALEAF>
<TOC1A>Subhead A1</TOC1A>
<BT>This is A1, from <CITATION>my
```

```
document</CITATION>.</BT>
<CC><LC>This is a listing</LC>
<CLINE>I don't know what to do in this program!</CLINE>
<CLINE>I don't know what to do in this program!</CLINE>
</CC>
<BT>You could have typed <USERACTION>exit</USERACTION>
instead of running the parser.</BT>
</ALEAF>
<ALEAF>
<TOC1A>Subhead A2</TOC1A>
<BT>This is A2. We'll start with a table, and move on to
a B leaf.</BT>
<TABLE><TBC>This is a sample table</TBC>
<TH><TBH>Column 1: Time</TBH><TBH>Column 2:
Money</TBH></TH>
<TR><TB>Never enough</TB><TB>Can always use
more</TB></TR>
<TR><TB>More than enough</TB><TB>Had enough to begin
with</TB></TR>
<SN>From <CITATION>The book of nonsense</CITATION></SN>
</TABLE>
<BLEAF>
<TOC2B>Subhead B1</TOC2B>
<BT>A C leaf will follow, after the bulleted list.</BT>
<BL>
<BLINE>This is the first item of a bulleted list</BLINE>
<BLINE>This is the second item of a bulleted list</BLINE>
</BL>
<CLEAF>
<C>Subhead C1</C>
<BT>This is a C leaf which contains a numbered list and a
figure.</BT>
<NL>
<NLINE>1. This is the first item.</NLINE>
```

```
<NLINE>2. This is the second item.</NLINE>
</NL>
<FIGURE><FIGREF SRC="image.tif" TYPE="tiff"/>
<FG><FIGNUM>101.12</FIGNUM><FDESC> - The wild boar at
rest.</FDESC></FG></FIGURE>
</CLEAF>
<CLEAF>
<C>Subhead C2</C>
<BT>This C leaf contains an unnumbered list and a
glossary item.</BT>
<UL>
<ULINE>This isn't in any order.</ULINE>
<ULINE>Who needs order?</ULINE>
<ULINE>Order just gets in the way.</ULINE>
</UL>
<GL><GLITEM>Order</GLITEM><GLDEFINITION> Something that
gets in the way frequently.</GLDEFINITION></GL>
</CLEAF>
</BLEAF>
<ICON TYPE="NOTE"><BT>Hope you enjoyed the
chapter!</BT></ICON>
</ALEAF>
</CHAPTER>
```

Though you can only see the top portion of it, Figure 6-6 shows the validated XML in the Internet Explorer 5.0 browser.

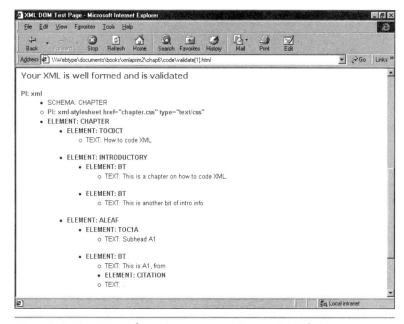

Figure 6-6 *A validated (though not necessarily meaningful) chapter*

A Style Sheet for the Chapter DTD

A style sheet for the Chapter DTD won't be too hard to develop in XML, even though the publishers may grumble about losing the fine control they had with previous desktop publishing tools, like QuarkXPress. Even though XML's supporting style technologies will enable some fairly intricate formatting, it's still not quite what print designers are used to. The format of this particular style sheet has very little to do with the way the document is presented in the final printing — it is just a generic representation that helps the author and the editors see the book. After the editing is over, the production staff could in theory just replace the style sheet with a style sheet customized for the look of a particular book and have the same elements fall into their proper place for printing.

Note

Documents created with the Chapter DTD will probably be combined with other chapters as part of a larger structure, which may have its own formatting rules. For the purposes of this style sheet, we'll assume that chapters start and end on their own pages, and that the larger document's structure will not interfere with any of the styling.

The style for the CHAPTER element marks itself as a block element, making itself a separate unit of text from any surrounding material. It also sets the default font information for the entire document:

```
CHAPTER {
        display:block;
        font-family:serif;
        font-size:12pt;
        font-weight: normal;
        font-style:normal;
}
```

I've avoided using actual font names throughout this style sheet, preferring to use the generic family names like serif and monotype. You can substitute real font names if you prefer, but keep in mind that not all computers will have your chosen set of fonts.

The TOC0CT opening headline is displayed in bold 24-point type. Note the padding-bottom attribute, which specifies the amount of space that should follow the headline.

```
TOC0CT {
        display:block;
        font-size:24pt;
        font-weight:bold;
        padding-bottom:9pt;
}
```

The CITATION and USERACTION elements will italicize words within the text, but they don't create separate blocks. Setting the display to inline (which is the default) makes it clear that these elements will not break up paragraphs.

```
CITATION {
    display:inline;
    font-style:italic;
}
USERACTION {
    display:inline;
    font-weight:bold;
}
```

BT is the primary element for displaying text. Each BT unit is the rough equivalent of a paragraph, so the BT element is clearly a block.

```
BT {
    display:block;
    line-height:24pt;
}
```

The XLEAF elements all share similar formatting. They each begin a block element, separated from the previous element by a preset amount of space, which is set in the padding-top value of CSS.

```
ALEAF {
    display:block;
    padding-top:12pt;
}

BLEAF {
    display:block;
    padding-top:9pt;
}
```

```
CLEAF {
    display:block;
    padding-top:9pt;
}

DLEAF {
    display:block;
    padding-top:9pt;
}

ELEAF {
    display:block;
    padding-top:9pt;
}
```

The headlines for the leaf elements are themselves block elements, each with their own set of formatting.

```
TOC1A {
    display:block;
    padding-bottom:6pt;
    font-size:18pt;
    font-weight:bold;
}

TOC2B {
    display:block;
    padding-bottom:6pt;
    font-size:14pt;
    font-weight:bold;
}

C {
    display:block;
    font-size:14pt;
    font-weight:bold;
    font-style:italic;
```

```
}

D {
    display:block;
    font-size:12pt;
    font-weight:bold;
    font-style:italic;
}

E {
    display:block;
    font-size:14pt;
    font-style:italic;
}
```

The code elements, the most dramatically simplified compared to the original chapter style sheet, take the most advantage of the power of CSS and XML. The extra spacing, which in Word required four different styles, is easily included in the definition of the CC element. Because the CC element encloses the caption and the code completely, it can supply the necessary padding at the top and bottom of the code listing without requiring that the author apply extra styling to the actual code.

```
CC {
    display:block;
    padding-top:9pt;
    padding-bottom:9pt;
    text-indent:.5in;
    font-family:monospace;
    line-height:18pt;
}
```

```
LC {
    display:block;
    padding-bottom:6pt;
    font-weight:bold;
}
```

```
CLINE {display:block}
```
The list elements can set the styles necessary for the list items
they enclose using Cascading Style Sheets' fairly comprehensive set
of list styles.

```
BL {
    display:block;
    text-indent:1in;
    line-height:18pt;
    list-style-type:disc;
    list-style-position:outside;
}
```

```
NL {
    display:block;
    text-indent:1in;
    line-height:18pt;
    list-style-type:decimal;
    list-style-position:outside;
}
```

```
UL {
    display:block;
    line-height:18pt;
    list-style-type:square;
    list-style-position:outside;
}
```

The content of those lists needs only to identify itself as a list item.

```
BLINE {display:list-item}
NLINE {display:list-item}
ULINE {display:list-item}
```

The GL element is a little more complex. Because glossary entries have a one-line item description followed by a multiline indented definition, the GL element sets its text indent to a negative 1 inch, which produces the required hanging indent.

```
GL {
    display:block;
    text-indent:-1in;
    padding-bottom:9pt;
    line-height:24pt;
}

GLITEM {
    display:inline;
    font-weight:bold;
}

GLDEFINITION {display:inline}
```

The ICON element simply indents its text one inch and applies appropriate padding and spacing. The NOTE, SHORTCUT, WARNING, and TIP elements don't need styles at this point because they have no content at all. In final production, they must be replaced with graphics.

```
ICON {
     display:block;
     text:indent:1in;
     padding-top:9pt;
     padding-bottom:9pt;
     line-height:18pt;
}
```

While Cascading Style Sheets Level 1 provided formatting only for text objects in the main flow of a document, relying on HTML's TABLE element and its children to build tables, CSS Level 2 provides a complete set of display properties for assembling tables from arbitrary elements. The table, inline-table, table-row-group, table-header-group, table-footer-group, table-row, table-column-group, table-column, table-cell, and table-caption values for the display property provide a construction kit much more flexible than the HTML model.

```
TABLE {display:table;
     padding-top:9pt;
     padding-bottom:6pt;
     }

TBC {
     display:caption;
     font-weight:bold;
     font-style:italic;
     padding-bottom:9pt;
}

TH{
     display:table-header-group;
     padding-bottom:9pt;
}

TBH {
```

```
        display:table-cell;
        font-weight:bold;
}

TR {
        display:table-row;
        line-height:18pt;
}

TB {display:table-cell}

SN {display:table-footer-group;
        font-size:10pt;
        padding-top:6pt;
        padding-bottom:6pt;
}
```

FIGURE elements are always centered on the page. The FIGREF element that actually places the figure picture doesn't need a style, unless extra padding is necessary. The FIGREF will inherit the centering from the FIGURE element. The figure caption (the FG element) will also inherit the centering, and the FIGNUM will appear in bold.

```
FIGURE {
        display:block;
        text-align:center;
}

FG   {
display:block;
font-style:italic;
}
```

```
FIGNUM {
display:inline;
font-weight:bold;
}

FDESC {
display:inline;
}
```

Eventually, we will be able to use styles like these to present complex XML documents in a browser with little difficulty. Changing styles with Cascading Style Sheets is extremely simple, making it easy to present documents in different formats aimed at different media. Although CSS doesn't provide all the answers, it provides enough structure to build a reasonably well-formatted XML document. More complex documents (such as those requiring transformations) may need XSL's more powerful tools, but for this level of formatting, CSS is just fine.

Pass 2: Toward a Cleaner DTD

The real test of the previous DTD will come as authors and the production department put it to use, stretching it and finding its weaknesses. Several significant weaknesses arose during the previous discussion but were overlooked for the sake of compatibility with the original Word-based version. A second round, unhindered by the political need of compatibility, may improve the DTD to make it more extensible. Three areas could definitely use some structural improvements — the leaf structure (ALEAF, BLEAF, and so on), lists, and icons — and many elements could use friendlier names.

Note

These improvements are mostly technical improvements that demonstrate some of the more interesting features of XML. They are not guaranteed to improve user productivity, however. Some users may find the older structures easier to understand. DTD developers will frequently need to compromise between a more "elegant" technical solution and a solution that is user-friendly. Automated tools for entering information will help bridge that gap, but their acceptance may take a while.

Even though the ALEAF/BLEAF/CLEAF structure makes sense to a reader who can scan through it, it requires a considerably larger number of elements than a more generic leaf version might. A more generic structure would use elements that behave similarly but aren't labeled A or B or C. Creating a generic leaf structure involves recursion — allowing an element to include another element of the same type within itself. Recursion has several meanings in different contexts, many of which lead to endless loops. XML permits elements to include themselves in the list of accepted child elements, but it does not, for example, permit entities to refer to files that then refer to the original file. For most purposes, the following recursion is the practical limit of recursion in XML.

In the following DTD, a LEAF element must contain a TITLE element and may contain additional LEAF elements and PCDATA.

```
<!ELEMENT TEST (LEAF+)>
<!ELEMENT LEAF (HEADER,(LEAF|CONTENT)*)>
<!ELEMENT CONTENT (#PCDATA)>
<!ELEMENT HEADER (#PCDATA)>
```

The following document takes advantage of the LEAF structure to create several layers of LEAF elements:

```
<?xml version="1.0" encoding="UTF-8"?>
<!DOCTYPE TEST SYSTEM "recurs.dtd">
<TEST>
<LEAF>
<HEADER>Top-layer Leaf 1</HEADER>
<CONTENT>This is a leaf.</CONTENT>
<LEAF>
<HEADER>Second-layer Leaf 1</HEADER>
<CONTENT>This is a leaf.</CONTENT>
</LEAF>
<LEAF>
<HEADER>Second-layer Leaf 2</HEADER>
<CONTENT>This is a leaf. </CONTENT>
<LEAF>
<HEADER>Third-layer Leaf 1</HEADER>
<CONTENT>This is a leaf.</CONTENT>
</LEAF>
</LEAF>
</LEAF>
<LEAF>
<HEADER>Top-layer Leaf 2</HEADER>
<CONTENT>This is a leaf.</CONTENT>
</LEAF>
</TEST>
```

Parsing this document reveals its layers of structure.

Figure 6-7 *Using a leaf structure provides a cleaner and more abstract means of nesting content.*

Using this structure enables us to simplify the following code from:

```
<!ELEMENT ALEAF (TOC1A,BT,(%content-elements;|BLEAF)*)>
<!ELEMENT BLEAF (TOC2B,BT,(%content-elements;|CLEAF)*)>
<!ELEMENT CLEAF (C,BT,(%content-elements;|DLEAF)*)>
<!ELEMENT DLEAF (D,BT,(%content-elements;|ELEAF)*)>
<!ELEMENT ELEAF (E,BT,(%content-elements;)*)>
<!ELEMENT TOC1A (#PCDATA)>
<!ELEMENT TOC2B (#PCDATA)>
<!ELEMENT C (#PCDATA)>
```

```
<!ELEMENT D (#PCDATA)>
<!ELEMENT E (#PCDATA)>
```

to this:

```
<!ELEMENT LEAF (HEADER,BT,( %content-elements;| LEAF)*)>
<!ELEMENT HEADER (#PCDATA)>
```

The LEAF element replaces all its predecessor leaf structures, and the HEADER element replaces TOC1A, TOC2B, and C, D, and E. Whenever an author creates a new leaf, it is assumed to be a subsection of the document. The level at which it appears (like A, B, C, D, or E) is determined purely by context. This may be disorienting at first, at least until the tools catch up to the possibilities.

This approach also creates some difficulties for style sheets, requiring some minor changes in the styles presented previously. The CSS specification allows for contextual selectors, which enable you to define styles based on the element type and also on the elements in which the element you're styling is nested. In our case, because all of the subleaves (below the AHEAD) use the same padding value, the new style for the LEAF element is reasonably simple.

```
LEAF {
    display:block;
    padding-top:12pt;
}

LEAF LEAF {
    display:block;
    padding-top:9pt;
}
```

This style definition states that all LEAF elements will start out with a default padding of 12 points on top. However, all LEAF elements that are enclosed by other LEAF elements (which includes all layers below the top) will have 9 points of padding on top. The headers are more difficult, but they use the same rule.

```
LEAF HEADER {
    display:block;
    padding-bottom:6pt;
    font-size:18pt;
    font-weight:bold;
}

LEAF LEAF HEADER {
    display:block;
    padding-bottom:6pt;
    font-size:14pt;
    font-weight:bold;
 }

LEAF LEAF LEAF HEADER {
    display:block;
    font-size:14pt;
    font-weight:bold;
    font-style:italic;
}

LEAF LEAF LEAF LEAF HEADER {
    display:block;
    font-size:12pt;
    font-weight:bold;
    font-style:italic;
}

LEAF LEAF LEAF LEAF LEAF HEADER {
    display:block;
    font-size:14pt;
    font-style:italic;
}
```

The top line of these style settings is the old TOC1A header — a header inside one layer of LEAF elements. The second line is TOC2B, and so forth. Instead of being tied to a specific named element, the style of the headline is dependent upon its position in the hierarchy of LEAF elements, as shown in Figure 6-8.

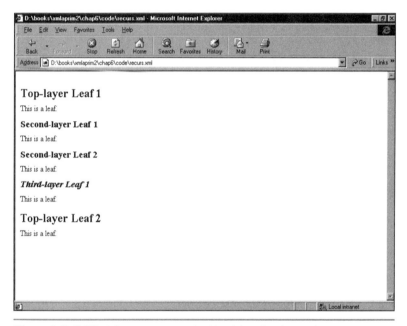

Figure 6-8 *CSS styles can use context to determine formatting.*

The lists could also stand significant improvement. For compatibility, we created three elements: BL, NL, and UL. These could be combined into a single LIST element with an attribute identifying the type of list.

```
<!ELEMENT LIST (LINE+)>
<!ATTLIST LINE
      TYPE CDATA (BULLETED|NUMBERED|UNORDERED)>
```

Even though this is tempting, for now it must depend on the ability of the processing application to keep up with the attribute.

Cascading Style Sheets, for example, can respond to element context, but can react to the CLASS attribute only. (Renaming TYPE to CLASS would, of course, solve this, but a CLASS attribute might need to reflect more than the type of list.) When XSL and other more context-sensitive style systems come into more general use, it may or may not be time for this change, depending to a large extent on the preferences of those using the tools.

At present, the list items all have their own elements — NLINE, BLINE, and ULINE. These can be combined into one LINE element as long as the processing software can keep up. This should not be as difficult as changing the announcement of the type of list it is from element to attribute status. The resulting declarations are:

```
<!ELEMENT BL (LINE+)>
<!ELEMENT NL (LINE+)>
<!ELEMENT UL (LINE+)>
<!ELEMENT LINE %textual-elements;>
```

This should make converting from one list type to another far more convenient. The BL, NL, and UL elements keep their previous style definitions, and the line element uses a style declaration very similar to its predecessors.

```
LINE {display:list-item}
```

The last improvement I suggest is using longer names for most of the styles. XML doesn't offer a SHORTREF declaration like SGML to provide for abbreviated versions of full names, so this will result in more markup and longer files. Still, if anyone must read the actual files, they'll have a much easier time figuring out what's going where.

Creating Wrapper Documents

While creating new XML formats for information seems like the right solution in many cases, moving from legacy formats to XML is a lot of work, and not something that will always have a return good enough to justify the effort. (I'm a very loud supporter of XML, and believe quite firmly that breaking documents down into the smallest possible components is a good idea, but even so, not every document is that valuable, and not every project can afford to throw away its legacy information.) In many cases, using an XML wrapper around the legacy information can be a good initial step. It isn't appropriate for all information — information that isn't easily represented as a series of letters and numbers should usually be left alone. That still leaves an enormous amount of information passed in various non-XML text formats available for processing.

The simplest kind of information to wrap is a plain text document. While WYSIWYG editing may have driven out many common uses of plain-text formatting, many documents (including Internet Engineering Task Force RFCs) are still distributed as plain text, formatted with whitespace — tabs, line breaks, and ordinary spaces. The old typewriter-based ways live on as the simplest format on the Web. Converting these documents to heavily marked-up XML is difficult, but the first level of conversion isn't that difficult:

```
<?xml version="1.0" encoding="UTF-8"?>
<?xml-stylesheet href="wrap.css" type="text/css"?>
<wrapper xml:space="preserve">


Text with line breaks goes here.


</wrapper>
```

The style sheet document is similarly simple:

```
wrapper {
    display:block;
    white-space:pre;
}
```

If the whitespace in the document isn't significant, the style-sheet processing instruction and the xml:space attribute can be dropped as well, making for a very simple wrapper. (Because the whitespace property won't permit automatic line breaking when whitespace is significant, like the HTML PRE element, displaying documents like this that don't include line breaks can be problematic.) Table 6-3 below lists the possible values of the whitespace property in CSS and their meanings. No 'wrap' value is available — in all cases where whitespace is treated as significant, line breaks must be stated explicitly.

Table 6-3 *Values for the CSS2 Whitespace Property*

Whitespace Value	Meaning
normal	Whitespace characters will generally be treated as insignificant; multiple consecutive whitespace characters will be condensed to a single space. (This is the default, whether or not the xml:space attribute was set to "preserve.") This behavior is the same as typical HTML browser behavior.
pre	All whitespace is treated as significant; lines only break at newline characters (or generated newline characters, like BR in HTML) within the text. No condensing of multiple whitespace characters will take place.
nowrap	Whitespace is treated as significant, but newline characters are ignored. Lines are only broken at generated newline characters (like BR in HTML).
inherit	This element will use the whitespace behavior of its parent element.

Wrapping entire documents in a single root element isn't a good long-term approach for document management — it loses nearly all of XML's advantages. Still, it can be a good starting place for further markup. Strategies that permit processing of different levels of markup, from almost none to heavy-duty content-based markup, make it possible for organizations and people with varying levels of commitment and resources to get started using a standard. (It can also make it difficult to get them to move beyond the lowest common denominator, so be careful.)

Leaving legacy data intact within a genuinely marked-up XML document may still be a good idea. The Weather Observation

Markup Format (OMF at `http://zowie.metnet.navy.mil/` `~spawar/JMV-TNG/XML/OMF.html`), for example, still keeps the text of the original legacy reports inside of its more thoroughly processed versions of that data, making it easier for the new systems and the old to communicate. In some cases, XML is great as a format for representing additional information about a document—metadata like author, date created, copyright, and so on—but isn't needed for the rest of the document, which already has its own encoding. While in the long run it may be more sensible to migrate to a single standard, such hybrid solutions are likely to be around for a number of years.

In the next chapter, we'll move from simple documents based on print and Web models to more complex documents intended to enhance commercial document interchange. We'll be using many of the same tools but expanding on XML's ability to create machine-readable documents.

Chapter 7

XML for Commerce

Perhaps the most important advantage of XML is that it enables people and companies to exchange information more clearly and completely than previous formats. Although this can improve the average home page as well as the efficiency of paper-document creation, XML has its greatest return on investment in more businesslike fields. XML promises to capitalize on two key trends in the electronic world: the growing use of Web sites for information distribution and the increasing use of electronic ordering and invoicing. XML can make Web sites more usable by making them more easily searchable, while simultaneously easing the difficult transition of business-to-business communication by providing intelligible standards for data interchange.

Caution

The first two examples provided in this chapter explore the process of using XML to create commerce-focused DTDs. While the prospect of creating your own DTDs for these functions may seem exciting, you should always check to make sure that an industry-standard DTD isn't already available. Creating your own DTD can give you a well-tailored solution to your system's particular needs, but it may also cut you off from the rest of your industry. XML markup is most useful when the same vocabulary (typically expressed in a DTD) is used by a number of people and tools. Commerce applications have the most at stake in standardization because search engines and other applications must be able to count on the same elements having the same meaning no matter what the source. Compatibility will be more important than a perfect solution in most cases involving multiple organizations. The final part of this chapter, which discusses industry initiatives already in progress, should give you a reasonable grasp of what's already out there.

Who (and What) Will Be Reading My XML?

The documents in the previous chapter were meant, in the end, for humans to read. XML makes the documents easier for machines to manipulate, providing a good way to apply formatting and possibly store the data, but in the long run, all those documents will be read by people. The applications in this chapter take advantage of several additional advantages of XML. First, XML enables developers to create documents that both humans and machines can read. Markup tags may look like labels in English (or another language) to the developer, but to the computer they're simply labels that help direct it to the data it needs for processing, which is stored neatly in nested structures. Second, XML offers considerably more flexibility than the other options currently available for data interchange between systems. XML can be used to represent the contents of a relational database, or it can represent the contents of an old hierarchical database or even the latest object-oriented database. At the same time, XML can easily represent document information, grouping information, or simple lists. Finally, XML provides a structure that is easy for programmers to manipulate using recursive structures that are widely available in most programming tools. Writing an XML parser isn't that difficult, especially if the parser foregoes validation and checks for well-formedness only.

These strengths give XML a range of capabilities far broader than those of other interchange formats. Although thousands of systems are already available for trading data between computers, none of them offers this much flexibility in a structure that is so easy to program. XML obviously won't solve all the problems of data interchange because not every program can handle every data structure XML can represent, but it still represents a major step forward. XML is definitely a generalist's tool. Given enough time and money, there will always be a more efficient or more beautiful way to perform the tasks described later, with customized database connections, exquisitely hand-crafted Web sites, or specially coded distributed components.

XML's combination of flexibility and structure suit it well to a group of applications that seeks out information. Search engines and agents can consider the information available in the DTDs and the tags of these documents when they try to categorize or index them. Making full use of these capabilities will require some standardization of tags — programs will have a hard time making sense of elements like <TODAYSSPECIALPRICE> and <SALETODAYONLY> (<PRICE> probably makes considerably more sense).

Search engines have an especially difficult task gathering and sorting information in its current amorphous state. The addition of meaningful standardized tags should make search engines better at finding relevant information. Agents usually operate on a smaller scale, typically seeking out choice bits of information for particular users, but they stand to gain in the same way, possibly achieving the status computers scientists have claimed for them for so long.

Automated search tools bring up an additional issue — the dangers of letting programs surf the Web. If your site generates XML documents from databases and could strain (or collapse) under the load created by these automated tools, you should definitely consider creating a robots.txt file for your site. When an agent or search engine visits a site, it should examine the `robots.txt` file to find out where on the site it is welcome and then avoid all proscribed areas. Details are available at `http://info.Webcrawler.com/mak/projects/robots/norobots.html`. Although robots.txt is not an "official" standard, it is widely accepted by search-engine developers and should help prevent programs from crawling all over your site, slowing it down, or possibly crashing it.

Developing documents for computers to read really isn't much more difficult than developing documents for people. Computers are fairly predictable, and the strong structures of XML should make it easier to create information that can be used by multiple processing applications, even extremely different processing applications.

A Better Electronic Catalog

Even though the HTML catalog in the previous chapter may have been acceptable as a way to present information on a page, and its XML transformation may have added some searchability, it can still stand some significant improvement. The main competitor to Joe's Catalog, Jane's Catalog, is embarking on this more difficult course. Building a new catalog format from the ground up may cost Jane some effort and adjustment, but it should create a more automatable catalog that is easier to manage.

As long as orders came in exclusively over the telephone, Jane was comfortable having a Web catalog that simply recreated her paper catalog. As the costs of her 800-number rose, she began to wonder whether she shouldn't revise her system and allow Web users to order over her cheaper Internet connection. At the same time, she's moving her catalog from the ragtag group of desktop publishing files they've used in the past, into a new database system capable of holding her items and all their associated data — even pictures! Because Jane doesn't spend much on advertising, she would like automated tools that easily understand her catalog, making it easier for users to find the items they want. XML sounds like it might give her a boost in that direction, and it should be a good fit for the database systems she's installing as well. The challenge is to create a catalog application that can present her data attractively to customers while easing the demands on her order-entry department.

Instead of working from the catalog as it is currently presented on the Web, we'll start by examining Jane's methods of assembling the catalog and processing orders. When Jane's computer receives an order (from a telephone operator at the moment), it processes payment, typically a credit card, and prints out a packing slip in the warehouse. Workers in the warehouse find the items and ship them out immediately. The order-entry department would like to see the Web application feed their computer a simple set of information: payment information, shipping information, and the list of products to be ordered (by item number) and quantities. This is a fairly easy set of data to deliver with existing Web tools. Eventually, on the customer side, Jane would like the application to display a full invoice to the customer, complete with shipping costs. Part of the motivation for moving to XML has to do with an interest in making the user's Web browser do as much work as possible, sparing her servers the trouble of processing information that client machines can handle just as easily. This saves Jane expensive bandwidth and processing effort. Even though XML may not be able to achieve this today, several other standards under development will soon make this much easier, as we'll see later in the chapter.

At this point, XML has several drawbacks for Web application development. Adding the necessary links for JavaScript code to read the XML information may complicate the clean structures Jane would like to produce. The DTD must provide support for scripting on some level without becoming too complex. Fortunately, Jane has already planned for her application to take advantage of frames, which will enable her to place code in another frame, safely outside the XML document. All the XML document needs to do is pass information regarding which item the user wants to a script in another frame, which will then store that information in a shopping basket and handle all the sales infrastructure Jane needs. The fact that Jane's computers will be generating static XML from a database will also ease the difficulties by allowing some repetitive information to appear in the XML markup.

Jane's Catalog is loosely organized into pages that group together related products. The groups are determined informally by the team that builds the paper catalog. The electronic catalog should preserve these groupings, making it easy for customers to flip back and forth between the two versions. All the grouping information is stored in the database as well, making it much easier for a script to churn out pages based on a set of queries. Jane just needs a set of elements that can present the catalog data elegantly, with minimal processing overhead, and that can easily adapt to the upcoming improvements in scripting and document object models while still accommodating the needs of the present.

The top level of this DTD is the group — all members of a group will be presented in the same document.

```
<!ELEMENT GROUP (GROUPNAME, ITEM+,LEGALNOTICE)>
<!ATTLIST GROUP
     GROUPLINK CDATA #IMPLIED>
```

The GROUPLINK attribute holds a key value that will make it easy for a parser at Jane's to link to the original database record for troubleshooting or other information gathering. The GROUP element begins with a GROUPNAME element, which is effectively a headline for the page, and ends with a LEGALNOTICE element, which will just contain the usual warnings about typos and pricing. It is probably unlikely that a search engine or agent would look for LEGALNOTICE as an element, but it does make formatting the fine print easier.

```
<!ELEMENT GROUPNAME (#PCDATA)>
<!ELEMENT LEGALNOTICE (#PCDATA)>
```

Under this headline are catalog ITEM elements. ITEM elements contain a variety of other elements, including ITEM subelements that represent products affiliated with their parent ITEM. Like the GROUP element, the ITEM element may have an attribute that connects it to its database entry.

```
<!ELEMENT ITEM (PRODUCTNAME, DESCRIPTION?,PRICING,
ITEM*)>
<!ATTLIST ITEM
     ITEMLINK CDATA #IMPLIED>
```

The PRODUCTNAME element, like the GROUPNAME element, is really just a headline. Because the elements receive different formatting and may need to be addressed differently through scripts, the two elements are created separately.

```
<!ELEMENT PRODUCTNAME (#PCDATA)>
```

The DESCRIPTION element must be able to handle a variety of content. (Remember that the DESCRIPTION element is optional — it won't get used for subitems.) Catalog entries don't often include italic or bold text, but periodically they do, mostly for book titles. Most product descriptions are just one paragraph, but occasionally an entry can go on for several paragraphs. Many descriptions even include pictures. As a result, the DESCRIPTION element must contain PARAGRAPH elements, which themselves contain a motley assortment of other elements, and IMG elements, modeled after the HTML version.

```
<!ELEMENT DESCRIPTION (PARAGRAPH | IMG)*>
<!ELEMENT IMG EMPTY>
<!ATTLIST IMG
    SRC CDATA #REQUIRED
    HEIGHT CDATA #REQUIRED
    WIDTH CDATA #REQUIRED>
<!ELEMENT PARAGRAPH (#PCDATA | CITATION | EMPHASIS |
HIGHLIGHT)*>
<!ELEMENT CITATION (#PCDATA)>
<!ELEMENT EMPHASIS (#PCDATA)>
<!ELEMENT HIGHLIGHT (#PCDATA)>
```

This simple set of markup tags should enable Jane and staff to recreate the descriptions for all the items in the catalog. Although this is exciting to the design staff, it doesn't have nearly the effect on the ordering processing as the contents of the PRICING element. The PRICING element contains all the price, shipping weight, delivery, availability, and warranty information, as well as the button that executes the script that adds the item to the shopping cart.

```
<!ELEMENT PRICING (PRODNUM,MARKER?,PRICE, MARKER?,
SHIPPING, MARKER?, DELIVERY, MARKER?, AVAIL, MARKER?,
WARRANTY, PURCHASE)>
<!ELEMENT PRODNUM (#PCDATA)>
<!ATTLIST PRODNUM
        ID      id      #REQUIRED>
<!ELEMENT MARKER(#PCDATA)>
<!ELEMENT PRICE(#PCDATA)>
<!ATTLIST PRICE
        ID      id      #REQUIRED>
<!ELEMENT SHIPPING (#PCDATA)>
<!ATTLIST SHIPPING
        ID      id      #REQUIRED>
<!ELEMENT DELIVERY (#PCDATA)>
<!ATTLIST DELIVERY
        ID      id      #REQUIRED>
<!ELEMENT AVAIL (#PCDATA)>
<!ATTLIST AVAIL
        ID      id      #REQUIRED>
<!ELEMENT WARRANTY (#PCDATA)>
<!ELEMENT PURCHASE (#PCDATA)>
<!ATTLIST PURCHASE
        onclick    CDATA    #REQUIRED>
```

Jane is reasonably confident that her warehouse will have the items listed in stock and uses the AVAIL element mostly to indicate when items are upcoming but haven't yet arrived in the warehouse, generating advance orders. A company that runs out of stock more frequently would probably need to generate its pages dynamically and reflect its current stock situation with more precise tags, like ONHAND for the number available or ONORDER to indicate when the item should arrive. Keep in mind, however, that you don't want to reveal your entire inventory to your competition.

Because this section's contents must be addressed by a script, it's picked up a lot of baggage. The following section on scripting with

XML will provide more detail on techniques for adding scripts and hooks for script to valid XML.

The PRICING element is a list of the parts required for order processing, including all of the noncustomer information needed to build a packing list. Optional MARKER elements are interspersed to enable descriptions like Price: to appear without cluttering the PRICE element. (When XSL appears in force, this may no longer be necessary.) The MARKER information is really just formatting and must be kept separate from the content of the other elements.

For now, all elements that may need to contribute information to a shopping cart are assigned ID values. The ID value in this case will be created using a naming convention that includes the product number (so as to avoid having duplicate ID values on the same page). This ID value enables scripts to "find" the element and extract its contents for processing. The PURCHASE element receives an on-click attribute, which enables it to call a script to add an item to the shopping basket. An actual PURCHASE element will look something like:

```
<PURCHASE onclick= "javascript:parent.cart.add('12323')">
Add to Cart</PURCHASE>
```

Using the event-handling attributes of HTML 4.0, this script will respond to clicks by calling the add method of the FRAME with the NAME attribute "cart."

Note

This EVENT model is supported by Internet Explorer 4.0 and 5.0 and will be supported by future versions of Netscape browsers as well.

Combining all of this information produces a DTD that encapsulates the information required for Jane's Catalog to present its information to the customer and return that data to the order department:

```
<!ELEMENT GROUP (GROUPNAME, ITEM+,LEGALNOTICE)>
<!ATTLIST GROUP
     GROUPLINK CDATA #IMPLIED>
<!ELEMENT GROUPNAME (#PCDATA)>
<!ELEMENT LEGALNOTICE (#PCDATA)>
<!ELEMENT ITEM (PRODUCTNAME, DESCRIPTION?,PRICING,
ITEM*)>
<!ATTLIST ITEM
     ITEMLINK CDATA #IMPLIED>
<!ELEMENT PRODUCTNAME (#PCDATA)>
<!ELEMENT DESCRIPTION (PARAGRAPH | IMG)*>
<!ELEMENT IMG EMPTY>
<!ATTLIST IMG
     SRC CDATA #REQUIRED
     HEIGHT CDATA #REQUIRED
     WIDTH CDATA #REQUIRED>
<!ELEMENT PARAGRAPH (#PCDATA | CITATION | EMPHASIS |
HIGHLIGHT)*>
<!ELEMENT CITATION (#PCDATA)>
<!ELEMENT EMPHASIS (#PCDATA)>
<!ELEMENT HIGHLIGHT (#PCDATA)>
<!ELEMENT PRICING (PRODNUM,MARKER?,PRICE, MARKER?,
SHIPPING, MARKER?, DELIVERY, MARKER?, AVAIL, MARKER?,
WARRANTY, PURCHASE)>
<!ELEMENT PRODNUM (#PCDATA)>
<!ATTLIST PRODNUM
     ID    ID    #REQUIRED>
<!ELEMENT MARKER(#PCDATA)>
<!ELEMENT PRICE(#PCDATA)>
<!ATTLIST PRICE
     ID    ID    #REQUIRED>
<!ELEMENT SHIPPING (#PCDATA)>
<!ATTLIST SHIPPING
     ID    ID    #REQUIRED>
<!ELEMENT DELIVERY (#PCDATA)>
<!ATTLIST DELIVERY
```

```
        ID    ID    #REQUIRED>
<!ELEMENT AVAIL (#PCDATA)>
<!ATTLIST AVAIL
        ID    ID    #REQUIRED>
<!ELEMENT WARRANTY (#PCDATA)>
<!ELEMENT PURCHASE (#PCDATA)>
<!ATTLIST PURCHASE
        onclick    CDATA    #REQUIRED>
```

The end result of this process is a structure Jane's Catalog can use both for transmitting information to users and processing this information to send orders back to the ordering system. (Those orders could be sent in an XML format, but that's the subject of the next system. The preceding DTD includes just the information that a client-side processor would need to build a full packing list and invoice of ordered goods).

A sample page from Jane's Catalog, generated by her database system, might look like the following:

```
<?xml version="1.0" standalone="no" encoding="UTF-8"?>
<!DOCTYPE GROUP SYSTEM "janes.dtd">
<GROUP GROUPLINK="23AA34FAB1">
<GROUPNAME>Pocket Calculating Devices</GROUPNAME>
<ITEM>
<PRODUCTNAME>Mortgage Calculator</PRODUCTNAME>
<DESCRIPTION><PARAGRAPH>Ever want to know precisely how
much of your house you own? What your monthly payments
would be if you refinanced? Mortgage-lovers will
appreciate this handy gadget. This calculator allows
comparisons between owning and renting, explores the
impact of inflation on your bank's profit margin, and
makes it easy to plan ahead.</PARAGRAPH></DESCRIPTION>
<PRICING><PRODNUM ID="I1024">1024</PRODNUM>
<MARKER>Price: $</MARKER>
<PRICE ID="I1024P">20.00</PRICE>
<MARKER>Shipping: $</MARKER>
```

```
<SHIPPING ID="I1024S">3.00</SHIPPING>
<MARKER>Delivery: </MARKER>
<DELIVERY ID="I1024D">Overnight</DELIVERY>
<MARKER>In Stock?: </MARKER>
<AVAIL ID="I1024A">Yes</AVAIL>
<MARKER>Warranty: </MARKER>
<WARRANTY>30 years</WARRANTY>
<PURCHASE
onclick="javascript:parent.cart.add('1024')">Add to
Cart</PURCHASE>
</PRICING>
<ITEM>
<PRODUCTNAME>Carrying Case</PRODUCTNAME>
<PRICING><PRODNUM ID="I1028">1028</PRODNUM>
<MARKER>Price: $</MARKER>
<PRICE ID="I1028P">2.00</PRICE>
<MARKER>Shipping: $</MARKER>
<SHIPPING ID="I1028S">1.00</SHIPPING>
<MARKER>Delivery: </MARKER>
<DELIVERY ID="I1028D">Overnight</DELIVERY>
<MARKER>In Stock?: </MARKER>
<AVAIL ID="I1028A">Yes</AVAIL>
<MARKER>Warranty: </MARKER>
<WARRANTY>2 years</WARRANTY>
<PURCHASE
onclick="javascript:parent.cart.add('1024')">Add to
Cart</PURCHASE>
</PRICING>
</ITEM>
</ITEM>
<LEGALNOTICE>Jane's Catalog is not responsible for
typographical errors. Prices and availability may change
at any time.</LEGALNOTICE>
</GROUP>
```

As you can see, nesting ITEM elements is simple. There is no need for the SUBITEM element we used in the last chapter, which makes for a more consistent structure. The ID elements duplicate information available elsewhere (the product number), but this evil is necessary only for the moment, as the next section will explain.

Adding Scripts to XML

SGML was developed in large part to encourage separation between programming logic and the data on which they worked. SGML does an excellent job of storing data in a structured format that programs can interpret, but it doesn't provide a mechanism for the kinds of "live" content that are rapidly spreading across the Web. XML's SGML inheritance in this field is something of a hindrance. Even tasks that are common HTML practice—like creating SCRIPT tags to hold the code needed to manipulate the document content—are frequently difficult in XML. JavaScript (a.k.a. the newly standardized ECMAScript) and VBScript both use the symbols &, <, and > for programming purposes. To either of these scripting languages, < means less than, not start a new markup tag here. A close examination of the HTML 4.0 DTD reveals that HTML uses SGML's CDATA type for element content, which enable these characters to appear:

```
<!ELEMENT SCRIPT - - CDATA  - script statements ->
 <!ATTLIST SCRIPT
    type        CDATA      #IMPLIED  - Internet content
type for script language -
    language    CDATA      #IMPLIED  - predefined script
language name -
    src         %URL;      #IMPLIED  - URL for an external
script -
    >
```

Because of assorted problems with SGML's implementation of it, XML doesn't offer the CDATA content model for elements—

only #PCDATA is available. Because the contents of the SCRIPT element in XML must be PCDATA, a parser will explode when it hits any code that uses &, <, or >. Developers must create a SCRIPT element that uses PCDATA and then converts that PCDATA space to CDATA by hand with a marked section: <![CDATA[...script...]]>. The SCRIPT element declaration will look similar to the preceding HTML DTD:

```
<!ELEMENT SCRIPT (#PCDATA)*>
<!ATTLIST SCRIPT
      type       CDATA        #IMPLIED
      language     CDATA        #IMPLIED
      src      CDATA      #IMPLIED>
```

Then, in all documents that use script, developers must convert this:

```
<SCRIPT LANGUAGE="JavaScript">
var x,y; x=1; y=2;
if x<y {alert ("X is less than Y!")}
</SCRIPT>
```

to this:

```
<SCRIPT LANGUAGE="JavaScript"><![CDATA[
var x,y; x=1; y=2;
if x<y {alert ("X is less than Y!")}
]]></SCRIPT>
```

This is the solution proposed by the HTML Activity's Voyager project for rebuilding HTML in XML. Another solution developers can turn to is the SRC attribute, which enables a page to load a separate file containing scripts. All the offending code can be stored in a separate file, avoiding the XML parser entirely.

Scriptlets — the latest Dynamic HTML tool from Microsoft — can also provide a place for scripts to hide, although at present they work only with Internet Explorer 4.0 and higher. Scriptlets use the OBJECT tag to import another file, which can then be used as an interface component. This might be useful for handling the shopping cart or cash register for an electronic catalog, but it remains to be seen how popular they will prove to be. A scriptlet OBJECT element might look like:

```
<OBJECT width=100 height=300 TYPE="text/x-scriptlet"
DATA="jsscriptlet.htm"></OBJECT>
```

Other tools for linking scripts to elements using style sheet-like syntax, based on proposals from Netscape and Microsoft, are under consideration by the W3C. The W3C's Document Object Model (DOM) enables scripts to access elements through the document structure as well as by ID. Unfortunately, full implementations of that model are still in development, though many XML parsers support the Core DOM.

Direct Connections: Business-to-Business Transactions

Electronic commerce over the Internet is just getting started, but it is rapidly becoming clear that retail sales over the Internet face security hazards and consumer skepticism. Instead of developing enormous systems for processing credit cards and handling customer inquiries, many Internet entrepreneurs have turned to the safer world of business-to-business transactions. Frequently, all parties involved in a deal already know and perhaps even trust each other, avoiding the anonymity issues associated with Internet commerce. Accounting systems already provide sales on credit to known customers, and shipping terms are already established. As we'll see in the next section, not all transactions are financial, either; many systems out there use similar connections to securely share private information.

Electronic data interchange (EDI) systems so far have tended to use structures from the database world: fixed-length or delimited fields ordered neatly into tables for processing. Transmission of this information has improved dramatically — companies used to mail tapes to each other regularly, but now they frequently connect over data networks — but the form of the information hasn't yet changed greatly. XML offers businesses more flexibility than their current systems can offer, along with an opportunity to create simple standards that can be extended to cover additional data structures as necessary.

The examples presented in this section provide only a very basic outline of what is necessary to create a full-fledged commercial interchange system. The standards proposed here will probably be superceded by recommendations from standards bodies and industry organizations.

EDI for commercial transactions has been expanding wildly over the last 20 years, and the structures it has created still have much to offer our XML examples. XML is not the answer to every aspect of electronic order placement. The businesses may trust each other enough to ship each other goods, but the orders must still be placed over a secure channel. This could be as simple as encrypting the XML document with public-key encryption tools and sending it via e-mail or as complex as sending it over a specially built private network. XML documents could also be sent on magnetic tape by private courier to companies uninterested in making network connections to their financial systems.

After that channel has been established, the businesses can begin considering the format for their orders. All orders still need ship-to and bill-to information, as well as contact information that can be used to reach a human if the computer fails. Dates are also critical, to give the recipient some idea of when the order was created and when it arrived. A priority level for the order might be useful in some situations, although there might be separate priorities for the order as a whole and for parts of the order. A listing of the items to be ordered will follow, concluding with an expected total number of items and total bill. The conclusion is a critical piece for making certain that items haven't been lost during processing. XML developers should probably look over their shoulder at the older forms of data interchange, if only to make certain that they haven't left out any key pieces that the older structures provided.

Our initial DTD for XML transactions, which provides a shell for the order, is deliberately abstract. At this level, it doesn't matter what kinds of items are being ordered — apples, tractors, and concrete beams are all just items to be transferred between companies. The second DTD, which defines the items, will be much more focused on the goods in question.

We'll start by defining the ORDER element, which encompasses the entire document:

```
<!ELEMENT ORDER (BILLTO, SHIPTO, CONTACT, PRIORITY,
ITEM+,TOTALS)>
```

The BILLTO and SHIPTO elements have similar contents:

```
<!ELEMENT BILLTO (REFERENCE | FULLADDRESS)>
<!ELEMENT SHIPTO ((REFERENCE |FULLADDRESS), SHIPVIA)>
<!ELEMENT SHIPVIA (REFERENCE | FULLADDRESS)>
<!ELEMENT REFERENCE (#PCDATA)>
<!ELEMENT FULLADDRESS (COMPANY, ADDRESSLINE+, CITY,
STATE, POSTALCODE, COUNTRY, CONTACT, PHONE, FAX?)>
<!ELEMENT COMPANY (#PCDATA)>
<!ELEMENT ADDRESSLINE (#PCDATA)>
<!ELEMENT CITY (#PCDATA)>
<!ELEMENT STATE (#PCDATA)>
<!ELEMENT POSTALCODE (#PCDATA)>
<!ELEMENT COUNTRY (#PCDATA)>
<!ELEMENT CONTACT (#PCDATA | REFERENCE)*>
<!ELEMENT PHONE (#PCDATA)>
<!ELEMENT FAX (#PCDATA)>
<!ELEMENT PRIORITY (#PCDATA)>
```

Most of this information is basic text, although the key REFERENCE element will probably be used for most transactions. By using a REFERENCE, an ordering company is announcing that it already has a record in the recipient's system. The processing application that receives this data will pass orders that use REFERENCE to the order system immediately—a relationship already exists. (If it's a bad relationship, because the company ordering doesn't pay the bills, or doesn't exist in the system, the order system can still reject the order.) Orders that arrive with full addresses will need further verification. Contacts will be called, credit checks run if necessary, and the new buyer will be entered into the order system and given its own REFERENCE information for future use.

The TOTALS element contains a summary that can be used to check the order.

```
<!ELEMENT TOTALS (TOTALITEMS, TOTALQUANTITY, TOTALCOST)>
<!-NOTE TOTALS ARE FOR CHECKING DATA ONLY AND DO NOT
REFLECT FINAL COSTS OR QUANTITIES ->
<!ELEMENT TOTALITEMS (#PCDATA)>
<!ELEMENT TOTALQUANTITY (#PCDATA)>
<!ELEMENT TOTALCOST (#PCDATA)>
```

This basic shell could be useful to a variety of businesses, even though they will probably want to customize it to some extent to reflect their needs. The most important feature of this shell, however, is what is left out. Because the ITEM element is never defined, this DTD is incomplete and needs a companion DTD to actually handle orders.

For this example, we'll use the publishing industry, the only industry in which I've encountered electronic ordering and all its associated benefits and costs. (Searching for hundreds of missing line items on thousands of orders of thousands of books each is not an experience I care to repeat, either.) The ITEM definition for this relatively simple industry will include only three pieces: BOOK, which carries the title information; QUANTITY, which specifies how many copies they want; PRIORITY, which enables the customer to request higher-priority treatment of certain titles; and EXTENDEDCOST, which provides the total cost the purchaser expects to pay if the other information is correct. EXTENDED-COST in this case acts like a checksum, making sure that the purchaser's information makes sense. (If they have the wrong price, they'll be billed for the correct amount, of course.)

```
<!ELEMENT ITEM (BOOK, QUANTITY, PRIORITY?, DISCOUNT,
EXTENDEDCOST)>
<!ELEMENT DISCOUNT (#PCDATA)>
<!ELEMENT EXTENDEDCOST (#PCDATA)>
```

The book industry standardized early on a notation for its products: the International Standard Book Number (ISBN). The ISBN for *XML: A Primer (Second Edition)*, for instance, is 0-7645-3310-X. The first digit indicates that the book is in English, and the next four digits indicate that the book was published by IDG Books. The next four digits (3310) uniquely identify the title for IDG Books, and the final digit (which could be a digit from 0–9 or an X) is a checksum. XML parsers won't process the ISBN to make sure the checksum is correct; that is the responsibility of the processing application. ISBNs uniquely identify books or book-related products, like boxed sets of books and other packages that range from books with stuffed animals to paper-making kits. Each ISBN is technically allowed to refer to only one item packaged as a unit for sale, although the contents of that package may include other items with their own ISBNs. (It's really a barcode standard that makes it easy for stores to order and sell books.) In theory at least, our DTD shouldn't even need to include title or pricing information because that should all connect to the ISBN. In reality, titles and prices change regularly, and customers aren't always notified. Adding titles and prices to the information transmitted also provides some extra insurance that the order will be processed correctly and can be used to generate warnings to customers that the information they have is outdated without stopping the order completely or requiring human intervention.

The BOOK element will include ISBN, title, and price. For most previous examples I've avoided using any element names that conflict with HTML. Although none of these orders should be going anywhere near a browser, this model could eventually be extended to retail, so it's probably best to rename the TITLE element.

```
<!ELEMENT BOOK (ISBN, BOOKTITLE, PRICE)>
<!ELEMENT ISBN (#PCDATA)>
<!ELEMENT BOOKTITLE (#PCDATA)>
<!ELEMENT PRICE (#PCDATA)>
```

The other critical part of a line item is the quantity. More than likely, the company placing the order wants more than one copy of the book. Some large wholesalers and distributors want to receive books only in whole, unopened cartons. Because books come in all kinds of shapes and sizes, the number of books to a box varies from book to book. The same title can even come in different carton quantities when a printer who uses a different size box reprints it! In any case, we must provide options for customers to specify whether they want whole cartons, the size of the carton they are expecting, and rough instructions for how to adjust to any differences in carton quantities. Most small customers won't care about cartons, since they'll be receiving repackaged boxes of mixed books from the warehouse.

```
<!ELEMENT QUANTITY (NUMBER, CARTON?)>
<!ATTLIST QUANTITY
        SHIPCQ     (NO | ROUNDUP | ROUNDDOWN |
ROUNDCLOSEST) "NO">
<!ELEMENT NUMBER (#PCDATA)>
<!ELEMENT CARTON (#PCDATA)>
```

Now that we have two complete DTDs, we can begin to create some orders. The first complete DTD provides the shell we'll use:

```
<!ELEMENT ORDER (BILLTO, SHIPTO, CONTACT, PRIORITY,
ITEM+,TOTALS)>
<!ELEMENT BILLTO (REFERENCE | FULLADDRESS)>
<!ELEMENT SHIPTO ((REFERENCE |FULLADDRESS), SHIPVIA)>
<!ELEMENT SHIPVIA (REFERENCE | FULLADDRESS)>
<!ELEMENT REFERENCE (#PCDATA)>
```

```
<!ELEMENT FULLADDRESS (COMPANY, ADDRESSLINE+, CITY,
STATE, POSTALCODE, COUNTRY, CONTACT, PHONE, FAX?)>
<!ELEMENT COMPANY (#PCDATA)>
<!ELEMENT ADDRESSLINE (#PCDATA)>
<!ELEMENT CITY (#PCDATA)>
<!ELEMENT STATE (#PCDATA)>
<!ELEMENT POSTALCODE (#PCDATA)>
<!ELEMENT COUNTRY (#PCDATA)>
<!ELEMENT CONTACT (#PCDATA | REFERENCE)>
<!ELEMENT PHONE (#PCDATA)>
<!ELEMENT FAX (#PCDATA)>
<!ELEMENT PRIORITY (#PCDATA)>
<!ELEMENT TOTALS (TOTALITEMS, TOTALQUANTITY, TOTALCOST)>
<!-NOTE TOTALS ARE FOR CHECKING DATA ONLY AND DO NOT
REFLECT FINAL COSTS OR QUANTITIES ->
<!ELEMENT TOTALITEMS (#PCDATA)>
<!ELEMENT TOTALQUANTITY (#PCDATA)>
<!ELEMENT TOTALCOST (#PCDATA)>
```

The second DTD includes the first DTD through a parameter entity and provides the information for the actual line items.

```
<!ENTITY % ORDER SYSTEM "order.dtd">
%ORDER;
<!ELEMENT ITEM (BOOK, QUANTITY, PRIORITY?, DISCOUNT,
EXTENDEDCOST)>
<!ELEMENT DISCOUNT (#PCDATA)>
<!ELEMENT EXTENDEDCOST (#PCDATA)>
<!ELEMENT BOOK (ISBN, BOOKTITLE, PRICE)>
<!ELEMENT ISBN (#PCDATA)>
<!ELEMENT BOOKTITLE (#PCDATA)>
<!ELEMENT PRICE (#PCDATA)>
<!ELEMENT QUANTITY (NUMBER, CARTON?)>
<!ATTLIST QUANTITY
        SHIPCQ      (NO | ROUNDUP | ROUNDDOWN |
ROUNDCLOSEST) "NO">
```

```
<!ELEMENT NUMBER (#PCDATA)>
<!ELEMENT CARTON (#PCDATA)>
```

Now that we have a framework, it's time to learn how to use it. Our order document calls only the book DTD directly. The order DTD is treated as a part of the book DTD and doesn't need to be called directly.

```
<?xml version="1.0" encoding="UTF-8"?>
<!DOCTYPE ORDER SYSTEM "book.dtd">
<ORDER>
<BILLTO>
<REFERENCE>8345A</REFERENCE>
</BILLTO>
<SHIPTO>
<REFERENCE>8345A</REFERENCE>
<SHIPVIA><REFERENCE>2A</REFERENCE></SHIPVIA>
</SHIPTO>
<CONTACT>Burnie Orange</CONTACT>
<PRIORITY>Normal</PRIORITY>
<ITEM>
<BOOK><ISBN>155828592X</ISBN><BOOKTITLE>XML:A
Primer</BOOKTITLE><PRICE>$24.95</PRICE></BOOK>
<QUANTITY
SHIPCQ="ROUNDDOWN"><NUMBER>100</NUMBER><CARTON>20</CARTON
></QUANTITY>
<DISCOUNT>.42</DISCOUNT>
<EXTENDEDCOST>$1447.10</EXTENDEDCOST>
</ITEM>
<ITEM>
<BOOK><ISBN>1558285288</ISBN><BOOKTITLE>MIME, UUENCODE,
&amp; ZIP</BOOKTITLE><PRICE>$24.95</PRICE></BOOK>
<QUANTITY
SHIPCQ="ROUNDDOWN"><NUMBER>100</NUMBER><CARTON>20</CARTON
></QUANTITY>
<DISCOUNT>.42</DISCOUNT>
```

```
<EXTENDEDCOST>$1447.10</EXTENDEDCOST>
</ITEM>
<ITEM>
<BOOK><ISBN>1558514716</ISBN><BOOKTITLE>Graphical
Applications with Tcl &amp;
Tk</BOOKTITLE><PRICE>$39.95</PRICE></BOOK>
<QUANTITY><NUMBER>16</NUMBER><CARTON>16</CARTON></QUANTIT
Y>
<DISCOUNT>.42</DISCOUNT>
<EXTENDEDCOST>$370.74</EXTENDEDCOST>
</ITEM>
<ITEM>
<BOOK><ISBN>155828480X</ISBN><BOOKTITLE>World Wide Web
Bible</BOOKTITLE><PRICE>$29.95</PRICE></BOOK>
<QUANTITY><NUMBER>10</NUMBER><CARTON>10</CARTON></QUANTIT
Y>
<DISCOUNT>.42</DISCOUNT>
<EXTENDEDCOST>173.71</EXTENDEDCOST>
</ITEM>
<ITEM>
<BOOK><ISBN>1558284783</ISBN><BOOKTITLE>Introduction to
CGI/Perl</BOOKTITLE><PRICE>$19.95</PRICE></BOOK>
<QUANTITY
SHIPCQ="ROUNDDOWN"><NUMBER>24</NUMBER><CARTON>24</CARTON>
</QUANTITY>
<DISCOUNT>.42</DISCOUNT>
<EXTENDEDCOST>277.70</EXTENDEDCOST>
</ITEM>
<TOTALS><TOTALITEMS>5</TOTALITEMS><TOTALQUANTITY>320</TOT
ALQUANTITY>
<TOTALCOST>$3716.35</TOTALCOST>
</TOTALS>
</ORDER>
```

Although this may not be as compact as the previous fixed-length or the more flexible delimited files, it's certainly more readable by humans. Its extra flexibility also gives it a significant advantage because it doesn't require that all information be present all the time. The spread of networks has lowered the costs of transmission, making this kind of verbosity acceptable. Building a processing application around this DTD and connecting it to the order system will take some effort, but hopefully the extra work will pay off in added flexibility, enabling customers to use any variety of XML processor they choose.

Direct Connections: Information Interchange

Even though orders are often the most important form of information exchanged between companies, other forms of information that aren't directly revenue-generating may also need to be shared, even among competitors. Situations where multiple firms must organize multiple parts provide fertile ground for information interchange systems. Establishing this interchange may be difficult because some companies may feel that they have much to lose by revealing their proprietary information, but often there is more to be gained than lost by sharing. Even though much of the work involved in creating these interchange systems is similar to that put into the documents described in the previous chapter, sharing documents between multiple companies creates additional challenges. This section of the chapter won't build any DTDs, which are likely to be even more industry-bound than the ordering processes already described. Instead, we'll explore some of the commerce-focused XML standards already in development.

Cross-Reference

To see a more comprehensive list of XML projects, visit http://www.oasis-open.org/cover/xml.html. For a directory of XML schemas, see http://www.schema.net.

ECIX: An Example from SGML

One of the most widely cited successes of SGML's commercial use, and an example worth pondering for XML, is the Pinnacles Electronic Component Information Exchange (ECIX) Group. Begun as a consortium of Hitachi, Intel, National Semiconductor, Phillips Semiconductors, and Texas Instruments, it is now part of the Silicon Integration Initiative (http://www.si2.org). ECIX began as a standard for electronic databooks, the documentation that accompanies electronic components. As the integration of multiple components on to chips progressed, the size of the average component grew rapidly, and documentation for electronic components exploded. Engineers trying to build new components were spending their time searching through documentation and recreating components in their CAD (computer-assisted design) software instead of building new chips. The semiconductor companies united to make exchanging electronic information about components easier. They built two separate pieces of the standard: the Pinnacles Component Information Standard (PCIS) and the Component Information Dictionary Standard (CIDS). PCIS provides component information in an electronic format that can be read by engineers or imported easily into a CAD system. CIDS provides a dictionary of component terms and definitions for easy lookup and standardization.

PCIS source documents provide detailed information about components including packages, functional descriptions, pin-outs, soldering and mounting, instruction sets, register sets, and memory maps. The PCIS source documents refer extensively to the CIDS dictionary, using a central, standardized source for definitions. As a result, engineers can query PCIS documents instead of endlessly flipping through pages in a databook. All definitions are standardized, making it much simpler for engineers to include components from other firms in their designs. By opening up their data to electronic search and manipulation, the industry has made it easier for competing firms to sell their goods to each other. Designers can find and use parts already suited to the task at hand and apply them immediately instead of redesigning them.

Cross-Reference

For more information on ECIX, see `http://www.si2.org/ecix/`.

Open Trading Protocol (OTP)

The Open Trading Protocol (OTP) provides an open XML format for handling commercial transactions over the Internet. OTP is being developed by the OTP consortium, a group of companies including systems, software, and network vendors and financial institutions. OTP hopes to create XML analogs to existing processing systems for purchases, whether between businesses or between retail customers and merchants. OTP provides tools for establishing that both parties in a transaction are bona fide, capable of supporting their obligations, and manages the transaction from the initial purchase through delivery and possibly also through record keeping and refund handling. OTP supports electronic cash mechanisms, and encourages more direct contact between customers and merchants for transaction handling. (It seems to be a step away from the current situation in which many customers turn to their credit card companies to resolve disputes rather than handling them directly.) OTP is designed to work with a variety of existing mechanisms, from the SET (Secure Electronic Transactions) protocol to HTTP.

Cross-Reference

For information on OTP, visit the OTP consortium at `http://www.ofx.net/ofx/ab_main.asp`.

Bank Internet Payment System (BIPS)

The Bank Internet Payment System (BIPS), a project of the Financial Services Technology Consortium (FSTC) is an XML-based system for supporting bank transactions like wire transfers and automated clearing house transfers. BIPS is not a complete system for building electronic commerce systems — instead, it focuses on one aspect of electronic commerce, payment systems, leaving other tasks to other protocols. (BIPS isn't even intended to handle all payment scenarios; the FSTC has another standard, "E-Check," for check payments.) BIPS is a component that can be built into other systems, such as those from CommerceNet (another industry association), rather than a stand-alone application.

Cross-Reference

For more information on BIPS, visit `http://www.fstc.org/projects/bips/`. For information on CommerceNet, visit `http://www.commerce.net/`.

XML/EDI

XML/EDI is an organization working to create mechanisms that use XML to support transactions that have been run over dedicated electronic data interchange (EDI) networks, primarily business-to-business transactions. XML/EDI is applying XML syntax, with its much more flexible data structures and generic tools, as a replacement for the formats (like X12 and EDIFACT) currently used for these transactions. While XML incurs certain costs (like more verbose messages because of the tagging), the XML/EDI group is a loud proponent of the argument that XML more than makes up for these costs. The ability to use off-the-shelf tools (like XML parsers and Internet protocols) can reduce the cost of transactions dramatically, while providing businesses with a richer vocabulary for describing their transactions.

Cross-Reference

For information on XML/EDI, visit `http://www.xmledi.net/`. An EEMA workgroup considering such proposals has a site at `http://www.edi-tie.nl/edifact/xml-edi.htm`, while information about integrating the X12 protocols and XML from the Data Interchange Standards Association (DISA) is available at `http://www.disa.org/x12/x12xmlfaq.html`.

Information and Content Exchange (ICE)

Information and Content Exchange is a difficult protocol to categorize. In some ways, it manages document content, including XML, but primarily, it uses XML to build a set of tools for managing business relationships, setting up a subscriber-syndicator model for content exchange. It doesn't handle secure transactions or financial obligations by itself; relying instead on HTTP, SSL, and other supporting structures to handle those issues. ICE focuses on managing the subscriber-syndicator relationship, simplifying the task of letting Web sites share their information through the application of clearly defined, previously agreed upon, and stable rules within a management framework supporting business needs. If a relationship goes sour, the syndicator can pull the plug on a subscriber, or a subscriber can stop making requests, without having to go to a lot of trouble. ICE is intended to move information sharing and reuse well beyond the framing that has appeared on the Web, reducing the costs of distributing information and at the same time making it more manageable and potentially billable.

Cross-Reference

To read the ICE Protocol, visit `http://www.w3.org/TR/NOTE-ice`. For more information on the latest developments, visit `http://www.vignette.com/CDA/Book/0,1038,S1-L1-173-174-156,00.html`. Robin Cover's bibliography page on ICE also brings together a number of resources, at `http://www.oasis-open.org/cover/ice.html`.

Newspaper Association of America – Standard for Classified Advertising Data

Classified advertisements are requests for transactions, though of a much more general sort than the specifications above are designed to accommodate. Classified ads are sometimes business-to-consumer, sometimes consumer-to-consumer, and come in an enormous variety from the help-wanted ads to real estate and vehicle sales to garage sale notices and legal notices. The Newspaper Association of America (NAA) is focusing on a few types of classifieds for its initial standard, starting with employment, real estate, and vehicles (including bicycles!). The NAA classified advertising exchange standard (which lacks an acronym, but uses "adex" as its root element) is designed to enable newspapers to share highly marked-up advertisements. This has promise in a number of areas. Highly marked-up ads make it possible to build search engines and processing around them that will reduce the need to scan miles of advertisements to find the right ones for a given reader. While newspapers can still print classified ads, this makes possible value-added services that newspapers may be able to charge for. Of more immediate commercial import, it should also enable newspapers to sell classifieds for a larger area than a single paper, building a larger national market in this kind of advertising. In the long term, classified advertisements could also be integrated with the transaction-focused systems above to create complete systems for handling small transactions.

 Cross-Reference

For the latest on the NAA's Classified Advertising Task Force's activities, visit `http://www.naa.org/technology/clsstdtf/`.

These initiatives are just a few of the publicly announced projects using XML for commercial applications. As more industry groups and companies start using XML, it will hopefully become ubiquitous, with many more standards arriving on a regular basis.

Chapter 8

XML for Document Management

XML promises a revolution in the way documents are managed. Document-management systems store documents, keep track of document contents, control access to them, and enable users to locate key information quickly. Many current document-management systems are just enormous electronic filing cabinets, storing documents with only a few keywords and a date provided for quick searching. XML documents carry within them the information and the structures needed to build more robust document systems, organizing collections of information that had previously been left to wither away in filing cabinets or trash cans.

Traditional file structures and even the Web have provided a minimum level of storage and accessibility, but more comprehensive systems are starting to become standard equipment in offices. By giving document-management systems a clearer picture of the contents of documents, markup languages make it possible to control larger sets of documents more efficiently. Searches can be limited to individual elements, reducing the amount of processing required to get to a document and reducing the number of false matches. If XML can bridge the extensive document systems already built using SGML and the ubiquity and ease of use of the Web, XML document-management may eventually replace the file system as it currently exists.

Achieving this promise will require significant changes in the way organizations look at their documents and the development of new (and friendlier) tools for managing information. A large part of the reason the paperless office has proven so difficult to achieve is the legacy that working with paper documents has left behind. Treating files as the basic unit for document management is much like treating single documents as the basic unit in a paper filing system. Documents, neatly stapled (or not), stored in file folders that group related documents. Sometimes the same file needs to be stored multiple places; sometimes the entire file folder must be searched to track down a single document. Treating documents as containers of information rather than as a fundamental unit in themselves is a huge first step toward moving past the antiquated tools most people currently use to manage their documents, even their computerized documents. By changing focus from the document to the information within the documents, management tools can finally provide the cross-referencing and searching tools needed to make computerized information systems genuinely useful.

XML's Inheritance: SGML and Document Management

XML inherits an enormous body of previous document-management development from SGML. (Indeed, many SGML vendors are hoping to reap a windfall of sales from people using XML for applications previously closed to SGML.) SGML found its most comfortable niche in large-scale document-management systems, often for publishers and government (especially defense) organizations, and notably for IBM, which originally developed markup. This core of users has widened slowly over the last 20 years, including more users in smaller organizations, academia, engineering, and distributed projects. Linux documentation, for instance, is shifting to an SGML format based on the DocBook DTD.

Note

For an excellent overview of SGML document-management scenarios, including case studies from Grolier Incorporated, Sybase, United Technologies, and Mobil, see Chet Ensign's *$GML: The Billion Dollar Secret* (Prentice-Hall, 1997).

SGML document-management systems tend to be fairly large, often employing conversion from SGML to another format for presentation, and combining tools from multiple vendors to create a complete solution. "SGML-in-a-box" isn't available; instead, a variety of authoring and development tools, consulting services, document repositories, search engines, and custom-built applications need to be integrated to provide a complete solution for shared document systems. Because SGML has remained a tool for custom-built solutions, the prices of those solutions and their components have remained extremely high, a significant barrier to widespread SGML adoption. Not every SGML product is expensive, however; James Clark's SP parser is freely available from `http://www.jclark.com/`, for instance, and Corel's WordPerfect 8 contains SGML tools, including a Visual DTD Builder.

Many SGML vendors are repositioning their products for use with XML. Although XML is technically a subset of SGML, some vendors are having an easier time than others. When buying these products for XML-focused solutions, always make certain that the output will be XML, without any of the many features of SGML that were removed in the XML creation process. The expertise gained from years of document design and information modeling, however, can be transferred directly from SGML to XML. After you've learned the basics of XML, and feel adventurous, exploring the resources available on SGML and data modeling can connect you to years of wisdom gained through hard work, helping you to avoid problems others have already solved.

Tip

A fantastic place to locate all kinds of SGML and XML resources is Robin Cover's extensive (indeed, overwhelming) SGML/XML Web page at `http://www.oasis-open.org/cover/sgml-xml.html`. The site lists books, papers, articles, software, and other resources in incredible detail.

The Future of XML Document Management

XML enables document-management systems to store documents as parts rather than as large clumps of often indecipherable information. Removing formatting information from the core of a document makes it far easier for search engines and similar tools to parse text without having to ponder formatting codes. Assigning element and attribute names that are meaningful in the context of information interchange is key to this process, as is the efficient storage and retrieval of the documents. A document-management tool written for XML from the ground up might even store documents as sets of elements within hierarchically organized databases. Instead of file systems, XML may force a move to more sophisticated repositories that store XML documents in a manner reflecting the structure of the document, a set of small pieces that can be manipulated, rather than a chunk of text that requires a full parsing every time it is accessed.

Cross-Reference

Repositories will receive more attention in Chapter 12, in the full context of XML's place in client-server applications.

XML is only getting started as a document format. A key piece of making the XML document-management dream real lies in the tools used to create the documents. If the XML tools are as clunky as the hand-coding we've done throughout this book, no one will want to use them. Even though XML tools may require significant interface changes, many WYSIWYG tools are already preparing for the transition. Microsoft has announced support for XML as a common file format for Microsoft Office, though in a limited capacity. Although the examples that follow are hand-coded, most of the people using them will not be entering tags directly. (Imagine an application...)

Building document-management applications is well beyond the scope of this book. The remainder of this chapter will explore ways to create DTDs that consider real business needs, creating centrally stored documents that can be easily searched and that meet the needs of more than one part of a company. The first example standardizes the memo, perhaps the most commonly used business document type. The second creates a custom solution to a problem common in larger companies, that of keeping track of completed projects. Both examples are small components of what will hopefully grow into large interlocking systems that store information so that it can be readily accessed and easily processed.

Small Steps toward the Paperless Office

Our first document-management DTD will address one of the largest paper-wasters in business environments: the memos that perpetually fill in-boxes. Many companies produce small weekly newsletters in a memo format; this DTD will disseminate chatty pieces of information as well as the boss' announcement that the company is cutting off the supply of free donuts. Although many people might question the wisdom of saving and managing memos, memos and other small-scale communications have grown dramatically in importance with the rise of litigation and the need to document processes. The Freedom of Information Act (FOIA), for example, requires that the federal government must maintain records of its activities and release them (in some form) to the public. At present, processing an FOIA request can take weeks or months as agencies contact their warehouses to gather old files. With an XML-based system based on DTD's like the one we're using for the memo, the time needed to locate documents could be greatly reduced. This DTD can be reused easily for a number of other tasks (for example, e-mail is typically formatted using a similar model).

Virtually no one will want to hand-code memos in XML. In the case of the memo, with its very simple structure, a program might be able to read the memo DTD and use it as a template, building a form around the needed information. XML parsers can use the information in a wide variety of ways, not just as document presentation information. An advanced XML processor might create the memo through an interview process rather than the usual clicking in fields in a document.

The first step in creating the memo DTD is interviewing people and collecting memos — lots of them — to examine how they are assembled. Most companies use a fairly standard format, with a letterhead of some kind at the top, followed by a distribution list, the source of the memo, a brief headline, and then the contents. In some cases, the typist is indicated at the bottom of the memo if the typist was someone other than the original author. For our example, we'll use an imaginary company — Jimmy's Delectable Car Parts Design (JDCPD). JDCPD is a successful firm that sells after-market high-performance parts for all kinds of cars and trucks. A typical memo might look like the one shown in Figure 8-1.

Jimmy's Delectable Car Parts Design

To: Accounts Payable
Cc: All Employees
From: Jimmy
Re: Donut Payments Prohibited
Date: October 10, 1997

Please note that all requests for donut reimbursement should be rejected in the future. Our health insurance company is protesting about the ever-growing size of the average employee. Given the difficult choice between getting our designers to exercise and denying them donuts, management has found it considerably simpler to the end the donut reimbursement program.

All protesting employees should be directed to my office, where rice cakes and herbal tea will be made available.

JD:tgk

Figure 8-1 *A typical memo*

Some memos are more complex like the one shown in Figure 8-2. Jimmy's Delectable Car Parts Design has a public relations office, which also puts out an internal weekly newsletter. The newsletter has short items of interest to JDCPD employees, that are presented in a friendly, informal style.

Jimmy's Delectable Car Parts Design

To: Jimmy
Cc: All Employees
From: Lois Turpin, PR Department
Re: JDCPD Today
Date: October 10, 1997

Design Contest Winner - Frank Kravitz of the fuel injection division has won the September award for best car part drawing. Frank's masterpiece, On to the Spark Plug II, will be on display in the lobby through November 12. Frank also won the award in January and July.

Donut Reimbursement Ends - To avoid a threatening doubling of health insurance premiums, JDCPD has ended its donut reimbursement program. "We are extremely sad to have to take such unpleasant measures," said Jimmy, "but we hope our employees will understand the difficult situation we face."

Rice Cakes Available - For a limited time, rice cakes and a variety of herbal teas will be made available in Jimmy's office. Employees needing a quick snack to get them charged up for a hard day of parts designing are welcome to stop by.

Remember - "Parts is parts!" Take pride in your work. The annual award for best design will be announced in December.

LT

Figure 8-2 *A more complex memo*

The public relations department would like to be able to use the memo format for other presentations as well, although they haven't planned anything specific yet. They know that in future editions of the newsletter, especially the upcoming Intranet newsletter, they would like to include thumbnails of the award-winning drawings and dress up the page a bit with more logos and assorted clip art. Press releases are also distributed in a similar format, although they probably won't be included in this project.

The human resources department has a few requests to make of the memo DTD project. Because all of these memos will eventually be going into a document-management system, the human resources director would like to be able to search the memo files for information by particular employees and about specified employees and projects. This feature could come in handy in case of a lawsuit, saving a tremendous amount of time and money spent searching through piles of memos for anything incriminating. Human resources obviously doesn't have time to read every memo in the firm, but this could help them to build an early warning system.

The mailroom is another critical customer for memos because they must distribute them. The mailroom's primary concern is that the distribution list receive a standard format, preferably one that can be switched over to e-mail painlessly so that they can get back to shipping packages instead of handing out memos. The rest of the company, including upper management, firmly believes that "memos are memos," although some of the designers would like to be able to add their drawings within the memos to provide reference material.

The humble memo apparently handles a variety of tasks, even though it does not need to carry much information. These tasks aren't all compatible, nor are they all likely to be accomplished on the first pass. Building a workable DTD will take some experimentation and approval from many people who do not wholly support electronic memos.

The best place to start on a document type definition is usually that area of a document that already has the most structure. In this case, that's the header area. The header always contains a distribution list, a source (the From: field), a topic, and a date. The distribution list at present can be anything the mailroom understands, but the prospect of using e-mail for all memos looms in the not-so-distant future. Initially, we'll create a memo DTD that includes very little detail:

```
<!ELEMENT MEMO (HEADER, MAIN)>
<!- MEMO DTD Version 0.1 - Experimental Use Only ->
<!ELEMENT HEADER (DISTRIBUTION, SUBJECT, DATE)>
<!ELEMENT DISTRIBUTION (TO+, CC?, FROM+)>
<!ELEMENT TO (#PCDATA)>
<!ELEMENT CC (#PCDATA)>
<!ELEMENT FROM (#PCDATA)>
<!ELEMENT SUBJECT (#PCDATA)>
<!ELEMENT DATE (#PCDATA)>
<!ELEMENT AUTHOR (#PCDATA)>
<!ELEMENT TYPIST (#PCDATA)>
<!ELEMENT MAIN (#PCDATA | AUTHOR | TYPIST)*)>
```

This is enough of a DTD for a simple demonstration of what is possible. To show what it can do, we create a sample document:

```
<?xml version="1.0" standalone="no" encoding="UTF-8"?>
<!DOCTYPE MEMO SYSTEM "memo.dtd">
<MEMO>
<HEADER>
<DISTRIBUTION>
<TO>To: Jimmy</TO>
<FROM>From: Simon</FROM>
</DISTRIBUTION>
<SUBJECT>Re: Sample Document Created with Memo
DTD</SUBJECT>
<DATE>Date: 10/11/1999</DATE>
</HEADER>
<MAIN>
```

I just thought you might like to see what a memo in XML looks like. Thanks for the vote of confidence at the last meeting. With any luck, this will make our transition to electronic documents reasonably painless.
```
<AUTHOR>SSL</AUTHOR>
</MAIN>
</MEMO>
```

Even though this parses well, it has some problems:

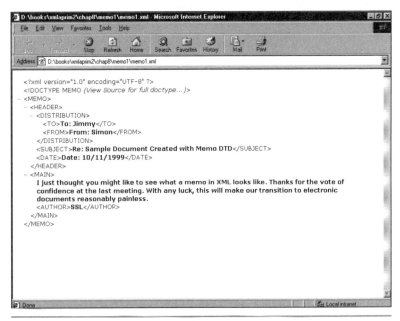

Figure 8-3 *The parsed memo*

The distribution fields are the main problem. Because they must include the "To:," "CC:," and "From:" headers, they don't quite make sense. This may be acceptable for paper documents, where humans can make sense out of the list just by reading it, but it will keep e-mail programs from working properly and make it difficult for the soon-to-arrive document-management system to keep track of senders and recipients. These fields all need to be broken down some more. Fortunately, they all use the same kind of information, referring to individuals or organizations within the company. Our solution clearly requires an extra element to identify senders and recipients. Because the two groups are composed of the same set of addresses of people and groups, they can share an element:

```
<!ELEMENT IDENTITY (#PCDATA)>
```

For now, it's not entirely certain what the address will be. The #PCDATA type lets us accept this uncertainty for the present, although JDCPD will probably want to move to a more specific model after they work out a directory structure. If they just need to combine name and e-mail address, they could use:

```
<!ELEMENT IDENTITY (NAME, EMAIL?)>
<!NAME (#PCDATA)>
<!ELEMENT EMAIL (#PCDATA)>
```

Better yet, if they start using some real directory-management tools, they might be able to use:

```
<!ELEMENT IDENTITY (#PCDATA)>
<!ATTLIST IDENTITY NAMEID CDATA #REQUIRED>
```

The information contained in the IDENTITY element could be a description humans can understand, whereas the NAMEID attribute of the IDENTITY element would provide a unique identifier for an individual that corresponds to a listing in a central directory system. People distributing memos on paper could read the IDENTITY element text easily, whereas e-mail and document-management systems could pick up the NAMEID attribute. This combination of human and machine-readable data would ideally suit the needs of the human resources department discussed earlier, because IDENTITY elements could be used anywhere in a document to identify individuals and company divisions.

Including the IDENTITY element also requires a reworking of the elements in the DTD for the header. Even though they could be mixed declarations and just include addresses with other data, this wouldn't require addresses in the format that the document-management system would like. (The content of the address element will still be PCDATA, but a list of acceptable attributes could force the NAMEID, if one existed, to be meaningful.) Enforcing these requirements requires creating another layer of elements. The "To:," "CC:," and "From:" headers and the information can remain in PCDATA. These items could also be made into entities, although they're short enough that that's probably overkill. It might also be smart to convert the author/typist material at the bottom to IDENTITY elements.

Note

XSL will be capable of handling the issue of text headers for a list of elements without needing extra text. E-mail systems won't be interested because they tend to provide that information automatically, and the document-management system won't need that extra text. For now, if the documents need to be viewed in browsers only supporting CSS, the documents will probably need to include the text. Later systems or dedicated applications can ignore it, but current systems may look better if it is included.

The last part of our document that may require significant improvement is the date. Dates have given programmers immense difficulty (for example, the Year 2000 problem) over the years because there isn't a single system for formatting them. 10/11/99 usually means October 11, 1999, to an American, but could mean November 10, 1999, to someone elsewhere in the world. Because the century (1900) isn't included, a computer will have difficulty determining the century when we hit the year 2000. To make sure that our system handles dates reliably, we need to separate year, month, day, and possibly hour, minute, and second to create date fields that can be easily sorted and interpreted. The program in which the memos are written and read must recombine the dates in a way that people find acceptable, but that task is generally trivial compared to building code that handles multiple date formats interspersed throughout a collection of data.

Depending on the processing application, it may be smarter to use a date field of some type rather than atomizing the year, month, and day information. This solution is presented to enhance compatibility with the widest number of document viewers, including viewers that will present only a styled version of the content. Recombining the atoms is generally easier than interpreting a date in an unfamiliar format. Given a smart enough processing application, date information can also be stored as attributes of the memo document rather than as sub-elements.

Note

This date solution is admittedly a kludge. Nonetheless, it seems like the safest route for now, requiring a minimum of parsing by the application as well as easy transformation later, to other formats. When XML has stronger support for data types, better alternatives may emerge. It may also be convenient to add an attribute to the DATE element that can hold the date in whatever format you like, provided that you stick with a standard format.

After taking all these considerations into account, our DTD looks like this:

```
<!ELEMENT MEMO (HEADER, MAIN)>
<!—MEMO DTD Version 0.2 - Experimental Use Only—>
<!ELEMENT HEADER (DISTRIBUTION, SUBJECT, DATE)>
<!ELEMENT DISTRIBUTION (TO, CC?, FROM)>
<!ELEMENT TO (#PCDATA |IDENTITY)*>
<!ELEMENT CC (#PCDATA |IDENTITY)*>
<!ELEMENT FROM (#PCDATA |IDENTITY)*>
<!ELEMENT IDENTITY (#PCDATA)>
<!—May add NAMEID attribute for easier connection to
directory structures later —>
<!ELEMENT SUBJECT (#PCDATA | DESCRIP)*>
<!ELEMENT DESCRIP (#PCDATA)>
<!ELEMENT DATE (YEAR, MONTH, DAY, (HOUR,MINUTE,SECOND)?)>
```

```
<!ELEMENT YEAR (#PCDATA)>
<!ELEMENT MONTH (#PCDATA)>
<!ELEMENT DAY (#PCDATA)>
<!ELEMENT HOUR (#PCDATA)>
<!ELEMENT MINUTE (#PCDATA)>
<!ELEMENT SECOND (#PCDATA)>
<!ELEMENT AUTHOR (IDENTITY+)>
<!ELEMENT TYPIST (IDENTITY+)>
<!ELEMENT MAIN (#PCDATA | AUTHOR | TYPIST)*>
```

The new document is considerably more marked-up:

```
<?xml version="1.0" standalone="no" encoding="UTF-8"?>
<!DOCTYPE MEMO SYSTEM "memo.dtd">
<MEMO>
<HEADER>
<DISTRIBUTION>
<TO>To: <IDENTITY>Jimmy</IDENTITY></TO>
<FROM>From: <IDENTITY>Simon</IDENTITY></FROM>
</DISTRIBUTION>
<SUBJECT>Re: <DESCRIP>Sample Document Created with Memo
DTD</DESCRIP></SUBJECT>
<DATE>
<YEAR>1999</YEAR><MONTH>10</MONTH><DAY>11</DAY></DATE>
</HEADER>
<MAIN>
I just thought you might like to see what a memo in XML
looks like. Thanks for the vote of confidence at the last
meeting. With any luck, this will make our transition to
electronic documents reasonably painless.
<AUTHOR><IDENTITY>SSL</IDENTITY></AUTHOR>
</MAIN>
</MEMO>
```

This parses well, although you can see that it has a few more layers:

Figure 8-4 *The more sophisticated version of the memo, parsed*

This model should work for most simple documents. The header will keep the memos filed properly, making it easy for a document-management system to track documents based on author, recipient, or title. The body content model remains a blank, however. The only kind of content that users can apply in the MAIN element right now is plain text. The body of the document needs some simple formatting elements to break up the text and provide a few options for breaking up the tedium of the ordinary memo. JDCPD needs only three options to produce the memos they have now:

PARAGRAPH, HIGHLIGHT (to give extra emphasis to important material), and HEADLINE.

```
<!ELEMENT PARAGRAPH (#PCDATA|HIGHLIGHT|IDENTITY)*>
<!ELEMENT HIGHLIGHT (#PCDATA)>
<!ELEMENT HEADLINE (#PCDATA)>
```

Note that the paragraph element enables writers to include
IDENTITY information. Sorting out IDENTITY information
from regular text is normally difficult, especially in informal documents. Encouraging the regular use of IDENTITY information
will make it far simpler. All of these elements make it much easier
for styles to connect to the users' documents.

The entire DTD now looks like this:

```
<!-MEMO DTD Version 0.3 - Experimental Use Only->
<!ELEMENT MEMO (HEAD?,HEADER, MAIN)>
<!-HEADER information for addressing ->
<!ELEMENT HEADER (DISTRIBUTION, SUBJECT, DATE)>
<!ELEMENT DISTRIBUTION (TO, CC?, FROM)>
<!ELEMENT TO (#PCDATA | IDENTITY)*>
<!ELEMENT CC (#PCDATA | IDENTITY)*>
<!ELEMENT FROM (#PCDATA| IDENTITY)*>
<!ELEMENT IDENTITY (#PCDATA)>
<!-May add NAMEID attribute for easier connection to
directory structures later ->
<!ELEMENT SUBJECT (#PCDATA | DESCRIP)*>
<!ELEMENT DESCRIP (#PCDATA)>
<!ELEMENT DATE (YEAR, MONTH, DAY, (HOUR,MINUTE,SECOND)?)>
<!ELEMENT YEAR (#PCDATA)>
<!ELEMENT MONTH (#PCDATA)>
<!ELEMENT DAY (#PCDATA)>
<!ELEMENT HOUR (#PCDATA)>
<!ELEMENT MINUTE (#PCDATA)>
<!ELEMENT SECOND (#PCDATA)>
```

```
<!ELEMENT AUTHOR (IDENTITY+)>
<!ELEMENT TYPIST (IDENTITY+)>
<!ELEMENT PARAGRAPH (#PCDATA|HIGHLIGHT|IDENTITY)*>
<!ELEMENT HIGHLIGHT (#PCDATA)>
<!ELEMENT HEADLINE (#PCDATA)>
<!ELEMENT MAIN ((PARAGRAPH | HIGHLIGHT | HEADLINE)*,
AUTHOR?, TYPIST?)>
```

This will work well for most memos, but it might be useful to allow content outside the confines of textual memo data to use the memo DTD. The public relations department, for example, would also like to use the memo DTD for its newsletters. Even though they could use PARAGRAPH, HIGHLIGHT, and HEADLINE, they would prefer to have something more specific for their newsletter, which would show up separately in the document-management system. More importantly, they would like to be able to modify their DTD later without creating repercussions throughout the company. The best solution for their situation appears to be a separate DTD that includes their elements, which can be combined with the main memo DTD when necessary. Their newsletter DTD will look like the following:

```
<!ELEMENT NEWSLETTER (STORY+)>
<!ELEMENT STORY (LEAD, PARAGRAPH*)>
<!ELEMENT LEAD (#PCDATA)>
```

Combining this with the memo DTD may be a bit of a problem. The easiest way to enable the NEWSLETTER element to replace the MAIN element in the memo is to change the MEMO element:

```
<!ELEMENT MEMO (HEAD?, HEADER, (MAIN | NEWSLETTER))>
```

Alternately, the MAIN element could be changed to include NEWSLETTER elements

```
<!ELEMENT MAIN (((PARAGRAPH | HIGHLIGHT | HEADLINE)*,
AUTHOR?, TYPIST?) | NEWSLETTER)>
```

If it turns out, however, that another part of the company also wants to repurpose the memo DTD, these declarations will grow incredibly unwieldy. If XML allowed a document to declare an element more than once (as it does with attributes), the solution would be simple: override MAIN in the newsletters by making a new MAIN declaration in another DTD. This isn't possible — declaring elements more than once is an error in XML that prevents the document from being valid. The easiest way to make this work is similar to our first attempt:

```
<!ELEMENT MEMO (HEAD?, HEADER, (MAIN | ALTERNATE))>
```

By using ALTERNATE, we've made it possible for multiple users to take advantage of our DTD and repurpose the memo for other applications. (ALTERNATE isn't a keyword — any element name, as long as the element is left undefined in that DTD, will do.) The public relations department can now create a DTD that uses and expands the memo DTD:

```
<!ENTITY % memo SYSTEM "memo.dtd">
%memo;
<!ELEMENT NEWSLETTER (STORY+)>
<!ELEMENT STORY (LEAD, PARAGRAPH*)>
<!ELEMENT LEAD (#PCDATA)>
```

The newsletter shown previously can be converted to XML in a fairly straightforward way:

```
<?xml version="1.0" standalone="no" encoding="UTF-8"?>
<!DOCTYPE MEMO SYSTEM
"http://127.0.0.1/newslet2/news.dtd">
<MEMO>
<HEADER>
<DISTRIBUTION>
<TO>To: <IDENTITY>Jimmy</IDENTITY></TO>
<CC>CC: <IDENTITY>All Employees</IDENTITY></CC>
<FROM>From: <IDENTITY>Lois Turpin, PR
Department</IDENTITY></FROM>
```

```
</DISTRIBUTION>
<SUBJECT>Re: <DESCRIP>JDCPD Today  - Sample Newsletter
Created with Memo DTD</DESCRIP></SUBJECT>
<DATE>
<YEAR>1999</YEAR><MONTH>10</MONTH><DAY>10</DAY></DATE>
</HEADER>
<ALTERNATE><!-BEGIN ALTERNATE CONTENT TO REPLACE MAIN ->
<NEWSLETTER>
<STORY><LEAD>Design Contest Winner -
</LEAD><PARAGRAPH>Frank Kravitz of the fuel injection
division has won the September award for best car part
drawing. Frank's masterpiece, <HIGHLIGHT>On to the Spark
Plug II</HIGHLIGHT>, will be on display in the lobby
through November 12. Frank also won the award in January
and July.</PARAGRAPH></STORY>
<STORY><LEAD>Donut Reimbursement Ends -
</LEAD><PARAGRAPH>To avoid a threatened doubling of
health insurance premiums, JDCPD has ended its donut
reimbursement program. "We are extremely sad to have to
take such unpleasant measures," said Jimmy, "but we hope
our employees will understand the difficult situation we
face."</PARAGRAPH></STORY>
<STORY><LEAD>Rice Cakes Available - </LEAD><PARAGRAPH>For
a limited time, rice cakes and a variety of herbal teas
will be available in Jimmy's office. Employees needing a
quick snack to get them charged up for a hard day of
parts designing are welcome to stop
by.</PARAGRAPH></STORY>
<STORY><LEAD>Remember - </LEAD><PARAGRAPH>"Parts is
parts!"  Take pride in your work. The annual award for
best design will be announced in December.</PARAGRAPH>
</STORY>
</NEWSLETTER></ALTERNATE>
</MEMO>
```

This newsletter XML file parses quite happily using the news DTD in combination with the memo DTD.

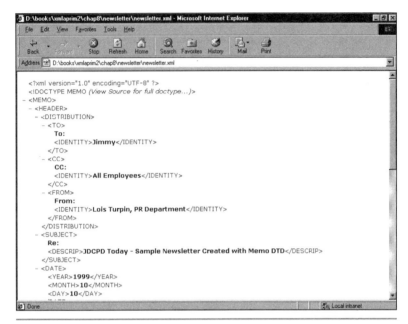

Figure 8-5 *The newsletter, parsed*

Using this model, other divisions can create their own ALTER-NATE content models. The designers, for example, could develop a design brief that included NOTATION elements that allowed them to include all kinds of drawings and additional information. The public relations department could do the same to include their extra logos and perhaps even create an electronic version of the company letterhead. Although the memo model won't be able to cope with everything, XML offers it a chance to expand into new fields without becoming completely overloaded.

This is by no means the only way to accomplish this task. Instead of using an ALTERNATE element to enable expansion, it might be more useful to move the entire MAIN element definition out of the main DTD and into another file. The memo's core functionality is primarily the header and its distribution mechanism, so this might make sense. In this case, because approximately 90 percent of the documents created with this DTD are simple memos, and because the newsletter DTD reuses parts of the DTD under the MAIN element (for example, PARAGRAPH), it seems simplest to keep the DTD for a simple memo in the memo DTD. Yet another option would be to move the distribution information out of the memo DTD, making it easier to reuse with other DTDs. Choosing between these options is frequently difficult and very dependent upon the particular needs of your document structures and management systems.

Even though the document-management system won't care directly about the style sheets, it can keep track of which style sheet was used where. After all, style sheets are just another link. Placing your style information into a document-management tool makes it easy to foresee the impact of significant changes because the tool can warn designers which documents are about to receive the new style. Best of all, the document-management system may to able to support some kind of versioning. Older documents can stay with their older style sheet, whereas newer documents receive a facelift. The capabilities of the management system, of course, may vary.

It's probably best to create a separate style sheet for each DTD, even if you combine DTDs on a regular basis. In that way, the user's machine doesn't waste cycles parsing style information it won't be using, and developers don't waste time searching through an enormous collection of styles. Choose a naming convention and stick with it. I tend to name my DTD files `name.dtd` and the corresponding CSS files `name.css`. You can keep them in separate directories if you like but try to maintain as much parallelism as possible between the two structures so parts don't disappear. When it's time to modify a DTD, create a new DTD file (and associated CSS or other style sheet file) so that older documents don't suddenly become invalid. Document-management systems require humans to behave systematically—changing a DTD significantly could leave the document system stranded with files of documents it can't parse. Although writing conversion programs is possible, it is rarely fun, and changing a significant library of documents by hand is even more tedious.

Building Histories: A DTD for Corporate Memory

History is rarely a favorite corporate subject. The future is always in sharp focus: companies strive to make the next quarter, the next year, or even the next decade their best one yet. Yesterday's sales figures may have paid for a new car or cost a promised bonus, but today's holdings and tomorrow's profits are of greater concern. As a result, companies often let their history slide. Memos and reports may accumulate in file cabinets, but periodically they get emptied or shipped to far-off storage, and key employees leave the company or retire. As employees have become more mobile, the odds of losing the person "who knows where all the bodies are buried" greatly increase. Most companies lack strategies for debriefing employees and organizing the information, costing wasted hours spent trying to determine what happened when a legal battle or a customer inquiry requires a reexamination of past activity.

The document structures we'll build in this example are designed expressly to keep some of that history alive and available at the end of a project or when an employee changes positions. Combined with a document management system, the information stored in that structure will make producing quick, comprehensive answers to questions about past projects easier. Large corporations that write proposals for large projects are often required to present past performance references; the information contained in this system will make it far easier for companies to describe their previous work, saving expensive resources for use on developing the forward-looking parts of the proposal.

This project and its associated DTDs could grow to be gigantic, especially if it expanded from project history into project management. This discussion will explore only some of the basic needs of the project and develop some of the core document types.

This project needs a considerable amount of political work before DTD design can even begin. Structured documents are useless if they aren't applied consistently. Even though it's easy to require that a particular element appear in a document, it's difficult to require that individuals who are on their way out the door fill out a few acres of paperwork. Building this document database successfully requires adding it to the process as a standard business procedure. The needs of that process will probably have direct effects on the nature of the DTD and the level of flexibility required. If this system is likely to be used on a regular basis, it might even be worthwhile to build a custom interview application to collect the information.

Each project will probably have a set of data associated with it, representing interviews and other documents collected over the life of the project. Projects that last for years could end up with sizable quantities of information under a single header. Even though it's conceivable for all of this information to be assembled in a single document, large projects will quickly amass too much information even for a document-management system. Although a single-document approach makes great sense for small projects, a larger set of documents will function more smoothly if information is broken into more manageable chunks. Even though the use of elements makes finding relevant information easier, documents with thousands or hundreds of thousands of elements have probably outgrown a single-document file structure. Our example will reflect that need for larger structures by building several document types, each of which can connect to a central project record.

We'll return to the need for compound documents, and to this example in particular, in Chapter 10 when we explore XML linking. For now, consider the links described as connections to information on a directory or database server, both of which are handled by the application, not the XML parser.

This project requires a set of DTDs, not just a single all encompassing DTD. Because it is possible that all the DTDs will be combined in a single document, designers must take care not to use the same element name twice. We'll begin by creating a set of common elements that may be used throughout all the documents in the set. IDENTITY is an even more important element in this situation than it was in the previous example because the participants on the project and their positions need to be clearly defined. IDENTITY in this case will carry an attribute value linking it to a centralized directory of employees, as well as providing space for the person's name, current title, and position:

```
<!ELEMENT IDENTITY (NAME,TITLE?,POSITION?)>
<!ATTLIST IDENTITY
     IDLINK CDATA #REQUIRED>
<!ELEMENT NAME (#PCDATA)>
<!ELEMENT TITLE (#PCDATA)>
<!ELEMENT POSITION (#PCDATA)>
```

Even though breaking the NAME element into first name and last name might be useful, it isn't really necessary because of the required IDLINK attribute of the IDENTITY element. IDLINK will connect the identity back to a directory, which includes a full set of information. IDENTITY isn't restricted to individuals; it could also refer to departments or even companies. The link to the directory will produce some extra overhead because all people and groups referenced through IDENTITY must be entered in the directory. Not all organizations store customer information in their directories, although it's become more popular as the computer encroaches on the turf of the Rolodex.

XML doesn't include a way to check the value of the IDLINK. It can require that it appear, but the parser will not itself check the value of IDLINK against the directory. That kind of logic must be placed in the application that processes the information returned by the parser. (The application could be the document-management system or another application preparing the information for display.) It should also be implemented in the program used to create the documents. Ideally, a simple lookup procedure would enable authors to select IDENTITY values from a list of names provided by the directory.

LOCATION elements are similar to IDENTITY elements — they refer to individual units and can be looked up in a directory server, probably the same server that stores identities. However, because companies may briefly use locations all over the world, it doesn't seem as worthwhile to require that all LOCATION elements have a link in the directory. Key locations, like company offices and places of work, should definitely be listed, but hotels are probably not be as important.

```
<!ELEMENT LOCATION (#PCDATA)>
<!ATTLIST LOCATION
     IDLINK CDATA #IMPLIED>
```

The next key element is the date. The documents themselves will be marked with the date they were written, and using a standard format for the date will make searching for information inside other elements much easier. The DATE element is the same as the DATE element used previously in the memo application, although it lacks the initial #PCDATA information:

```
<!ELEMENT DATE (YEAR, MONTH, DAY, (HOUR,MINUTE,SECOND)?)>
<!ELEMENT YEAR (#PCDATA)>
<!ELEMENT MONTH (#PCDATA)>
<!ELEMENT DAY (#PCDATA)>
<!ELEMENT HOUR (#PCDATA)>
<!ELEMENT MINUTE (#PCDATA)>
<!ELEMENT SECOND (#PCDATA)>
```

This DTD will undoubtedly explode with additional elements for formatting and notation, but we'll start simple. The four elements we'll include for content are EMPHASIS, RUMOR,

QUOTE, and PARAGRAPH. EMPHASIS will enable authors to hit certain points harder; RUMOR will enable authors to include content that isn't certain, but may be useful (and which probably should not be repeated); and QUOTE enables them to include material from customers and others. PARAGRAPH just provides a basic grammatical structure. These elements may all contain mixed content, including their counterparts, represented by the parameter entity %TEXTELEMENTS;:

```
<!ENTITY % TEXTELEMENTS "(#PCDATA | EMPHASIS | RUMOR |
QUOTE | IDENTITY | LOCATION | DATE)*">
<!ELEMENT EMPHASIS (%TEXTELEMENTS;)>
<!ELEMENT RUMOR (%TEXTELEMENTS;)>
<!ELEMENT QUOTE (%TEXTELEMENTS;)>
<!ELEMENT PARAGRAPH (%TEXTELEMENTS;)>
```

Now that we have a set of elements we can use within the text, let's define some document-level structures. The information in this dataset will be stored in several different kinds of documents. Project managers will have different information to report than field technicians or accountants, and this will be reflected by a wide range of different document structures. For our example, we'll use a project completion report, which provides a general report by the project manager on the work performed after a project is finished. Our root element is FINALREPORT, which contains elements identifying the project, the author, the date of the report, and the classification of the document. It also provides elements in which the author can add an overview of the project, financial information, schedule information, detailed information regarding completed work, and lists any commendations from the customer.

```
<!ELEMENT FINALREPORT (PROJECT, IDENTITY, DATE,
CLASSIFICATION, OVERVIEW, FINANCIALS, SCHEDULE, DETAIL,
COMMENDATIONS?)>
```

The PROJECT element, like the IDENTITY and LOCA-TION elements, links to other sources of information. This saves the author the effort of re-describing the project, the customer, the type of contract, and other stable information such as the start date of the project. (Start dates are not always stable, but they should be pretty firm by the time the project is completed.) As a result, the PROJECT element can remain simple, storing the name of the project in #PCDATA and linking to more detailed information through the PROJLINK attribute:

```
<!ELEMENT PROJECT (#PCDATA)>
<!ATTLIST PROJECT
     PROJLINK CDATA #REQUIRED>
```

The IDENTITY and DATE elements that follow the project indicate the author of this document and the date of its writing, respectively. Their position in the PROJECT element is the only thing that identifies them as such; developers who want to make this more explicit (for example, to help out weaker search tools) could create wrappers for them:

```
<!ELEMENT AUTHOR (IDENTITY)>
<!ELEMENT REPORTDATE (DATE)>
```

This would require a small change in the FINALREPORT element:

```
<!ELEMENT FINALREPORT (PROJECT, AUTHOR, REPORTDATE,
CLASSIFICATION, OVERVIEW, FINANCIALS,SCHEDULE, DETAIL,
COMMENDATIONS?)>
```

CLASSIFICATION is designed to help the document management system control access to the document. Some documents may be OPEN, available to the public without restriction (which means they're handy for the public relations office), others may be PROPRIETARY (for use only within the company), some may even be SECRET (which limits access to particular readers within the company), and others may be SPECIAL. SPECIAL can be a classification above SECRET, or it can just be a general classification that requires the application to check the identity of the reader against a list someplace else.

No matter how this element is created, remember that the application, not the parser, must enforce security. XML has no built-in tools for providing security; document management systems and other tools must take this responsibility, locking users out of documents until their identity and permissions have been validated.

Implementing this kind of element requires making some choices. The easiest way to implement this is by making CLASSIFICATION an element that uses #PCDATA as its data type. In this way, new types can be added easily, but the parser won't check the type. An adventurous author could add GOOFY as a security classification.

```
<!ELEMENT CLASSIFICATION (#PCDATA)>
```

Another way to implement this element would be to make CLASSIFICATION an empty element with attributes that indicate the level of security:

```
<!ELEMENT CLASSIFICATION EMPTY>
<!ATTLIST CLASSIFICATION
    SECLEVEL (OPEN | PROPRIETARY | SECRET | SPECIAL)
"SPECIAL"
    SECLINK CDATA #IMPLIED>
```

The SECLEVEL attribute indicates the level of security, whereas SECLINK makes linking to an outside security directory for SPECIAL situations easy. (Depending on the type of application, the developer might want to set the default to a different value, or simply to #REQUIRED.)

We've finally reached the meat of the document—what was actually accomplished on this project, how much it cost, and how long it took. Because this document is a summary document, all this information can be easily stored. Heavy-duty accounting and schedule information can be stored in other documents (or even databases) and linked to the project through a centralized system, in much the same way that the PROJECT element is connected by the PROJLINK attribute. The FINALREPORT document is here for quick reference, not a line-by-line account of every widget purchased and sold. The overview section begins the summary:

```
<!ELEMENT OVERVIEW (PARAGRAPH+)>
```

The FINANCIALS element is a little more broken down but still presents only a general explanation of the project's costs:

```
<!ELEMENT FINANCIALS (ORIGINALQUOTE, FINALCOST,
EXPLANATION?)>
<!ELEMENT ORIGINALQUOTE (#PCDATA)>
<!ELEMENT FINALCOST (#PCDATA)>
<!ELEMENT EXPLANATION (PARAGRAPH+)>
```

The SCHEDULE element provides a similar broad description of the project schedule and uses the EXPLANATION element created for FINANCIALS:

```
<!ELEMENT SCHEDULE (ORIGINALSCHEDULE,ACTUALSCHEDULE,
EXPLANATION?)>
<!ELEMENT ORIGINALSCHEDULE (STARTDATE, ENDDATE?)>
<!ELEMENT ACTUALSCHEDULE (STARTDATE, ENDDATE?)>
<!ELEMENT STARTDATE (DATE)>
<!ELEMENT ENDDATE (DATE)>
```

In many cases DTDs can be simplified by using elements in more than one context, but this can create problems for simple processing applications. If someone wants a list of all the explanations for financial transactions, they need a processor smart enough to separate EXPLANATION elements nested inside of FINANCIALS elements from those nested inside of SCHEDULE elements. Developers should find out the limitations of the planned processing application early. That way, creating separate FIN-EXPLANATION and SCHEDEXPLANATION elements is easy.

Despite its name, the DETAIL element receives a very simple XML declaration. DETAIL is the area in which the project manager enters detailed information, but from the perspective of the parser, all that information uses PARAGRAPH elements, which can contain all the elements listed in the %TEXTELEMENTS; parameter entity. The COMMENDATIONS element is likewise a container for text elements:

```
<!ELEMENT DETAIL (PARAGRAPH+)>
<!ELEMENT COMMENDATIONS (PARAGRAPH+)>
```

Now that we have all the parts defined, it's time to combine them into DTDs. Our first DTD contains all the text elements needed in documents in this system, providing basic text content types:

```
<!-TEXT CONTENT ELEMENT INFORMATION ->
<!-IDENTITY INFORMATION ->
<!ELEMENT IDENTITY (NAME,TITLE?,POSITION?)>
<!ATTLIST IDENTITY
     IDLINK CDATA #REQUIRED>
<!ELEMENT NAME (#PCDATA)>
<!ELEMENT TITLE (#PCDATA)>
<!ELEMENT POSITION (#PCDATA)>
<!-LOCATION INFORMATION ->
<!ELEMENT LOCATION (#PCDATA)>
<!ATTLIST LOCATION
     IDLINK CDATA #IMPLIED>
<!-DATE INFORMATION ->
<!ELEMENT DATE (YEAR, MONTH, DAY, (HOUR,MINUTE,SECOND)?)>
<!ELEMENT YEAR (#PCDATA)>
<!ELEMENT MONTH (#PCDATA)>
<!ELEMENT DAY (#PCDATA)>
<!ELEMENT HOUR (#PCDATA)>
<!ELEMENT MINUTE (#PCDATA)>
<!ELEMENT SECOND (#PCDATA)>
<!-OTHER TEXT CONTENT ->
<!ELEMENT EMPHASIS (%TEXTELEMENTS;)>
<!ELEMENT RUMOR (%TEXTELEMENTS;)>
```

```
<!ELEMENT QUOTE (%TEXTELEMENTS;)>
<!ELEMENT PARAGRAPH (%TEXTELEMENTS;)>
<!ENTITY % TEXTELEMENTS "(#PCDATA | EMPHASIS | RUMOR |
QUOTE | IDENTITY | LOCATION | DATE)*">
```

The second piece, which actually defines our project report, includes the preceding DTD using a parameter entity:

```
<!-DTD for Final Project Reports ->
<!ELEMENT FINALREPORT (PROJECT, AUTHOR, REPORTDATE,
CLASSIFICATION, OVERVIEW, FINANCIALS,SCHEDULE, DETAIL,
COMMENDATIONS?)>
<!-Link to text content declarations ->
<!ENTITY % TEXTDECLARATION SYSTEM "textelem.dtd">
%TEXTDECLARATION;
<!-Project Identification ->
<!ELEMENT PROJECT (#PCDATA)>
<!ATTLIST PROJECT
      PROJLINK CDATA #REQUIRED>
<!-AUTHOR AND REPORT DATE WRAPPERS, FOR EASIER SEARCHING
->
<!ELEMENT AUTHOR (IDENTITY)>
<!ELEMENT REPORTDATE (DATE)>
<!-CLASSIFICATION. ENFORCED BY DOCUMENT MANAGEMENT SYSTEM
->
<!ELEMENT CLASSIFICATION EMPTY>
<!ATTLIST CLASSIFICATION
      SECLEVEL (OPEN | PROPRIETARY | SECRET | SPECIAL)
"SPECIAL"
      SECLINK CDATA #IMPLIED>
<!-REPORT ELEMENTS ->
<!ELEMENT OVERVIEW (PARAGRAPH+)>
<!ELEMENT FINANCIALS (ORIGINALQUOTE, FINALCOST,
EXPLANATION?)>
<!ELEMENT ORIGINALQUOTE (#PCDATA)>
<!ELEMENT FINALCOST (#PCDATA)>
```

```
<!ELEMENT EXPLANATION (PARAGRAPH+)>
<!ELEMENT SCHEDULE (ORIGINALSCHEDULE,ACTUALSCHEDULE,
EXPLANATION?)>
<!ELEMENT ORIGINALSCHEDULE (STARTDATE, ENDDATE?)>
<!ELEMENT ACTUALSCHEDULE (STARTDATE, ENDDATE?)>
<!ELEMENT STARTDATE (DATE)>
<!ELEMENT ENDDATE (DATE)>
<!ELEMENT DETAIL (PARAGRAPH+)>
<!ELEMENT COMMENDATIONS (PARAGRAPH+)>
```

This DTD is only a possible beginning for a much larger and more elaborate structure. With a well-built document management system, multiple document types could be constructed around a database of PROJECT information. Document types for drawings, detailed reports of tasks carried out, customer orders, time spent on projects, status reports, and even project management information could be kept in the same system, enabling secure but easy access and the ability to cross-reference. These systems have yet to appear, and most of them will undoubtedly need a considerable amount of customization, but they will probably be the most efficient keepers of XML information. With any luck, document management systems will replace the file cabinets and file systems of today, keeping track of large numbers of documents and their components and making them readily accessible.

Chapter 9

XML for Data-Driven Applications

The documents in the preceding chapters have mostly corresponded to real paper documents, the kind of documents that people can pick up (or load in a Web browser) and read. XML isn't limited to this kind of information; indeed, many of its earliest applications have supplied information in forms not readily presentable to humans. The field in which XML may make the greatest strides is communication between computers and between computers and other devices. This has proven a difficult affair so far. The DTDs and examples in this chapter provide solutions for what I call non-traditional documents — data structures for which XML is very appropriate but not documents humans would normally read. Instead of presenting information to people, these documents present information to programs, which use that information to determine their behavior, not just present information on a screen or a page.

 Cross-Reference

This chapter presents an introduction to data-focused XML documents and their uses, including some applications that you might construe as programming. But it isn't a guide to XML processing in general. See Chapter 12 for more information on models and tools for processing XML.

Data for Interchange

The simplest (though in some ways most complicated) use of XML is as an interchange format for transmission between unlike systems. The concepts involved are fairly simple, though they offer infinite variations. (Some of those variations tie into the commercial dreams explored in Chapter 7.) As was briefly shown in Chapter 4, XML can serve as a container for nearly any text-based information, simplifying the task of shipping information from one application to another, even if the application designers know nothing about the other's products and know only the rules for the file format. The tabular data commonly transferred among relational databases may not seem like a natural fit for XML's hierarchical structures, but XML can flexibly handle tables without a hitch, and database vendors (like Oracle and IBM) are adding XML parsers and interfaces to their existing products. Nearly any application, not just databases, that needs to transfer information among formats can put XML to use as a commonly understood layer.

Making this work requires more than dumping information out of one application and pouring it into another verbatim. Both applications need to include components capable of parsing XML and relating the file contents to their internal data structures and/or taking their internal data structures and exporting them to XML files. Figure 9-1 demonstrates this process.

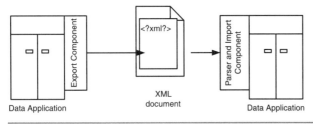

Figure 9-1 *Importing and exporting using an XML file for interchange*

Presently, database vendors are announcing tools that should make this process easier, but most current implementations involve an XML parser that uses SQL (through JDBC or ODBC, typically) to add information to a database or Common Gateway Interface (CGI)-style programming to export database information into a template. Non-database applications typically require some custom programming, much like the tools used to import and export plain text and delimited text versions of information. Though the techniques appear primitive (and currently tend to produce fairly verbose output), XML's structures are well-matched to raw-data interchange. Its use of Unicode as a foundation for text processing simplifies many of the chores involved in exchanging information among sources that use different character sets. Its structures promise more reliability and more manageability than the current delimited formats that provide baseline interchange services.

A few XML-centric database tools are starting to emerge. Object Design (`http://www.objectdesign.com`) has created eXcelon, a front end to relational databases that provides XML services. Bluestone's XML-Server (`http://www.bluestone.com/xml/XML-Server/`) is intended more as a standalone database that can be integrated with client-server architectures. Older hierarchical databases, still a significant in mainframe computing, may be making a comeback in XML as vendors recast their products into XML-focused toolkits like SoftwareAG's Tamino (`http://www.softwareag.com/tamino`).

Data for Control

Many applications perform a limited number of tasks and need only a set of data to send them on their way. Programming a consumer VCR, for instance, means giving it start and stop times for recording, a channel, and possibly information about the way in which the information records, like tape speed. In no case (unless there are some *very* unusual VCRs out there) does a user have to write the code that actually tells the VCR to check the time and compare it to a table, select the channel, move the mechanisms to start the recording process, and check the time until the stop time is reached.

Running a House

Our first example applies XML to a rather different computing field: device control. Given a system that responds to a small set of inputs without requiring processing of return values, you can write a "program" purely in data. For starters, we'll build a DTD able to control a set of light switches (or other electrical devices). Light switches are an extremely simple example, but many situations require the control of hundreds or thousands of lights. Our example will begin with the lighting in a typical house, but it could extend to cover display lights or even stage lights.

My parents used to receive a catalog from DAK (a direct marketer selling electronics of all sorts) every few months; it was crammed with odd and unusual stereo equipment and gadgetry. One of the weirdest items DAK carried was the X-10 system, which enabled you to control electrical devices by remote control. Originally it came with a controller unit and modules that plugged in between the electrical socket and the plug of a lamp or other electrical device. The controller unit sends signals over the electrical wires to the individual boxes (up to 256 of them) telling them to turn on and off or dim to a particular level. Eventually, it sprouted a serial computer interface, which made it easy to program devices to turn on and off at various times of day - a more expensive, but more accurate, device timer than the boxes with dials on them. Now, it's grown considerably more elaborate (see `http://www.x10.com` for details). Remote controls that can run a house rather than a TV make it easy for the ultimate couch potatoes to run significant portions of their houses without getting up.

Although the DTD we'll develop isn't designed expressly for the X-10 interface, you can easily build an interface that converted the data in these documents into the signals controlling electrical devices. The X-10 system actually uses a limited set of commands to control its devices, but our DTD doesn't need to worry about specific commands. It will just define particular states that the control system should achieve. A processing application would take the information returned by the parser and determine the necessary commands to achieve the state desired. Instead of giving the controller a sequence of steps, our document will give it a desired result and enable the controller to figure out how best to get there. We will control two different categories of equipment: lights and appliances. Lights can turn on and off and dim, whereas appliances can only turn on and off. (If someone wants to extend this to controlling appliances via remote controls and not just their power, extending the DTD shouldn't be too difficult.) Lights and appliances are identified by addresses that effectively represent hexadecimal numbers. The address begins with a house code, A–P. Generally, users set up an entire system on one letter, which limits them to 16 devices but avoids conflicts with neighbors. Users without gadget-minded neighbors can use more than one house code. The unit code identifies the controlling module. It's a number from 1 to 16. Device modules can be set to the same address; all device modules with the same address will respond simultaneously to commands. A set of three lamps on address B10 will all turn on or off or dim as requested in response to commands sent to B10.

Our DTD will enable users to create documents to give orders to this system. A computer will process all these documents, but we'll keep them human-readable for easy editing. To help with this, our documents may include a description of all the modules on the system, followed by the states desired and the conditions that set them off.

```
<!ELEMENT CONTROLSCHEDULE (MODULE*, STATE*, TRIGGER*)>
```

Our modules need several identifiers. For now, we'll stick with the system that X-10 uses to build an address, adding two pieces that provide additional information to the processing application and human editors:

```
<!ELEMENT MODULE (ADDRESS, TYPE?, DESCRIPTION?)>
<!ELEMENT ADDRESS (HOUSE, UNIT)>
<!ELEMENT HOUSE (#PCDATA)>
<!ELEMENT UNIT (#PCDATA)>
```

```
<!ELEMENT TYPE (#PCDATA)>
<!ELEMENT DESCRIPTION (#PCDATA)>
```

We give the MODULE element a little bit of extra flexibility by enabling it to contain ADDRESS and TYPE elements. We could require the user or the program creating these files to track whether the module at a particular address is a light module or an appliance module and to identify the modules purely through addresses. Adding TYPE increases flexibility and makes these documents more portable. A processing application that doesn't care about TYPE can strip it out, whereas a new application set up for the first time might use the TYPE element to import more complete information about the control modules. TYPE also adds a bit of flexibility in case new varieties of a module appear because commands may vary depending on the kind of module receiving them. (At present, the X-10 system doesn't, but a more advanced future system might.) DESCRIPTION gives the humans programming these devices a description of the device and its location.

The ADDRESS element enables us to identify modules uniquely (or in sets, as described previously). A developer impatient with the A-P, 1-16 identifiers of the X-10 system could convert them to their hex equivalents easily and represent them in the DTD like this:

```
<!ELEMENT ADDRESS (HEXADDRESS | (HOUSE, UNIT))>
<!ELEMENT HEXADDRESS (#PCDATA)>
```

For now, we'll stick to using the HOUSE and UNIT identifiers.

Even though the MODULE element includes ADDRESS elements, it won't be that useful for issuing commands because multiple modules can share a single address. ADDRESS will be the key element for issuing commands. After a document's initial MODULE declarations, a series of STATE declarations may follow. STATE declarations define a final position rather than a means of getting there. We'll provide names for our STATEs, as well as a description and list of component parts:

```
<!ELEMENT STATE (NAME, DESCRIPTION?, COMPONENT+)>
```

The NAME element provides a reference our programs will use to find and implement this STATE. The DESCRIPTION element, the same one used previously for modules, provides descriptions to human users. The COMPONENT element defines the final position for the devices on modules at a single address:

```
<!ELEMENT COMPONENT (DESCRIPTION?, ADDRESS, POSITION)>
<!ELEMENT POSITION (#PCDATA)>
```

ADDRESS elements are the same elements defined previously for identifying modules. POSITION holds the data defining the position to which you should set the module. For appliance modules, it could be ON or OFF; for the lamp module, it could be ON, OFF, or a dimmer position defined by a percentage. If new modules came on the market, the POSITION element could hold new values as necessary, because only the processing application interprets the meaning of this element.

Telling the system to move to one of these states is more complicated because a user might want to select a particular state for several different reasons. Timers control many of the home automation uses for these modules. Lights can turn on and off depending on the time of day. This can make a house appear occupied while the owners are away, or it can just make sure that the lights are on when people come home from work. Users may also want the ability to select a state by flipping a (specially wired) light switch. Motion detectors and remote consoles can also select a state. This requirement makes constructing our TRIGGER element a little tricky.

```
<!ELEMENT TRIGGER (STATENAME, TIMED*, SWITCH*)>
<!ELEMENT STATENAME (#PCDATA)>
```

STATENAME is just a reference to a previously defined STATE element. TIME elements define a time for implementing the

chosen STATE. Because users may need a variety of timing mechanisms, several options are available for daily events, weekly events,
and events taking place on a particular day:

```
<!ELEMENT TIMED ((DAILY | WEEKLY | DATE), TIME)>
<!ELEMENT DAILY EMPTY>
<!ELEMENT WEEKLY (WEEKDAY*)>
<!ELEMENT WEEKDAY (#PCDATA)>
<!ELEMENT DATE (DAY,MONTH, YEAR)>
<!ELEMENT DAY (#PCDATA)>
<!ELEMENT MONTH (#PCDATA)>
<!ELEMENT YEAR (#PCDATA)>
<!ELEMENT TIME (HOUR, MINUTE, SECOND?)>
<!ELEMENT HOUR (#PCDATA)>
<!ELEMENT MINUTE (#PCDATA)>
<!ELEMENT SECOND (#PCDATA)>
```

As mentioned in the previous chapter, many available date formats don't require atomizing the day, month, year, etc. For an application like this one, you might prefer those formats.

The SWITCH element contains a description — a name or
address understood by the processing application — of the switch
triggering the implementation of the state:

```
<!ELEMENT SWITCH (#PCDATA)>
```

The processing application for this document must parse the
document and set up an internal timer as well as the serial connection to the modules and switches. When any of the trigger conditions are met, it will send out the appropriate commands to the
control modules, setting the lights and other devices to their appropriate positions.

Most wall and remote switches in these systems are hard-coded
to particular modules. Users who need to connect only one switch to
one device could still use direct calls to the module and bypass this
processing system directly. The system that makes a later call to a
module will simply override previously issued commands. Of

course, if someone turns a light off or leaves it unplugged, nothing will visibly happen.

Assembling our DTD produces the following:

```
<!ELEMENT CONTROLSCHEDULE (MODULE*, STATE*, TRIGGER*)>
<!ELEMENT MODULE (ADDRESS, TYPE?, DESCRIPTION?)>
<!ELEMENT ADDRESS (HOUSE, UNIT)>
<!ELEMENT HOUSE (#PCDATA)>
<!ELEMENT UNIT (#PCDATA)>
<!ELEMENT TYPE (#PCDATA)>
<!ELEMENT DESCRIPTION (#PCDATA)>
<!ELEMENT STATE (NAME, DESCRIPTION?, COMPONENT+)>
<!ELEMENT COMPONENT (DESCRIPTION?,ADDRESS, POSITION)>
<!ELEMENT POSITION (#PCDATA)>
<!ELEMENT TRIGGER (STATENAME, TIMED*, SWITCH*)>
<!ELEMENT STATENAME (#PCDATA)>
<!ELEMENT TIMED ((DAILY | WEEKLY | DATE), TIME)>
<!ELEMENT DAILY EMPTY>
<!ELEMENT WEEKLY (WEEKDAY*)>
<!ELEMENT WEEKDAY (#PCDATA)>
<!ELEMENT DATE (DAY,MONTH, YEAR)>
<!ELEMENT DAY (#PCDATA)>
<!ELEMENT MONTH (#PCDATA)>
<!ELEMENT YEAR (#PCDATA)>
<!ELEMENT TIME (HOUR, MINUTE, SECOND?)>
<!ELEMENT HOUR (#PCDATA)>
<!ELEMENT MINUTE (#PCDATA)>
<!ELEMENT SECOND (#PCDATA)>
<!ELEMENT SWITCH (#PCDATA)>
```

We can use this DTD to create files that a processing application uses to control a small set of lamps and a radio:

```
<?xml version="1.0" encoding="UTF-8"?>
<!DOCTYPE CONTROLSCHEDULE SYSTEM "controller.dtd">
<CONTROLSCHEDULE>
```

```
<MODULE>
<ADDRESS><HOUSE>B</HOUSE><UNIT>2</UNIT></ADDRESS>
<TYPE>APPLIANCE</TYPE>
<DESCRIPTION>Radio in livingroom</DESCRIPTION>
</MODULE>
<MODULE>
<ADDRESS><HOUSE>B</HOUSE><UNIT>10</UNIT></ADDRESS>
<TYPE>LAMP</TYPE>
<DESCRIPTION>Lamp in entryway</DESCRIPTION>
</MODULE>
<MODULE>
<ADDRESS><HOUSE>B</HOUSE><UNIT>10</UNIT></ADDRESS>
<TYPE>LAMP</TYPE>
<DESCRIPTION>Light outside front door</DESCRIPTION>
</MODULE>
<MODULE>
<ADDRESS><HOUSE>B</HOUSE><UNIT>11</UNIT></ADDRESS>
<TYPE>LAMP</TYPE>
<DESCRIPTION>Lamp in livingroom</DESCRIPTION>
</MODULE>
<STATE>
<NAME>AFTWORK</NAME><DESCRIPTION>Come home to a friendly
house.</DESCRIPTION>
<COMPONENT>
<DESCRIPTION>Turn the radio on</DESCRIPTION>
<ADDRESS><HOUSE>B</HOUSE><UNIT>2</UNIT></ADDRESS>
<POSITION>ON</POSITION>
</COMPONENT>
<COMPONENT>
<DESCRIPTION>Turn on the living room light</DESCRIPTION>
<ADDRESS><HOUSE>B</HOUSE><UNIT>11</UNIT></ADDRESS>
<POSITION>ON</POSITION>
</COMPONENT>
</STATE>
<STATE>
```

```
<NAME>AFTDINNER</NAME><DESCRIPTION>turn on front light,
dim lights</DESCRIPTION>
<COMPONENT>
<DESCRIPTION>Turn on porch, front lights</DESCRIPTION>
<ADDRESS><HOUSE>B</HOUSE><UNIT>10</UNIT></ADDRESS>
<POSITION>ON</POSITION>
</COMPONENT>
<COMPONENT>
<DESCRIPTION>Dim livingroom</DESCRIPTION>
<ADDRESS><HOUSE>B</HOUSE><UNIT>10</UNIT></ADDRESS>
<POSITION>80%</POSITION>
</COMPONENT>
</STATE>
<STATE>
<NAME>POWERSAVE</NAME><DESCRIPTION>Dim front
lights</DESCRIPTION>
<ADDRESS><HOUSE>B</HOUSE><UNIT>10</UNIT></ADDRESS>
<POSITION>40%</POSITION>
</STATE>
<STATE>
<NAME>MORNING</NAME><DESCRIPTION>Turn off front
lights</DESCRIPTION>
<ADDRESS><HOUSE>B</HOUSE><UNIT>10</UNIT></ADDRESS>
<POSITION>OFF</POSITION>
</STATE>
<TRIGGER>
<STATENAME>AFTWORK</STATENAME>
<TIMED>
<WEEKLY><WEEKDAY>MON</WEEKDAY><WEEKDAY>TUES</WEEKDAY><WEE
KDAY>WED</WEEKDAY><WEEKDAY>THURS</WEEKDAY><WEEKDAY>FRI</W
EEKDAY></WEEKLY>
<TIME><HOUR>17</HOUR><MINUTE>00</MINUTE></TIME>
</TIMED>
</TRIGGER>
<TRIGGER>
```

```
<STATENAME>AFTDINNER</STATENAME>
<TIMED>
<DAILY/><TIME><HOUR>20</HOUR><MINUTE>00</MINUTE></TIME>
</TIMED>
</TRIGGER>
<TRIGGER>
<STATENAME>POWERSAVE</STATENAME>
<TIMED>
<DAILY/><TIME><HOUR>23</HOUR><MINUTE>00</MINUTE></TIME>
</TIMED>
</TRIGGER>
<TRIGGER>
<STATENAME>MORNING</STATENAME>
<TIMED>
<DAILY/><TIME><HOUR>7</HOUR><MINUTE>00</MINUTE></TIME>
</TIMED>
</TRIGGER>
<TRIGGER>
<STATENAME>AFTWORK</STATENAME>
<SWITCH>RMT01 - ON</SWITCH><!-Remote Control in case we
get home early -->
</TRIGGER>
<TRIGGER>
<STATENAME>MORNING</STATENAME>
<SWITCH>LT01 - OFF</SWITCH><!-If you don't want to leave
lights on all night -->
</TRIGGER>
</CONTROLSCHEDULE>
```

This document tells the controller of the existence of several modules controlling some lights and a radio. At 5 p.m., or when someone pushes a remote control button, the living room lights up, and the radio turns on. At 8 p.m., the living room lights dim a bit (for better television viewing, perhaps) and the front porch light turns on to welcome visitors or frighten away thieves. At 11 p.m., the front lights dim to save a few dollars on power. In the morning (or when someone flips a switch off), the porch lights go off.

This is a fairly elaborate exercise for rather small results. The real power of this example, however, comes in situations involving more widespread automation. Although writing XML directly like this is tedious and error-prone, it could serve well as a file format for control data produced by a friendlier GUI application. File formats like this make it easier to exchange data written for a particular control program to a different program, without losing all the logic. Because the information is presented as a series of states rather than direct commands, it doesn't matter what mechanism underlies those states. These files could work with an X-10 system, a different system that uses radio frequencies, a manual system that prints out instruction cards for lamplighters, or a much larger system controlling hundreds or thousands of lights. XML's easy-to-parse structure makes it a reliable tool for exchanging information among systems of every size.

Use DTDs like this one for simple control situations where the expected results are easily defined, and it doesn't matter very much if something fails. XML is obviously not a programming language, rather a delivery vehicle for data. Situations where the flow of data is essentially one-way are ideal for this application of XML, but more complex situations that produce exceptions or errors demand a much richer set of commands delivered in a more interactive fashion. XML can transmit data between processing applications on different nodes on a network, where all nodes can send and receive XML responses, but the core logic must remain in the processing application. XML just provides a structured way of storing and communicating data.

Controlling Instruments with Instrument Markup Language

Instrument Markup Language (IML) and an implementation of IML, Astronomical Instrument Markup Language (AIML), are both projects under development by NASA's Goddard Space Flight Center and Century Computing, a division of AppNet, Inc. These two markup languages take the basic concepts described in the example above and apply them to more difficult (and more useful) situations. Astronomers regularly deal with equipment kept in remote and inhospitable locations, from telescopes located far from urban light pollution to metering stations in uninhabited areas to satellites and spacecraft. AIML and IML use XML as a container for descriptions of instruments and commands to control them, giving astronomers and the engineers supporting them ready access to remote control for instruments anywhere. AIML's first project will provide support for instruments on the SOFIA (Stratospheric Observatory for Infrared Astronomy) project, which uses a Boeing 747 modified to carry a 2.5 meter reflecting telescope to make observations.

 Cross-Reference

Both AIML and IML are still in development. For the latest on AIML, visit `http://pioneer.gsfc.nasa.gov/public/aiml/`. To access the latest information on IML, visit `http://pioneer.gsfc.nasa.gov/public/iml/`.

IML is a very general markup language for describing and controlling instruments, while AIML is an implementation of that language that you may customize for astronomical needs. IML and AIML documents are parsed and fed into Java applications, which then present an interface to the controls and send information and orders to and from the controls. Hardware designers can create AIML documents that describe their instruments, and the software will configure its display and controls to reflect that description, greatly simplifying the task of integrating hardware and software. The general software that understands the AIML vocabulary can present detailed information about the instruments, without being directly tied to code specific to that instrument. The fragment below, which describes a refrigeration component of the High Resolution Airborne Wideband Camera (HAWC), provides information about two ports (one for outgoing commands, one for incoming data) on the instrument using XML syntax.

```
<Instrument id="ADR"> <!- subsystem ->
  <Port name="ADR" function="command" number="2201"
type="ASCII" serverPort="false" >


    <Command name="HouseKeeping" >
      <Argument name="tag"      type="java.lang.String"
required="true" hidden="true" />
      <Argument name="Command" type="java.lang.String"
required="true" hidden="true" />
      <Argument name="RATE"
type="java.lang.Integer" required="true" >
        <ValidRange low="0" high="120000" />
      </Argument>
    </Command>


        <!- Note the special XML decimal-like encoding
for NEWLINE terminator ->
<RecordFormat name="HouseKeeping" size="-1"
ordered="true" terminator="&#10;" attributeSeparator=" ">
      <Format name="tag"      format="%s" size="16"
ordered="true" />
      <Format name="Command" format="HOUSEKEEPING"
size="-1" />
      <Format name="RATE"      format="%s"
ordered="false" header="RATE=" />
```

```
      </RecordFormat>
    </Port>
    <Port function="data" name="ADR" number="2200"
type="BINARY" serverPort="false" >

        <Telemetry name="Status" >
          <Field name="tag"       type="java.lang.String"
required="true" />
          <Field name="Time"      type="java.lang.Integer"
required="true" />
          <ArrayField name="Temperatures" required="true"
dimensions="10">
              <Field name="dataElement"
type="java.lang.Float" required="true" />
          </ArrayField>
          <Field name="Heat Switch"
type="java.lang.Integer" required="true" />
        </Telemetry>

        <RecordFormat name="Status" size="64"
ordered="true" >
          <Format name="tag"       format="%s" size="16"
ordered="true" />
          <Format name="Time"      format="%d" size="4"
ordered="true" />
          <ArrayFormat name="Temperatures" size="40"
ordered="true" >
              <Format name="dataElement" format="%f"
size="4" ordered="true" />
          </ArrayFormat>
          <Format name="Heat Switch" format="%d" size="4"
ordered="true" />
        </RecordFormat>
    </Port>
  </Instrument>
```

Tip

Note the use of Java types to identify the format of the information going to and returning from the instruments. Until XML gets a type vocabulary of its own, expect to see a lot of borrowing from other vocabularies.

This information will configure the software used to control the instrument. If the instrument gets another port, or if more commands become available for controlling the instrument, the hardware engineer simply adds that to the interface by modifying this file. The next time the updated file loads into a Java program that presents an interface to the instruments, the interface will reflect the new information. Making small changes quickly makes it much easier to run projects on an iterative basis, starting with a foundation and moving forward in small steps, rather than laying out the complete vision at the start of a project and making drastic changes throughout should that vision prove faulty.

Object Documents

XML's nested structure bears a strong resemblance to the hierarchies of data that appear in object-oriented programming's data structures. XML and object-oriented programming fit well because both systems typically store datasets within datasets within datasets. Storing the information contained in object structures has been difficult, because the linear and tabular file types most commonly used for documents fit poorly for this kind of hierarchical structure. This section of the chapter won't produce any specific DTDs, because they vary radically from program to program. Instead, we'll examine a few general examples of projects that may help developers create complementary objects and file structures.

Bean Markup Language (BeanML)

The Bean Markup Language, a development of IBM's AlphaWorks (`http://www.alphaWorks.ibm.com/formula/bml`) reads very much like a command language, using a simple set of tags and attributes to instantiate Java Beans and add properties and event handling to them. BeanML doesn't really create new objects — it just enables you to describe the properties of Java Beans and connect them using a simple XML syntax. BeanML documents use a Bean element as their root element and then use child add, args, bean, call-method, cast, event-binding, field, property, and string elements to properly instantiate the Bean and connect it to other objects.

A very simple BeanML document might look like:

```
<?xml version="1.0" encoding="UTF-8"?>
<bean class="java.awt.Panel" id="mainPanel">
   <add>
         <bean class="java.awt.Label">
            <property name="text" value="This is a
label"/>
         </bean>
   </add>
</bean>
```

This creates a Panel using the Java AWT libraries, containing a Label announcing that "This is a label." You can use BeanML with any Java Beans, providing an XML vocabulary for building complex applications out of Beans without the need to write extended and repetitive Java code. BeanML documents can even be compiled, eliminating the delay caused by parsing XML when the program starts.

 Caution

BeanML is still a work in progress, like most things at alphaWorks. The material presented above is subject to change, and may no longer be accurate. Check the alphaWorks site (http://www.alphaWorks.ibm.com/) for the latest details.

MDSAX and Coins

MDSAX and Coins are two Java-based open source projects that help developers process XML and make XML immediately useful to Java developers as a means of serializing Java objects. MDSAX is a framework that helps developers create chains of processors for XML documents, while Coins is a set of tools for feeding the data stored in XML documents into Java objects and back out again. Both use XML documents as a key tool for controlling (indeed, creating) Java applications, sparing developers the code-compile-debug cycle for many cases where such coding is repetitive. Developers can specify how MDSAX should process XML documents using a Context Markup Language, which references Java classes (typically filters that process the XML documents). When a program sets up MDSAX, it passes it a ContextML document, which tells it how to set up the processing tree. A simple ContextML document might look like:

```
<context>
    <documentRouter>
        <elementRouter key="context">
            <x key="context"
factory="com.jxml.mdsax.MDContextFactoryImpl"/>
            <x key="documentRouter"
factory="com.jxml.mdsax.MDDocumentRouterFactory"/>
            <x key="stack"
factory="com.jxml.mdsax.MDFilterStackFactoryImpl"/>
            <x key="elementRouter"
factory="com.jxml.mdsax.MDElementRouterFactory"/>
            <x key="trace"
factory="com.jxml.mdsax.debug.MDTraceFilterFactory"/>
            <x key="display"
factory="com.jxml.mdsax.debug.MDDisplayFilterFactory"/>
            <x key="results"
factory="com.jxml.mdsax.debug.examples.counter.
ResultsFactory"/>
            <x key="element"
```

```
factory="com.jxml.mdsax.debug.examples.counter.
ElementFactory"/>
        </elementRouter>
    </documentRouter>
</context>
```

The keys connect through this document to Java classes. After this initial boot process (which can be left to a default document), the ContextML document that describes how those classes should be arranged can appear much simpler, as in this context document from a counter example.

```
<context>
        <results/>
        <element/>
</context>
```

Coins uses XML documents for similar tasks, though with a much broader scope and with the ability to write back to a file. Coins uses binding documents to specify how classes should connect with XML document content. The processor loads the binding document, then loads an XML document and connects the information in that document to Java objects as appropriate. This is useful for a large number of programming cases, from XML document processing (where each element needs particular processing) to Java graphical interface development, where even Sun's newest and friendliest interface tools still require a considerable amount of redundant code. Coins provides a set of tools that work for developers building XML processing applications, and (perhaps more importantly) provides a framework for building Java programs with XML documents.

 Cross-Reference

For more information on ContextML, MDSAX, or Coins, visit http://www.jxml.com.

XML-RPC

XML-RPC uses XML syntax to describe remote procedure calls between computers over a network, transporting the calls and the responses to those calls over the ubiquitous HTTP protocol. Calls are made as XML documents, which are sent using POST HTTP requests. The header tells the receiving Web server where to direct the RPC call. For example, an XML-RPC request might look like:

```
POST /rpchandler  HTTP/1.0
User-Agent: MyClient/1.0 (WinNT)
Host: mycomputer.simonstl.com
Content-Type: text/xml
Content-length:169

<?xml version="1.0" encoding="UTF-8"?>
<methodCall>
   <methodName>test.returnId</methodName>
   <params>
        <param>
             <value><string>ASCII</string></value>
        </param>
   <params>
</methodCall>
```

The Web server receiving this request passes it to /rpchandler, which could be a servlet, a CGI script, or a program set up to answer at that URL. It receives the XML, calls the method named "test.returnId" with the string parameter "UTF-8", and then responds with its own XML-RPC document, possibly the one shown below.

```
HTTP/1.1 200 OK
Server: JavaWebServer/1.1
Content-Length:
Content-Type: text/xml
Date: Fri, 12 Feb 1999 19:01:32 GMT
```

```
<?xml version="1.0?>
<methodResponse>
   <params>
       <param>
            <value><string>Server
12345</string></value>
       </param>
   </params>
</methodResponse>
```

It's a long route to get a server identification (or a Hello World), but XML-RPC has a lot to offer, especially in cross-platform coordination. UNIX servers, Windows 95 desktops, Macintoshes, System/390 mainframes, and any other networked system or environment can connect using this system, sharing processing over the network transparently. It doesn't matter what kind of computer it is, running what kind of operating system — as long as it has an HTTP connection and the capacity to process XML, it can connect to a larger network of XML-RPC enabled computers.

Developers used to the more complicated approaches of CORBA and COM may find this a useful alternative for simple solutions, though it doesn't yet have the level of support of those more established technologies. In the long run, XML's easy interchange and hierarchical structures may pose a significant challenge to the two current kings of the object world.

 Cross-Reference

For more information on XML-RPC (including information on error messages, data types, and many other issues), visit http://www.xmlrpc.com.

Metadata-Describing Resources Using XML

The information inside of documents is important, but knowing which document to search can make that information more accessible. Metadata — data about data — can make information more accessible. Even before XML was finalized, a number of proposed standards that used it for metadata appeared. Microsoft's Channel Definition Format (CDF) was one of the first XML implementations to achieve widespread use, through the Channel Bar that has been a part of the Internet Explorer browser since version 4. More tools for describing documents, like the W3C's Resource Description Framework (RDF) and the Dublin Core Metadata Initiative's Element Set are on the way, providing a common vocabulary for describing the incredible quantity of resources available on the Internet and elsewhere. XSA, a completely separate initiative, is a simple but very useful specification that developers can use to describe the latest version of their software.

Channel Definition Format

CDF is the first XML-based standard to receive anything resembling widespread use. Microsoft submitted the proposal to the W3C in March 1997, but CDF will probably remain primarily a Microsoft standard. CDF contains a standard set of tags for defining push content channels. Channels automate the flow of data from Web server to Web browser, providing the browser with a schedule for downloading new content from the channel's server and labeling that content with a button and some brief descriptions. CDF documents, like the one shown below, display information pointing the browser to the source of the information, descriptive information (like the logo, an abstract, and a title), and a schedule for regular downloads. When the user wants to visit the channel, the information is already loaded for them, avoiding waiting for downloads and making it easy for users to reference Web information offline.

```
<CHANNEL HREF="http://www.simonstl.com/index.html">
<TITLE>Simon St.Laurent's Ravings</TITLE>
<ABSTRACT>Collected essays, projects, and book
information for Simon St.Laurent</ABSTRACT>

<LOGO HREF="http://www.simonstl.com/craneico.gif"
STYLE="ICON"/>
<LOGO HREF="http://www.simonstl.com/logo.gif"
STYLE="IMAGE"/>

<SCHEDULE>
<INTERVALTIME DAY="14">
</SCHEDULE>

<ITEM HREF="http://www.simonstl.com/articles/index.html">
<TITLE>Articles</TITLE>
<ABSTRACT>Articles on XML</ABSTRACT>
</ITEM>

<ITEM HREF="http://www.simonstl.com/projects/index.html">
<TITLE>Projects</TITLE>
<ABSTRACT>Projects, including open-source software
development</ABSTRACT>
</ITEM>

<ITEM HREF="http://www.simonstl.com/xmllinks.html">
<TITLE>XML Links</TITLE>
<ABSTRACT>Links to XML Resources, from specifications to
news sites to mailing lists.</ABSTRACT>
</ITEM>

</CHANNEL>
```

Channel content is still in HTML, not XML. XML just provides a framework that enables the browser to find and describe the content. Users can explore that content through the channel bar, even (as far as the browser collected) when not connected. The schedule can have odd effects on computers that use dial-up connections; since most schedules are designed to download data at off-peak times (midnight to 4 a.m.), Internet Explorer 4.0 users may wake up in the middle of the night to the cheerful sound of their modem dialing out to their Internet Service Provider.

 Cross-Reference

You can access CDF information from several sources. View the submission to the W3C, which includes a full description of the DTD, at `http://www.w3.org/TR/NOTECDF-submit.html`. Microsoft has white papers and other information available through its Site Builder (`http://www.microsoft.com/sitebuilder`) and Internet Explorer (`http://www.microsoft.com/ie`) Web sites. For more information on CDF and push technologies in general, see Ethan Cerami's *Delivering Push* (McGraw-Hill, 1998).

XML Software Autoupdate (XSA)

XSA enables software designers to create description files for their software, making it possible for sites to poll those files and keep track of updates. XSA was created by Lars Marius Garshol, keeper of a list of XML tools (at `http://www.stud.ifi.uio.no/~larsga/linker/XMLtools.html`), with help from James Tauber (keeper of `http://www.xmlsoftware.com`) and Robin Cover (the keeper of `http://www.oasis-open.org/cover/`). An explosion of free (and not-so-free) software tools in various stages of development marks XML's early development period. The "release early and often" strategy typical of open source development made it difficult for the keepers of XML sites to keep up with the constant changes, and XSA seeks to ease their difficulties while helping developers announce new software.

XSA files are pretty simple. An XSA document wizard remains in development, but creating XSA files by hand is fairly easy. The XSA element contains a vendor and multiple products. The vendor element contains name, e-mail, and URL information, while the products contain an ID, version information, the date of last release, an info URL for the product, and information about changes since the last version. (XSA makes no provision for describing multiple versions of a product, though they can store as multiple products.) For example, the XSA file describing the author's XLinkFilter might look like:

```
<?xml version="1.0" encoding="UTF-8"?>
<xsa>
    <vendor>
        <name>Simon St.Laurent</name>
        <email>simontl@simonstl.com</email>
        <url>http://www.simonstl.com</url>
    </vendor>
    <product id="xlinkfilter">
        <version>0.20</version>
        <last-release>19981227</last-release>
        <info-url>
http://purl.oclc.org/NET/xlinkfilter</info-url>
        <changes>XLinkFilter 0.20 includes an image map
demo, more documentation, and support for generating
XPointers through a LocationFilter.</changes>
    </product>
</xsa>
```

The XSA file must then post someplace public — probably on the vendor's Web site — and register with sites, which will then check back periodically to see if anything has changed and update their own information.

Cross-Reference

For more information on XSA, including a DTD, documentation, and examples, see `http://birk105.studby.` `uio.no/www_work/xsa/`.

Resource Description Framework (RDF)

The W3C's Resource Description Framework (RDF) started at about the same time as XML, and solves many similar problems in a different way. RDF is an extremely general tool for representing metadata. RDF provides tools for describing entities and relationships between them, while XML's background comes from the SGML project of document representation. RDF uses XML as its 'serialization syntax', but doesn't use an XML DTD. From RDF's perspective, attributes are the same as sub-elements with text (but not sub-element) content, resulting in a very different approach to information. You can, in theory, use RDF with nearly any kind of information presented as a directed graph or set of graphs, from simple information about a resource to complex relationships describing a matrix of content — even, perhaps, a document. Nonetheless, XML is the document syntax (it's both more convenient for many document applications and much more familiar) and RDF will be used for metadata, providing descriptions for those documents.

RDF performs as a key component in many of the W3C's plans, including the Digital Signature Initiative (DSIG), the Platform for Internet Content Selection (PICS), and the Platform for Privacy Preferences (P3P). RDF provides its own tools (schemas) for specifying the structure and content of RDF material. RDF by itself is fairly useless — sort of like XML by itself, before someone creates a vocabulary — and RDF's formal structures look more complicated than those of XML, largely because of the more flexible syntax. An RDF example will appear below, in the section on Dublin Core, using a predefined vocabulary, but RDF, with all of its implications, really deserves its own book — or three or four. The interactions between RDF processing and XML processing will undoubtedly grow, but currently (while RDF is still in working drafts), the applications haven't sprouted widely.

Cross-Reference

For a good tutorial on the graph theory underlying RDF, see `http://www.utm.edu/departments/math/graph/`. For an excellent (free) tool that will help you create RDF documents, explore Reggie at `http://metadata.net/dstc/`. The W3C has an RDF validation service available at http://jigsaw.w3.org:8000/description with a Java graphical viewer you will have fun exploring.

Dublin Core

The Dublin Core Metadata Initiative began long before either XML or RDF appeared on the W3C's radar screen, and provides a vocabulary for describing Web (and other) resources. The Dublin Core vocabulary is based on the information long stored in library card catalogs, helping readers find the information they need. The Dublin Core Metadata Element Set recently released as RFC 2413, and more descriptive tools will surely come from this project. The Dublin Core Metadata Element Set is *only* a vocabulary, with no dependencies on either XML or RDF. The RFC doesn't include either a DTD or an RDF schema (though an appendix of the RDF schema draft includes a schema for Dublin Core). Nonetheless, the Dublin Core information perfectly complements RDF, giving it a vocabulary you can instantly apply to a wide variety of Web documents.

Dublin Core uses the elements Title, Subject, Description, Type, Source, Relation, Creator, Publisher, Contributor, Rights, Date, Format, Identifier, and Language. Not all of the elements will be needed for every document, though the more specific the information, the more useful it will be. If these headings feel like the information on a library card catalog card, that's because the Dublin Core group is composed primarily of librarians and their successors in information management. Making good use of this opportunity helps to create catalogs that can find information more reliably than today's full-text search engines explored on the basis of much more tightly defined criteria. A sample Dublin Core document that describes the author's Web site appears below.

```
<?xml version = "1.0"?>
<rdf:RDF xmlns:rdf = "http://www.w3.org/TR/WD-rdf-syntax"
     xmlns:DC = "http://info.internet.isi.edu/in-
notes/rfc/files/rfc2413.txt">

<rdf:Description xml:lang="en"
about="http://www.simonstl.com">
  <DC:Title>
    Simon St.Laurent's Web Site - Articles, Projects, and
Books
  </DC:Title>
  <DC:Creator>
    Simon St.Laurent
  </DC:Creator>
  <DC:Description>
    This Web site contains pointers to XML information,
as well as articles by Simon St.Laurent and links to
books he has written.
  </DC:Description>
      <DC:Subject>
            XML XLink XLinkFilter DDML XSchema CSS
      </DC:Subject>
  <DC:Publisher>
    simonstl.com
  </DC:Publisher>
  <DC:Identifier DC:Scheme="URI">
    http://www.simonstl.com
  </DC:Identifier>
  <DC:Rights>
```

```
   Copyright 1998-9 by Simon St.Laurent
 </DC:Rights>
</rdf:Description>
</rdf:RDF>
```

I hope that standard vocabularies for the Subject area will arrive soon, though that seems a much larger task in some ways than determining the broad categories and always open to new interpretations. With luck, however, the Dublin Core project and its vocabularies will make the Web a more searchable and more useful place.

 Cross-Reference

For more information on the Dublin Core Metadata Initiative, see http://purl.org/DC/. For RFC 2413, describing the Dublin Core Metadata Element Set, visit http://info. internet.isi.edu/in-notes/rfc/files/rfc2413.txt.

Futures

XML's popularity for data applications will depend heavily on how much use developers find for its combination of structure, flexibility, machine-readability, and human-readability. Unlike most documents in the previous chapters, these applications aren't intended for direct consumption by human users. Readability is maintained to make documents easier to examine and debug, but few of the documents will ever see a style sheet or directly reach human readers. Even though XML does incur more overhead than traditional binary files, its verbosity and emphasis on nested structures give programmers new tools for communications between computers and applications. As XML spreads, we may see more programs based on shared architectures, all using a common set of file formats for wildly different projects.

Chapter 10

The XPointer Specification

XML's cleanly defined structures make it possible to describe portions of documents easily without having to litter the document with identifiers. Taking advantage of the nested structures and the potentially greater meaningfulness of element names, XPointers specify paths you can follow to extract a portion of a document. When combined with the XLink specification described in the next chapter, XPointers are powerful tools for precisely specifying links between documents.

Note

The discussion in this chapter is based on the 3 March 1998 draft of the XPointer specification, available at http://www. w3.org/TR/1998/WD-xptr-19980303. Work on XPointer (and XLink) has been extremely slow, though the signs for 1999 look more promising. The Working Group should release a requirements document in February 1999. Check the W3C XML site at http://www.w3.org/XML/ for the latest information. XSL and XPointer are supposed to be unifying some terms, so checking the XSL area (http://www.w3.org/Styles/XSL/) may also be useful.

311

Pointing vs. Querying

XPointers have considerable powers to search documents and return subsets of information as fragments of documents. While XPointers aren't really a query language (they're more like a set of directions for a road map), they have many of the same capabilities, optimized for use in document navigation. XPointers focus more on location than on content, however, and don't really specify what the results of an XPointer look like. Typically they'll appear as an easily processed tree structure (like a subset of the trees created with the W3C's Document Object Model, or DOM), but in some cases they might include parts of elements, or even just attributes. While this makes sense for the linking applications XPointers are meant for, it can wreak havoc when introduced into scenarios that call for a more structured approach.

The W3C held a Query Languages Workshop in December 1998, where 94 participants discussed 66 different position papers on querying for the Web, mostly about XML. (You can access a list of position papers at http://www.w3.org/TandS/QL/ QL98/pp.html.) A variety of developers and organizations are creating query languages, some based on the Structured Query Language (SQL) used by relational databases, some based on the query tools for object databases, others based on set notation, and undoubtedly many more. Tools for querying XML will probably reveal an important story over the next few years, but (apart from XPointers) there isn't much to see yet.

XPointers: An Introduction

The XPointer (an abbreviation for Extended Pointer) is derived from the Text Encoding Initiative (TEI) standards described above in Chapter 4. XPointers designate resources using location terms, which are grouped into locators. An XPointer may contain a single locator (though some locators may contain other locators). We'll build simple locators first and then combine them.

Locators may contain absolute, relative, spanning, attribute, or string-matching location terms. String-matching terms have the most limited vocabulary, but they provide a degree of precision the other terms can't match. Attribute terms make it possible to retrieve attribute values as well as element content. Spanning terms refer to the information between two locators. Relative terms enable links to refer to document content by its position within the element tree of a document and by its content. Absolute location terms identify elements using the more conventional ID and NAME addressing schemes, as well as some other basic locations.

Absolute Location Terms

Absolute location terms provide ready access to a few key pieces of an XML document. The root(), origin(), id(*id*), and html(*name*) keywords make it easy to address the root element of a document, the element using the keyword, an element with a given id, and a "classic" HTML A element with a NAME attribute value. Absolute location terms must appear at the beginning of a locator; if you do not specify an absolute location term, the default of root() will be assumed.

The root() term specifies the root element of the document, the outermost element of the document tree. root( ) effectively refers to the entire content of the document. The origin( ) keyword refers to the linking element itself and frequently provides an absolute position for subsequent relative terms. This enables an XPointer to specify content like "2 paragraphs below the link element," for example. The empty parentheses following the root( ) and origin( ) keywords are required.

The other two absolute keywords reference elements by names assigned to them by authors, for both HTML and XML. The html(*name*) keyword takes a value that matches an HTML A element's NAME attribute, providing exactly the same service for fragment identifiers as was available in HTML. Mostly, this will get used in XML documents that refer to HTML documents, because

XML documents should use the ID attribute instead. The id(*name*) keyword provides similar but improved functionality. Every element in a document may have an ID value; this means that you can quickly reference any element this way. By default, as described in the next chapter, XLink will treat all fragment identifiers that aren't otherwise marked this way. The fragment identifier "#*fragmentidentifier*" gets treated as id(*fragmentidentifier*) automatically.

Relative Location Terms

Relative location terms are more complicated, although considerably more flexible. The keywords for relative location terms are tools for navigating the document tree, as listed in Table 10-1.

Table 10-1 *Relative Location Terms*

Keyword	Effect
child	Selects child elements of the location source (must be elements nested directly under the source).
descendant	Selects elements appearing in the content of the location source (may be nested more than one level).
ancestor	Selects elements in whose content the location source is found (parent elements).
preceding	Selects elements that appear before the location source.
psibling	Selects sibling elements that appear before the location source. (Sibling elements share the same parent element.)
following	Selects elements appearing after the location source.
fsibling	Selects sibling elements that appear after the location source. (Sibling elements share the same parent element.)

All the relative keywords use the same set of arguments, enclosed in parentheses:

```
(Instance, NodeType, Attribute, Value)
```

You must always include *Instance* (which is a numeric value, or 'ALL') and *NodeType*; *Attribute* and *Value* are optional and used only when needed to identify an element by the value of one of its attributes. The *Instance* enables developers to specify elements in positions relative to the location source. *NodeType* defines the candidate type of the location term.

Instance and *NodeType* enable developers to specify the *n*th appearance of a certain node in the structure described by the relative location keyword, making it easy to specify relative position using position in a document. The value of *Instance* may be either a positive or negative integer (for example, 2, -12, +4) or the keyword "all". Using all will return all nodes that meet the criteria specified by the rest of the location term, while the numbers indicate moves along the document tree in the manner specified by the location term. Positive numbers count from the first appearance of a structure matching the location term, while negative numbers count from the last appearance. For example, CHILD(3,QUOTE) refers to the third appearance of the QUOTE element within the location source element. CHILD(5,EXPLANATION) refers to the fifth appearance of the EXPLANATION element within the location source element. Using negative numbers for the instance value counts backward, CHILD(-1, PRICE) refers to the last PRICE element within the location source, whereas CHILD(-3,PRICE) refers to the third-from-last, and so on.

Typically, *NodeType* will appear as the name of an element. However, developers may not always know, or need to know, the name of the target to which they should point. To accommodate this, XML enables the *NodeType* to take three values that aren't element names. The value #element enables the location term to accept all elements as candidates for a match. CHILD(2,#element) refers to the second element within the location source element. The #text value tells the location term to accept text nodes as candidates for a match. Text nodes are composed of the character data that combines with markup in a mixed declaration. For example, in:

```
<CASE>Name:<NAME>Jim</NAME>
Fish bonker:<BONKER>01234</BONKER>
Crime:<CRIME>Fishing without mowing the lawn
first</CRIME>
Status:<STATUS>Dismissed</STATUS></CASE>
```

the first pseudo-element (child(1,#text)) contains the text "Name:", the second (child(2,#text)) contains a newline character (remember, XML preserves whitespace) and "Fish bonker:", and so on.

XPointers may also reference comments, processing instructions, and CDATA sections. The #comment value refers to comments, while #pi refers to comments and #cdata to CDATA sections. Finally, #all indicates the last available value for *NodeType*. This *NodeType* enables both elements and pseudo-elements to count as candidates. If applied to the previous example, using the CASE element as the location source, CHILD(1,#all) would refer to "Name:", whereas CHILD(2,#all) would refer to the NAME element following it.

Adding the *Attribute* and *Value* arguments to perform attribute matching enables another level of precisely specifying locations. Both the *Attribute* and *Value* arguments are optional. But if the *Attribute* argument appears, the *Value* argument must follow. CHILD(1,*,TARGET,ME) refers to the first element within the locator source that contains an attribute TARGET with the value ME. CHILD(2,QUOTE,SPEAKER,ROOSEVELT) refers to the second QUOTE element with a SPEAKER attribute set to ROOSEVELT. Both of these arguments will accept the value * in place of a specific argument. If you substitute * for the *Attribute* argument, any attribute whose value matches the value argument matches. If you use * for the *Value* argument, the attribute named by the attribute argument may have any value. CHILD(1,QUOTE,SPEAKER,*) refers to the first QUOTE element that has a SPEAKER attribute declared, no matter what the value. CHILD(3,QUOTE,*,ROOSEVELT) refers to the third QUOTE element that has any attribute with a value set to ROO-SEVELT. The attribute could be named PRESIDENT, SPEAKER, or Q2FD - it doesn't matter.

The *Value* argument also accepts the value #IMPLIED. Like the attribute list declaration default type it resembles, it refers to attributes that are declared but have no assigned default value. In this case, it only refers to attributes in the document that were declared but left unspecificied — if an element provided a value for an attribute, even one declared #IMPLIED, an XPointer using #IMPLIED as a *Value* will not recognize it.

Attribute Location Term

The attribute location term may appear simpler than most of the other terms, though its use (in linking at least) remains somewhat mysterious. Used in combination with terms identifying an element, it "takes only an attribute name as a selector and returns the attribute's value." This is somewhat unique, as the other XPointers designate locations rather than return values per se, but you can quickly realize uses for this term. It uses the syntax:

```
attr(AttributeName)
```

For example, attr(id) would return the value of an attribute named id from the currently identified element (or the root element, if no other declarations preceded it).

Spanning Location Term

The span() keyword enables the combination of XPointers to collect everything from the beginning of one XPointer to the end of the second. (It's not clear from the specification what happens if the location referenced by the first XPointer appears after the second argument.) Spanning makes it easy to create "combination"

XPointers that simplify the creation of links used for a variety of tasks, from annotation to transclusion. (Transclusion means roughly the inclusion of one document or a part of a document inside another.) The syntax for span() looks like:

```
span(XPointer1, XPointer2)
```

The two XPointers get interpreted separately; the selection made by the first XPointer has no effect on the selection made by the second. The span() term then selects all of the content starting at the first and ending at the second.

```
<CASE>Name:<NAME>Jim</NAME>
Fish bonker:<BONKER>01234</BONKER>
Crime:<CRIME>Fishing without mowing the lawn
first</CRIME>
Status:<STATUS>Dismissed</STATUS></CASE>
```

Referencing the document above, the XPointer (span(child-(NAME,1),child(BONKER,1)) identifies the fragment:

```
<NAME>Jim</NAME>
Fish bonker:<BONKER>01234</BONKER>
```

Similarly, the XPointer (span(child(NAME,1),child(#text,2)) identifies this fragment:

```
<NAME>Jim</NAME>
Fish bonker:
```

String Location Term

String location terms are the last set of available location terms. The string keyword is used with the following syntax:

```
string(Instance, String, Position, Length)
```

The *Instance* argument works the same way it did with the relative terms. The *String* argument is just the string to match. (In searching for a match, the processor should ignore all markup characters, so string values can cross element boundaries.) *Position* provides an offset from the precise character position identifying the location returned, measured as characters from the first character of the found string. If *Position* is 0 (or missing), then the location will be the position of the first character of the string when found; if it is 2, it will be the third character from the start, and so on. *Length* tells the processor how many characters to include, and only appears when you use position. (If *Position* and *Length* are missing, the locator refers to the string as found.) In the code,

```
<LINE>The worms crawl in and the worms crawl out</LINE>
<LINE>The ones that crawl in are lean and thin</LINE>
<LINE>The ones that crawl out are fat and stout</LINE>
```

the term string(1,worms,4,1) returns the location of the letter s in "worms" in the first appearance of the word in the first line. The string (2,worms,3,1) returns the location of the letter m in "worms" in the second appearance of the word. String (1,crawl,1,1), string (2,crawl,1,2), and string (3,crawl,1,3), and string (4,crawl,1,4) returns the location of the letter c in the first appearance of the word "crawl," the letters "cr" in the second, "craw" in the third, and "craw" in the fourth.

Combining Location Terms

Much of the power of location terms comes when used in combination. Absolute location terms make it easy to specify a new default locator element instead of the default root( ). Relative location terms can combine to enable you to specify the element directly above the fifth appearance of the FRAB element whose FLIPGELLY attribute is set to "postmaster." Combining terms is simple — just list them in sequence. Terms will evaluate from left to right. For example, given the fragment:

```
<BOOKSHELF ID="history">
```

```
<BOOK><TITLE>The Shaping of America, Volume 2:
Continental America,
1800-1867</TITLE><AUTHOR>Meinig</AUTHOR></BOOK>
<BOOK><TITLE>That Noble Dream: The Pursuit of Objectivity
in the American Historical
Profession</TITLE><AUTHOR>Novick</AUTHOR></BOOK>
<BOOK><TITLE>The Origins of the Korean War, Vol.
II</TITLE><AUTHOR>Cumings</AUTHOR></BOOK>
<BOOK><TITLE>Nature's Metropolis: Chicago and the Great
West</TITLE><AUTHOR>Cronon</AUTHOR></BOOK>
</BOOKSHELF>
```

the locator id(history) selects the entire BOOKSHELF element. id(history).child(3,BOOK) selects our third BOOK element. The AUTHOR element, in this case "Cumings," is selected by id(history).child(3,BOOK).child(1,AUTHOR).

id(history).child(3,BOOK).psibling(1,BOOK) selects the second BOOK element. Finally, both the third and fourth book elements, and their content is selected by span(id(history).child(3,BOOK), id(history).child(4,BOOK)). The possibilities seem endless, giving developers all kinds of power for creating chunks, even when the chunks don't neatly match single elements.

XML enables a shorthand notation for multiple argument lists (unusual in itself because XML allows very little abbreviation). id(history).child(3,BOOK).(1,AUTHOR) equals id(history).child(3,BOOK).child(1,AUTHOR); XML understands that the keyword repeats between steps.

Note

While XPointer makes it easy to identify document fragments of all kinds, difficulties arise when processing them. A separate working group is addressing these issues, figuring out exactly how to present document fragments of many different (and not well-formed) kinds. See http://www. w3.org/XML/Activity.html for more information.

Now, we can create some rather powerful references that surpass the naming powers granted developers by the HTML A element. Our references can cruise through document structures to precisely locate their targets. The next step combines these references with new linking technologies, expanding the toolbox further and bringing linking to a whole new level.

Note

Because of XPointer's serious instability, there aren't very many implementations. For a current list, see Steve DeRose's "XPointer and XLink Implementation links" at `http://www.stg.brown.edu/~sjd/XML-Linking/xptr-implementations.html`.

Chapter 11

The XLink Specification

HTML's explosive growth probably had more to do with its linking than with any other single factor. Hundreds of people and organizations worked simultaneously on hypertext systems, some even using SGML, but none of them had the simplicity of HTML's convenient linking system. <A HREF="*targetURL*"> has strung millions of pages together and built the World Wide Web. Still, there's definitely room for improvement. Hypertext specialists and other developers complained loudly about the limited abilities of these basic links, and at least some HTML developers looked at SGML's more complete (indeed, just about all-inclusive) HyTime specification and wished for some of its power, though not its complexity. XML presents a chance to do things better, and the XML working group has focused on linking early. XML linking builds on HTML's success and provides more powerful, yet more complex tools.

Note

I base the discussion in this chapter on the 3 March 1998 draft of the XLink specification, available at `http://www.` `w3.org/TR/1998/WD-xlink-19980303`. Work on XLink (and XPointer) has been extremely slow, though they show more promise for 1999. The Working Group should release a requirements document in February 1999 – check the W3C XML site at `http://www.w3.org/XML/` for the latest information.

Simple Links

After six years of extensive use, HTML's linking systems are under mounting criticism for providing only the simplest of links. Conversely, many developers seem perfectly content with the current linking syntax, and a small army of development tools and Web-mapping tools have grown up around this key standard. HTML's HREF attribute has done well enough for most developers. Why break it? XML doesn't break the previous standard, it just adds to it. It adds a lot in fact, but the basic HTML link structure is still preserved, and certain aspects of it grandfathered into the XML standard to make it easier for XML documents to link to HTML. We'll start by examining the kinds of links available in HTML documents, and then we'll look at how we can implement them in XML.

Links in HTML

The A element is the key to nearly all HTML linking, although the LINK element plays a limited role. Figure 11-1 displays a simple HTML link created with an A element.

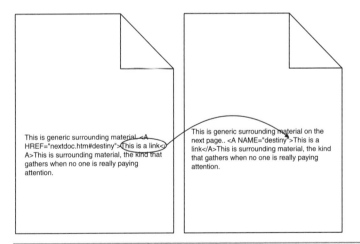

This is generic surrounding material. <A HREF="nextdoc.htm#destiny">This is a link</A>This is surrounding material, the kind that gathers when no one is really paying attention.

This is generic surrounding material on the next page.. <A NAME="destiny">This is a link</A>This is surrounding material, the kind that gathers when no one is really paying attention.

Figure 11-1 *Simple unidirectional in-line link, HTML*

The A element has several attributes, only one of which gets constant use from HTML developers: the all-powerful HREF (soon to be href, if the W3C's early plans for the next version of HTML hold up). HREF usually takes a URL (Uniform Resource Locator) for its value, which represents the target of the link. URLs may be absolute or relative. Absolute URLs begin with a scheme, which describes the protocol used to interpret the URL. Commonly used schemes include http:, ftp:, gopher:, mailto:, nntp:, file:, and javascript:. The information applicable to the scheme follows the scheme. In most cases, this will appear as a reference to a server or a file on a server, prefixed with two slashes. For example, an absolute URL using the HTTP protocol implements the following syntax:

```
http://hostcomputer:port/path?query
```

The port and query are optional. The host computer must contain a valid DNS name or IP address, and the port optionally specifies a port on the hostcomputer (80 is the default for http). Path specifies a path to a particular file on the host computer; only numbers, letters, and $, -, _, +, !, *, ', (,), and the period and comma can appear in the path. Other characters may be escaped by the % sign, followed by their hexadecimal value. The optional query provides additional information to the server, enabling it to respond appropriately to form or other information. The content of query is limited to the same characters as path.

Note

For the javascript: scheme, the value after the colon can be any valid javascript code. The javascript: scheme is on the way out - HTML 4.0 provides the onclick attribute to enable elements to activate scripts without placing javascript in the HREF attribute.

Relative URLs use the URL of the current page (or, if it exists, the URL set by the BASE element in the HEAD element of the page) as a prefix to their information. Relative URLs do not include a scheme.

Cross-Reference

See the complete official syntax for URLs defined in RFC 1738 (http://www.w3.org/Addressing/rfc1738.txt) and RFC 1808 (http://www.w3.org/Addressing/rfc1808.txt).

Both absolute and relative URLs may include a fragment identifier at the end in place of the query. Fragment identifiers in HTML include a pound sign (#) and a value that should connect to the NAME attribute of an A element in the target document. For example, in

```
<A HREF="#laterlink">Skipping around is fun!</A>
...
...
<A NAME="laterlink">Aren't you glad you skipped ahead?
```

clicking on "Skipping around is fun!" would scroll the document to the location of the A element with the NAME attribute "laterlink." Of course, you can also use fragment identifiers in combination with URLs.

```
<A HREF="zip.html#nothingness">
```

would take a user who clicked it to the line in the zip.html file that contained

```
<A NAME="nothingness">
```

Note

More recent specifications (including XLink) refer to URIs (Uniform Resource Identifiers) rather than URLs. URIs supplement URLs with additional tools for identifying resources, like Uniform Resource Numbers (URNs). In common usage, however, the extra features URIs provide typically get ignored because they require additional tools (usually directories) to resolve their contents to locations. Though you may use URIs with XLink, this chapter will use the more common URL terminology.

The A element also allows for REV and REL tags, intended to show the relationship between the anchor and the target URL. REL indicates the relationship of the URL to the anchor (moving forward along the link), whereas REV indicates the relationship of the anchor to the URL (moving backward along the link). Neither of these is widely used in anchor tags. The LINK element, which appears in the HEAD element of HTML documents, also supports the HREF, REL, and REV attributes. In the case of LINK (as we saw in Chapter 2), REL does get used to indicate that the target URL represents a style sheet. LINK also provides a TYPE attribute to indicate the MIME type of the target URL. Unlike an A element, the LINK element doesn't take the user anywhere — it just connects outside resources to the document, in much the same way that the IMG, APPLET, SCRIPT, or OBJECT elements can, using their SRC attributes.

Simple Links in XLink

In XML, we call typical HTML links simple in-line links. Links connect resources — "anything which happens to be reachable by the use of a locator in some linking element", according to the XLink working draft. (Resources include documents, but they also include graphics and other files.) The locator is a URL, defined the same way as URLs for HTML, and equally (actually more) capable of using fragment identifiers. For in-line links, the element defining the link counts as one of those resources, and the target as the other. The classic HTML href link is a unidirectional link because it points only one direction: from the element that provides the link to the target location, and an in-line link because the A element is involved as a resource. (The "Back" button doesn't count, in this example, as providing two-way linking.) Traversing describes the action taken when a link is actuated, even if the link doesn't "take" the actuator (which may be a user or a program) any place new.

A simple link in XML carries all its linking information in the linking element. You do not need in a simple link for the application

to search out other elements carrying information about the locators —
all the locator information rests in the href attribute. Building a true
XML link isn't exactly simple, however; it takes more than an href
attribute for an element to be a link. A sample declaration for an
element using simple links follows:

```
<!ELEMENT simple ANY>
 <!ATTLIST simple
     xml:link      CDATA                    #FIXED "simple"
     href          CDATA                    #REQUIRED
     role          CDATA                    #IMPLIED
     title         CDATA                    #IMPLIED
     inline        (true|false)             "true"
     content-role  CDATA                    #IMPLIED
     content-title CDATA                    #IMPLIED
     show          (embed|replace|new) #IMPLIED
     actuate       (auto|user)              #IMPLIED
     behavior      CDATA                    #IMPLIED
 >
```

You don't have to call link elements simple — any element can be
a link element. The simple element declaration is used, both here
and in the Working Draft, only for illustration. In fact, any element
can be a link — you do not need to create separate elements like the
HTML A that exist solely to implement simple links.

The familiar href attribute, still there, works the same way as it
did in HTML, although, as we'll see later, it too has extended. The
rest of the attributes are new. The first attribute, xml:link, announces to the processing application that this element represents a
linking element that is a simple link. All links require the xml:link
attribute; defining it with a fixed value in the DTD usually proves a
better solution than spelling out this attribute in every single
instance of the element.

Avoid the temptation to create documents and DTDs that use an
href attribute without declaring xml:link. Even though they might

work in HTML browsers, xml:link compliant processing applications will ignore the href attribute if missing the xml:link attribute.

The role attribute is optional (as are all the attributes marked #IMPLIED or provided with a default value here), enabling the link to specify the "meaning" of the link to the application processing the link. The role attribute is intended for use only by machine processors — information meant for humans to read should reside in the title attribute. The href attribute provides the link with a locator, a URL as already described. The title attribute, also optional, includes information that could, for example, pop up as the user rolls the mouse over a link much as the ALT tags for clickable images appear during rollovers in the latest versions of the Netscape and Microsoft browsers.

Note

The title attribute in XML has nothing to do with the title element in HTML; it's just an unfortunate overlap in name.

The inline attribute, when set to "true", declares all links built on this element as in-line links. In a simple link, inline becomes "true" by default. The Working Draft states that simple links are "usually in-line and always one-directional," but it's difficult to think of scenarios where a simple out-of-line link could be useful. (One possibility uses links to highlight information without expecting any real traversal.) Simple links will point forward to a single locator, without the use of the more complex tools needed for multidirectional or out-of-line links. Even though simple links could conceivably point to other links, XLink (as we'll see later) has better mechanisms for achieving that result.

The next two attributes presented here, content-role and content-title, perform similar functions to role and title; however, they describe the content to which the locator points rather than the link. While role and title describe the link element as a resource, content-role and content-title describe the target resource.

The show attribute represents one of XML's greatest improvements on HTML linking. The show attribute accepts, replace, new, and embed as values. Replacement is the standard practice in HTML: links replace the current resource in the processing application (the browser window, for instance) with the target resource. New provides similar functionality to that available through HTML's TARGET attribute: the ability to open the target resource in a new context. Within a browser, that new context would probably be a new window; within a processing application, that new context could be an additional process operating in parallel. Embed adds an entirely new dimension. When the link is traversed, the resource designated by the href attribute should embed in the body of the originating resource. In other words, it should embed in the element acting as the link. Embed enables XML developers to create links that act more as if they have SRC attributes than href attributes. In fact, XML documents that need to create equivalents to HTML's SRC attributes should probably use embed in combination with the automatic traversal made possible by the actuate attribute.

The actuate attribute accepts the values auto and user. User requires an external action (for example, a user clicking) before the link becomes traversed. The user, again, may be a human viewing the document or another processing application exploring or otherwise using it. Auto requires that the link be traversed by the processing application as soon as it encounters the resource. When combined with the show attribute's embed value, auto acts like a client-side include, requiring the processing application to seek out the resource and include it in the linking element. Processing applications will need versatility to support this because of the varied content of those resources.

The last attribute available to simple links, behavior, provides another place for developers to place information directing programs how to traverse this link. Unlike role and content-role, it does not link to a particular side of the connection and may describe the link as a unit. The XLink specification provides no example values for behavior — interpretation of this attribute is entirely up to document authors and application developers.

Figure 11-2 shows the kind of link created by the simple element.

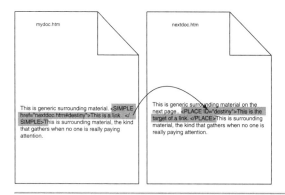

Figure 11-2 *Simple in-line link, XML*

Now that I've described all these attributes, we'll create a simple element using the preceding declaration element, which uses all of these attributes and describes what the parts might do.

```
<simple role="emptiness"
href="http://www.simonstl.com/zero/zero.html"
title="zero" content-role="cliff" content-title="last
stop before nothingness" show="replace" actuate="user"
behavior="gotozero"/>
```

The href attribute identifies the targeted resource. The role attribute provides our processing application with information about our target's role in this link — in this case, "emptiness". Content-role provides that same processing application with information about this resource, a "cliff" in this instance. The behavior attribute describes the link as a whole — gotozero. The title describes the target element as "zero," whereas the content-title provides users with a description of this resource as "last stop before nothingness." Because the actuate attribute is set to "user," the processing application will do nothing to the link until directed to act on it, typically by a user clicking a link. When the link is traversed, the target document will replace the linking resource (technically the element, but quite likely the entire document) because the show attribute is set to "replace."

Reconstructing HTML with XML

Now that we've gone through the entire gamut of simple link possibilities, you can now reconstruct the A element in XML. We'll begin with a simple version and add features so that it becomes clear how XML differs from HTML. Our first version of the A element declares a minimum set of attributes:

```
<!ELEMENT A ANY>
<!ATTLIST A
      xml:link    CDATA                   #FIXED "simple"
      href        CDATA                   #REQUIRED
      title       CDATA                   #IMPLIED
      inline      (true|false)            "true"
      show        (embed|replace|new)     "replace"
      actuate     (auto|user)             "user">
```

Tip

Technically, you do not have to provide the options lists for the inline, show, and actuate attributes, but it is generally good practice and may save some processing application confusion down the line.

Our XML A element will now work like its predecessor in the form <A href="target.html"> or <A href="target.html" title="My Link!">. The xml:link, inline, show, and actuate values already have default values specified and don't need to be declared explicitly. The A element demonstrates a classic example of a user-actuated, simple in-line link that by default replaces the content of the originating resource with the content of the target resource. So far, so good.

The REV and REL attributes have been replaced for the most part by role and content-role, respectively. Although we could plow ahead and just create REV and REL attributes for our A element (since they rarely get used), it's probably a better idea to move them into XML compliance. XML provides a mechanism for remapping the xml:link attributes to other attribute names. You will discover frequent use for this in situations where an element already has an attribute named role or title that has nothing to do with linking, and also in creating backward-compatible attributes. Using this remapping requires the addition of an xml:attributes attribute. The value of this attribute is a list of attribute names in pairs. The first member of a pair must be the standard name of an xml:link attribute; the second member is the name of the attribute to which it will be mapped. In our case, this means that we will need to add the following attribute listing to our attribute declaration for the A element:

```
xml:attributes      CDATA #FIXED "role REL content-role
REV"
REV     CDATA    #IMPLIED
REL     CDATA    #IMPLIED
```

The xml:attributes declaration requires that the value of the REL attribute be treated as the value of the usual XML role attribute for linking, whereas the value of the content-role attribute equal the value of the REV attribute.

 Warning

When remapping attributes, never assign attributes names beginning with XML-. These are reserved for the future use of the XML standard. The examples in the standard use xl- as an alternative prefix.

The HTML version of the A element includes one feature that cannot carry over directly into XML. The TARGET attribute, although unavailable, might produce similar results by giving show a value of "new".. In combination with the show attribute, the TARGET attribute can map to the behavior attribute, but the success of that tactic will depend completely on the ability of the processing application to interpret the behavior. Web browsers will probably cope with this problem, but XML parsers may not.

The last attribute of the HTML A element that needs addressing in XML is the NAME attribute, used to create fragment identifiers in HTML. xml:link takes a somewhat different approach to
creating fragment identifiers, although it isn't that hard to create an
A element that looks like HTML but behaves like XML. For now,
you can create a NAME attribute for your A element of type ID.

```
NAME           ID      #IMPLIED
```

Generally, a good idea to call your ID-type attributes ID. This
makes it easier to use Cascading Style Sheets and other mechanisms
that expect to find ID attributes. In the long term, you'll want to
rename your NAME attributes ID.

XLink, confronted with a simple *#fragmentidentifier*, will check
the list of ID values in a document. The ID values include all attributes defined as type ID, not just those named ID. (Always remember to declare the ID attribute as type ID; otherwise, XLink will
ignore it.) In this case, XML can use the NAME attribute, since it
is of type ID, as a fragment identifier. This produces HTML syntax
that smoothly provides XML functionality. Our (mostly) complete
A element now looks like the following:

```
<!ELEMENT A ANY>
<!ATTLIST A
      xml:link        CDATA               #FIXED "simple"
      xml:attributes  CDATA               #FIXED
          "role REL content-role REV"
      href            CDATA               #REQUIRED
      title           CDATA               #IMPLIED
      inline          (true|false)        "true"
      show            (embed|replace|new) "replace"
      actuate         (auto|user)         "user"
      REV             CDATA               #IMPLIED
      REL             CDATA               #IMPLIED
      NAME            ID                  #IMPLIED
      TARGET          CDATA               #IMPLIED>
```

Locators and Fragments

Even though XLink can use the simple fragment identifier notation of HTML, it is capable of far more interesting things using XPointers. Many of the tasks XPointer performs prove quite useful even in simple links, enabling authors and developers to treat elements, rather than documents, as the primary unit involved in linking. Because it can use XPointers, XLink's locator syntax is considerably more robust than that of HTML, providing a number of tools that can address parts of documents by structure, ID, HTML anchor, or even text content.

Note

While XPointer makes it easy to identify document fragments of all kinds, processing them is more difficult. A separate working group addressing these issues, formed to figure out exactly how to present and process document fragments of many different (and not necessarily well-formed) kinds. See `http://www.w3.org/XML/Activity.html` for more information.

HTML enabled fragment identifiers to follow a URL using the following syntax for the href attribute:

```
href="url#fragmentidentifier"
```

XML enables a similar syntax but typically uses its more developed XPointers in place of HTML's fragment identifier:

```
href="url#XPointer"
```

or

```
href="url|XPointer"
```

or

```
href="url?XML-XPTR=XPointer"
```

In the first case, using #, the location referenced by the URL is to be fetched as a whole document by the processor (replacing the current document, if the show attribute is set to "replace"). Then the location referenced by the XPointer is to be located by the client. Secondly, using the | connector, according to the XLink standard, "no intent is signaled as to what processing model is to be used to go about accessing the designated resource." The final version, using the standard query syntax, provides a means for the server to handle the XPointer processing, cutting down on the bandwidth needed for transmission because the server can return only as much of the document as needed.

XPointers give the embed value of the show attribute considerably more power because it enables a link to refer to a section of a document — and present it in the context of the current document — rather than replacing the current document completely. This use of ID values makes it very easy for authors to subdivide a document into more manageable chunks with well-structured elements. You can display a long file containing many smaller chunks broken down into those chunks rather than as an enormous file. This makes it easy to excerpt other documents using links-a feature known in other systems, notably Ted Nelson's Xanadu, as transclusion.

Cross-Reference

For more on transclusion and Xanadu, see the article entitled "Embedded Markup Considered Harmful," in the Winter 1997 issue of *World Wide Web Journal,* available from O'Reilly and Associates.

For this to work efficiently, file structures will need to change to avoid making the processing application load the entire document rather than just the desired chunk. The file system itself would have to be an XML processor (perhaps even an object database), storing XML documents as elements rather than as a single file that must parse sequentially. For more about what this might look like, see my article "Building the File System into the File," at http://www.simonstl.com/articles/filesys.htm.

More Complex Links

Extended links give the world of linking entirely new geometries, making possible new architectures and new interfaces. Even though the "I am here — click to go there" model of the HTML A element has done an excellent job getting the Web started, it's time to move on to "I am one part of a set —0 treat me as such and explore." Extended links, multidirectional links, and out-of-line links will enable developers to build more intricate structures that make managing links easier in the long run.

Extended links enable developers to create groups of links, effectively providing the user (or a processing application) with a set of choices from a link rather than a single target. Even though the requirements for how an extended link must be treated by a processing application remain very loose in the Working Draft, you can easily picture an extended link as a set of choices that will appear on a pop-up menu (or other interface) to enable the user to select a direction. The classic application for this is a thesaurus. When the user clicks a word, a set of synonyms will appear on a pop-up menu. The user chooses from among the words and can view further information on the word chosen.

Implementing these links is a bit complex. As we did with simple links, we'll start by examining some sample declarations, in this case for an element which can represent an extended out-of-line link:

```
<!ELEMENT extended ANY>
<!ATTLIST extended
  xml:link        CDATA              #FIXED "extended"
  inline          (true|false)       "true"
  content-role    CDATA              #IMPLIED
  content-title   CDATA              #IMPLIED
>
```

As with the previous simple example, elements implementing extended links do not need to be named extended. They simply need the xml:link attribute set to "extended".

Our extended element closely resembles the simple element, with two changes. First, the xml:link attribute value is now "extended" instead of "simple." Second, the extended element has no href attribute, or indeed any description of the targets. The extended element must rely on a set of sub-elements to contain its locators. A locator element might look like:

```
<!ELEMENT locator  ANY>
  <!ATTLIST locator
      xml:link  CDATA                   #FIXED "locator"
      role      CDATA                   #IMPLIED
      href      CDATA                   #REQUIRED
      title     CDATA                   #IMPLIED
      show      (embed|replace|new)     "replace"
      actuate   (auto|user)             "user"
      behavior  CDATA                   #IMPLIED
  >
```

The locator element (which, again, you don't need to call locator) carries key linking information. The href carries the locator for use with an activated link. The title provides information that will be presented to human users, whereas role carries information for the processing application. Every locator has its own show, actuate, and behavior as well. If the locator doesn't specify these attributes, it should use the attribute specified in the extended element by default. This makes creating groups of links that point to different locations but share the same behavior easier, while preserving the right of individual links to behave differently when needed.

You will find extended links, both in-line and out-of-line, useful in a great number of situations. An in-line extended link might use the DTDs presented previously and look something like this:

```
<extended>History Texts
<locator title="African" href="african.xml"/>
<locator title="Asian" href="asian.xml"/>
```

```
<locator title="European" href="european.xml"/>
<locator title="North American" href="namerican.xml"/>
<locator title="Pacific" href="pacific.xml"/>
<locator title="South American" href="samerican.xml"/>
</extended>
```

This link accomplishes several things. First, if a user encounters it in a document, this element represents a live in-line link. Clicking the words "History Texts" might bring up a menu that offers the titles of the choices listed in the locator elements. Choosing one of those titles takes the user to the referenced document. Second, because this is an extended link, it sets up links that can connect all these documents. The documents listed in the locators, if they have encountered this declaration at some point (we'll see how later), all link to each other at the document level. Right-clicking in the margin of any of them, for example, could bring up a menu of the other documents to which the document clicked links. We'll cover that again in a moment, when we reach the document value of the xml:link attribute.

Extended out-of-line links resemble the preceding links, except that the content of the extended link element is not itself a part of the link. Clicking the content of an extended link element, if it has any, won't call up a menu. Extended out-of-line links just set up the connections between other elements. For example:

```
<extended inline="false">
<locator title="Overview" href="#overview"/>
<locator title="Architecture" href="#architecture"/>
<locator title="Detailed Design" href="#details"/>
<locator title="Parts List" href="#parts"/>
</extended>
<SECTION ID="overview"><title>Overview</title>
...
</SECTION>
```

```
<SECTION ID="architecture"><title>Architecture</title>
...
</SECTION>
<SECTION ID="details"><title>Detailed Design</title>
...
</SECTION>
<SECTION ID="parts"><title>Parts List</title>
...
</SECTION>
```

The extended element in this case has no content apart from links. It creates links between the SECTION elements that follow. A reader who doesn't care about the Overview SECTION can click it and get a menu of the more detailed descriptions available. Similarly, someone who stumbled into the parts list can use that same menu to return to the Overview or Architecture SECTION elements. These links may serve a truly multidirectional function (if the application supports it) because users can navigate between multiple locations without regard for moving forward or backward in the senses Web users have come to expect. These links can traverse in either direction — clicking the target document (or using its linking interface) will bring up a list of links that include the document from which the user came. This added flexibility will no doubt confuse many users who already get lost in the web of HTML links, but gives power users a great new tool for navigation.

For comparison, I display an extended in-line link in Figure 11-3, and its equivalent extended out-of-line link in Figure 11-4. Note that all links may traverse in either direction.

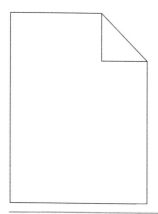

Figure 11-3 *Extended in-line link, XML*

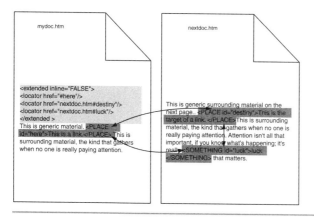

Figure 11-4 *Extended out-of-line link, XML*

As exciting as these new tools seem, they may make it even more difficult to manage links. An XML document cannot always "know" of other documents with which it shares links, especially if those links are stored in content owned by other people. Managing the mazes of links created by the ability to include more than one location in a link presents a logistical challenge that calls for centralization of linking information. Fortunately, xml:link provides some basic tools that address both of these issues. group and document values for the xml:link attribute can create extended link groups-elements that help to manage links, telling documents to check each other for relevant links and enabling the creation of centralized link clearinghouses for sets of related data.

Using extended link grouping requires the creation of two elements — one to define a group and the other to identify the documents in the group. The declarations for those elements look like:

```
<!ELEMENT group (document*)>
   <!ATTLIST group
             xml:link   CDATA    #FIXED "group"
             steps      CDATA    #IMPLIED
   >
   <!ELEMENT document   EMPTY>
   <!ATTLIST document
             xml:link   CDATA    #FIXED "document"
             href       CDATA    #REQUIRED
   >
```

These declarations are far simpler than their fellows. In the group element, all that needs declaring in element instances is the steps attribute, which tells the processing application how many layers of links to follow before stopping its search for related links. (This keeps endlessly deep searches from tying up machines.) The document elements just contain hrefs that will take the processing application to the documents you want searched for links. When the processing application comes across one of these elements, it will load the documents specified by the href attributes of the document elements in the group. It then checks those documents for links to the original document, building a table of links. The processing application will load all the documents and process the linking information in them — that counts as step 1. If the steps attribute is greater than 1, the processing application will load documents to which the original document was linked by the first round of documents loaded.

Tip

Generally, the value of steps should be kept low to keep documents from loading in hundreds of other documents and chewing up bandwidth.

The initial advantage of extended link groups is that they make it easy for a processing application to obtain reasonably complete information about the documents to which an initial document is linked, instead of "discovering" links only when you open the new documents. You can arrange sets of documents in groups, making discovery of related links easy:

```
<group steps=1>
<document href="cousin2.xml"/>
<document href="cousin3.xml"/>
<document href="cousin4.xml"/>
<document href="cousin5.xml"/>
</group>
```

When the processing application reaches this group of elements in the file `cousin1.xml`, it will open the documents `cousin2.xml`, `cousin3.xml`, `cousin4.xml`, and `cousin5.xml`. After parsing them, it will determine whether they have any links to the `cousin1.xml`. If they do, the processing application will add those links to the list of links for cousin1.xml and make them available to users. Without these declarations, a user of the `cousin1.xml` would see only those links that originated in the `cousin1.xml` file itself, which is probably a much more restricted set of links.

The implications of this change are profound. Extended link groups make it possible to centralize link information, replacing a maze of links (shown in Figure 11-5) with a centralized hub-and-spoke system (shown in Figure 11-6) that enables developers to examine and manage links without having to read endless documents. It also reduces the bandwidth overhead, enabling developers to require an XML document to download only one extra document (or perhaps a few) to create a complete list of links.

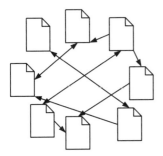

Figure 11-5 *Old-style linking, connecting a set of documents through decentralized links*

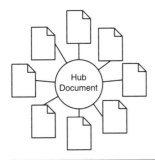

Figure 11-6 *Centralized linking, providing a hub for easy management of links*

Extended link groups also make it possible to add links from other documents to your own effectively. As long as the other document recognizes your document (that is, your document referenced from a document element or connected through a number of links no greater than the steps attribute allows), links from your document to the target document will be recognized by the target document and may appear as outgoing links. Even if the target document does not recognize your document, links from your document may still be "remembered" by the processing application when traversed, enabling documents to reference each other easily. If the processing application remembers the links from document to document, the target document will become linked to your document, although only within the context of the processing application. This makes annotating documents much simpler than it has been in the past.

Beyond Traversing: The Mysteries of Links

While it may seem like the XLink spec brings incredible power to the Web, it still has a long way to go — and it's hardly clear that the Web represents the target application for those designing the XLink specification. Several communities have intersected in the creation of XLink, all demanding different things and with a different set of rules and preferences. Many people in the process like to cite "established practice" and "years of hypertext experience," but much of that experience conflicts at best, confuses at worse, and yet an enormous number of possibilities remain open.

A number of key issues remain unresolved, the most basic of which is: What is a link? Is a link a set of resources, or a connection among those resources? While simple links have an easily determined unidirectional traversal path, extended links may be multidirectional. However, no mechanism currently exists to identify which paths among resources are actually traversable. (In other words, extended links use the same vocabulary as simple links, but are otherwise completely different.) Developers can implement this any way they like. The attributes that could give hints — particularly role, content-role, and behavior — have no specified values. Some developers have proposed using style sheets, probably XSL, to determine link traversal paths, but so far, no development has occurred in that direction.

Traversal does not apply to every application. Many developers who see links as sets treat them as amorphous sets without traversal paths because traversal isn't important to their applications. You may find link sets extremely useful for many modeling applications that have nothing to do with Web browsers, describing resources and their behavior in completely different contexts. Specifying traversal behavior — in fields where traversal may not exist — can prove a distraction at best and a hindrance at worst to these developers. Other developers insist on the primacy of arcs connecting resources. (See the XArc proposal at `http://www.jfinity.com/xarc/` for one example of this.)

 Cross-Reference

Have a question about the XLink or XPointer spec? Want to make a contribution? You can access a public XLink/XPointer mailing list at `http://collie.fujitsu.com/xlxp-dev/threads.html`. A form for signing up (for this and many other lists) is available at `http://metalab.unc.edu/xml/mailinglists.html`.

XML links may seem complicated, but further development of the specification and use will make them friendlier. As we'll see in the following chapters, the implications of these linking schemes may prove as dramatic as the implications of XML itself.

Chapter 12

Processing XML: Repositories, Processors, and Gateways

Even though this book focuses primarily on how to write XML documents and create XML DTDs, creating documents and DTDs is only a part of XML. Documents without applications may be useful for learning syntax, but aren't very appealing otherwise. A full-scale treatment of parsing and processing applications would take another book (or, more likely, a set of books), but a basic understanding of how these applications work is critical to creating usable XML. Many of the teams working on XML development will have separate groups building document types and creating processor applications because the two kinds of work demand different sets of skills. Still, both groups need to share a common vocabulary. In this chapter, we'll examine the new vocabularies and architectures that XML is creating and some of the implications XML has for data processing.

Building Distributed Architectures with XML

Many developers won't need to touch a line of code to make XML work for them — shrink-wrapped servers and browsers can do a perfectly adequate job of storing and presenting XML information, along the lines of current Web servers and Web browsers. Creating a simple Web site with XML is about the same as creating a simple Web site with HTML, except for the extra work of defining your vocabulary (for the elements) and building a style sheet that tells the browser how to present the XML information. The same tools that have been used for HTML, like CGI, Active Server Pages, Servlets, and Cold Fusion, can all be used with XML. It's a change of format, so some extra attention to syntax is definitely required, but the transition doesn't have to be painful. XML opens new possibilities that developers can take advantage of as they find it necessary or appropriate. The next few sections will explore key aspects of the existing infrastructure and the changes that infrastructure may face in the next few years, as "XML support" becomes more widespread.

Repositories (Servers)

The early Web servers were extremely simple. They were built on top of existing file system and network infrastructures and provided users access to information that was stored in very traditional ways. As more and more structured information, particularly information stored in relational databases, became a part of the Web, servers also spawned some sophisticated tools for presenting information. Server-side development enabled site managers to provide users with controlled access to sensitive information, giving them a mediated and (usually) secure presentation of information. At present, much of that server-side processing is moving either to other server-side computers (which then access remote databases and sometimes file servers) or to the client (as with Java applets and sometimes XSL). Because processing of information can take place at any point between the traditional client and server, this section will focus on the repository portion of servers — file systems and databases — and the next section will address processing, wherever it may take place.

In the HTML world, most of the information is stored in one of two kinds of architectures: databases and file systems. Typically, relational databases are connected to the Web through a program that accepts users requests, makes a query against a server, and returns results formatted using HTML. Files have an easier path — the Web server translates the URL it received from the client into a path to a file, and sends the client the information it finds in that file. There are times when databases lurk behind file-like URLs and times when files are actually stored (usually as Binary Large Objects, or BLOBs) in databases, but generally the distinction between the two forms is fairly clear. Putting files into databases is rarely more efficient than putting them into file systems, and putting database information into files is almost always a losing proposition.

XML threatens to add stress to the file-request structure by making much heavier demands of files in order to fulfill its validation and linking requirements. Although the extra transmission costs of DTDs and style sheets may not hit the ceiling of the current capabilities of file-based Web servers (they can be easily cached and used for multiple documents in most cases), the new linking features may. The new embed functionality will encourage developers to create documents that include parts of other documents. XPointers make describing chunks of documents easy. If all the XPointer processing takes place on the client, servers will spend considerable amounts of effort sending files to clients that can be used only in part. Documents that link to multiple documents this way could increase the load dramatically — especially if the processing applications are other programs voraciously seeking out key bits of information. While extended link groups may provide delightful functionality to the client by creating true multidirectional links, they promise an enormous traffic jam at the server, especially if developers keep their links distributed across multiple files rather than consolidating them in centralized link clearinghouse files.

XML also promises to blur the formerly clear distinction between file systems and databases because its sharply hierarchical structures are good candidates for storage inside of databases and good carriers of information typically stored within databases. XML stored as a serial file can present a good representation of a table or even a set of tables, though there are significant processing costs in parsing such a file that continue to give relational databases a significant edge. While XML files are great for interchange between databases and for archival storage of database information, using an XML file as a database itself is probably not the best idea when large amounts of information are involved. At the same time, complex XML documents can seriously tax the resources of a relational database that maps XML's hierarchical structures to its own internal tabular structures, making the storage of XML in a relational repository an equally chancy proposition, loaded with extra processing costs. (Many newer relational databases, object-relational databases, provide additional facilities that help with these issues.) While database information can flow smoothly into an XML document, treating XML documents as databases or putting XML information into a relational database may not be the best idea.

Still, there are many cases in which a more flexible approach to XML document storages would have significant benefits. Cases in which the client only needs a fragment of a document (specified through an XPointer or another query), or where the document must be parsed and transformed before being sent to a client application are both something of a hassle if XML documents are stored as long chains of bytes in serial order. Putting XML documents into a repository that can reflect (without breaking) their internal hierarchical structures is one answer that promises both efficient handling of XML document information and ready access to whatever pieces of information are needed at a given moment. Two kinds of databases, object stores and hierarchical databases, promise to streamline this process. (Neither of them is as efficient as a relational database at manipulating tabular data, so relational databases will still definitely continue to fill their niche.)

Object stores, like those available from POET Software (http://www.poet.com) and Object Design Inc. (http://

www.odi.com) store objects (like those created in Java, C++, and other object-oriented languages) in a hierarchical format that is readily fed back to the programs that created them. Hierarchical databases (like ADABAS, at http://www.softwareag.com) are older, early competitors of relational databases, but are highly optimized to store hierarchically structured data, like XML documents. While the details vary among the various database environments, the general effect for XML processing is that a pre-parsed version of the documents is available, reducing or removing the overhead of serializing and parsing XML. Instead of loading a document, parsing it, and extracting the needed pieces, a Web server could just execute a query against the database, which would then return the needed pieces — as XML fragments, or possibly as a complete document. Knitting the pieces together is usually less costly than taking them apart.

Building efficient repositories out of this system is going to take considerable work; ideally, the interfaces could be much like those on a Web server, with a file system-like structure for organizing documents and a query language (XPointer and/or something else) to retrieve specific information when the entire document is not needed. Adding information to these systems will require a little more than today's file system-based File Transfer Protocol (FTP) tools can handle, but hopefully successors (like the IETF's Web Distributed Authoring and Versioning, (WebDAV)) can fill in the gaps and make the use of these systems both transparent and efficient.

Processors (CGI, Middleware, and Beyond)

All but the most basic of Web servers perform some processing on the documents they serve. Some processing on the Web is done on servers, providing users access to repositories that store information in non-HTML formats. The servers can manage security, collect information, and perform other tasks. Other processing is done in

Web browsers and other applications, using scripts, applets, and other objects, like browser plug-ins. As support for XML grows, some of this processing will grow easier. In any case, more of it will become distributable, capable of moving from the repository server to a middleware server to the client, blurring the meanings of client, server, and middleware. The basic paradigm of Web servers storing information and passing it to Web clients (browsers) that display that information is in for a change. Unlike HTML documents, XML documents are easy to tear apart and reassemble, and transformation and processing can both take place while the document is torn apart. In the HTML world, a flexible application that used both client and server processing might involve a script that built an HTML document, which was then transmitted to a browser, which used a different script to animate the document according to the user's needs. In the XML world, a processing module could assemble an XML document from a relational database, and pass that document to another module for reassembly as a table in a document. When it reaches the user, another processing module a mouse-click away could transform that same information into a graph, a form letter, or an entry in a local database.

This flexibility is part of what makes XML so powerful as an interchange format, but it really demands a change in the way we view documents. XML documents are not just a series of bytes (though they definitely are a series of bytes). Rather, they are a set of structures that can be presented, modified, manipulated, and extracted from. The style of markup will definitely have an impact on how much processing flexibility is available, but the processors can build on the structures inside of the documents, transform those structures, and represent the new structures as new XML documents. While the cost of repeated parsing and document reconstruction can become significant, especially if repeated across too many structures, tools like MDSAX (`http://www.jxml.com/mdsax`) are designed to integrate multiple layers of document processing, making it possible to create efficient structures that need to parse a document only once and perhaps construct it again at the end (if it isn't simply mapped to application data structures). Middleware tools that apply generic processing to particular documents based on their structure and content make it possible to build very specialized applications using generic components. The shared structures of XML documents enable developers to create tools that work across vocabularies.

XSL is a good example of a generic application that has been built with processing on both the client and the server in mind. Browsers that support XSL can perform its transformations and formatting at the client, but the server can perform the needed transformations (typically, to HTML) for clients that can't process XSL themselves. This flexibility provides site designers a good way to take advantage of the capabilities of the newer browsers, while still supporting (at a fairly low cost) legacy browsers that have no understanding of XML, much less XSL. XSL transformations can even be stacked — the results of an XML transformation are XML, which can then be processed for another round.

Gateways (Browsers, Editors, and Other Applications)

Getting information into and out of these repositories and processors requires another kind of application, which interacts with the outside world. These *gateways* can be a browser, transforming an XML document into a set of pixels on a user's screen, an editor, enabling users to create new XML documents and modify old ones directly, or a gateway to another system, like an instrument controlled by commands contained in an XML document. Input and output make storage and processing worthwhile. Like the other areas, this remains a field where the technology is in development, and no best solution to XML has yet emerged.

Typically, gateways are built on a parser, which passes the information in the XML document to the application. The application then shows that information to the world in some non-XML format (possibly after some additional processing like that described in the previous section.) In some cases (like editors), that information can be mapped back to an XML document and shipped back to the repository; in others, it takes a one-way road from the gateway application to a user's screen or some code controlling a device, for instance. Some gateways just collect information that isn't in an XML format and convert it to XML, providing a one-way path for input. The next two sections will take a close look at two key applications for everyday human interaction with information stored in XML, browsers, and editors.

Browsers: Anatomy and Futures

For the most part, I've used browsers throughout this book to bring XML to life, making it visible and presentable. Grossly simplified, browsers consist of four key parts: a communications engine that can send requests and receive information using HTTP and other network protocols, a parser that interprets that information, a presentation engine that displays the elements found by the parser, and an interface that controls user interaction with the information provided. A simple model of how a browser processes HTML documents appears in Figure 11-2.

The communications engine gets HTML files from Web servers and passes them to the parser, which breaks them down into a tree of discrete elements. The presentation engine examines the contents of those elements and formats them properly for the screen, downloading additional materials as necessary. The interface provides the browser window in which the document is displayed, with its menus, navigation aids, scroll bars, and other features. It handles user actions and opens new pages when necessary, which go through the same communications — parsing and processing.

Browsers today are far more complicated than this simple model. They include scripting engines, style sheet interpreters, Java Virtual Machines, plug-in interfaces, and all kinds of graphics engines, along with an ever-growing number of attachments to provide mail, news, groupware, HTML editing, and other integrated features. The channel features described in Chapter 9 have added some extra overhead. Handling all of those parts has exploded the browser out from its original origin as a very small, simple program. Browsers now are growing as large as full-scale office applications, eating up more hard-drive space and consuming more download time with every new version release.

Competition between the browser vendors has also changed the rules for parser, presentation, and interface: documents are becoming dynamic. We touched on this in Chapter 7, but the impact on the browser deserves more attention. Documents are no longer static entities incapable of changing after they've reached the browser. Scripts can add and remove elements, change their appearance, modify their contents, and move them around the screen. The parsing engine still reads in code as it arrives, but the resulting tree it produces is now open to manipulation and modification. Effectively, scripts have been given read and write access to the document tree, making possible a whole new category of browser-based interfaces.

The W3C is currently in the process of standardizing the competing approaches to this technique. The Document Object Model Working Group is creating an Applications Processing Interface (API) for accessing and manipulating the contents of HTML and XML documents. Level 1, which provides a foundation, is now a W3C Recommendation, and work on Level 2 has begun. Their abstract presents neatly the impact the Document Object Model will have on the simplified model presented in Figure 12-1.

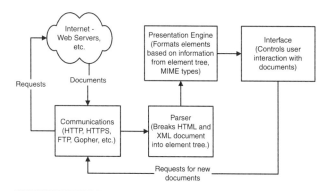

Figure 12-1 *The structure of a simple browser*

Note

The Document Object Model (DOM) Level 1 provides a mechanism for software developers and Web script authors to access and manipulate parsed HTML and XML content. All markup as well as any document type declarations are made available. Level 1 also enables the creation "from scratch" of entire Web documents in memory; saving those documents persistently is left to the programmer. DOM Level 1 is intentionally limited in scope to content representation and manipulation; rendering, validation, externalization, etc. are deferred to higher levels of the DOM.

The parser creates an initial state for the browser, after which the element tree it creates may be modified, reorganized, or even rebuilt. Our XML documents, and even their document type declarations, may change shape (which may cause problems, at least until higher levels of the DOM appear to clarify validation).

These developments are the latest stimulus for the continuing expansion of the browser. Netscape's long-held dream of creating a browser that provides a complete interface is on the verge of being realized, although battles between Netscape and Microsoft continue. The implications of this extreme new flexibility are enormous. The browser environment is reaching the point where it is rich enough to handle a variety of data presentation and processing jobs, most of which used to be the field of applications built with specialized client-server tools. Although it remains to be seen if the DOM will provide enough flexibility for developers to write a word processor in a browser, it certainly promises enough flexibility to make it possible to create far more powerful client interfaces than the forms we have at present.

In addition to opening up these possibilities for the major browser vendors, these developments open up larger possibilities for a wider audience of developers. While recreating the capabilities of

Netscape Navigator or Microsoft Internet Explorer is well beyond the capacity (or interest) of most programmers and companies, XML opens up new possibilities for small browsers targeted at particular niches. Perhaps the first true XML browser is Jumbo (`http://www.xml-cml.org/jumbo/`), built to demonstrate the possibilities of Chemical Markup Language (CML). Jumbo is a Java application that combines a parser, the Java Swing classes, and some custom code to display XML both generically, as a tree, with further information available in a right-hand pane (as shown in Figure 12-2), and as an application object, to do things like draw molecule structures in a panel (as shown in Figure 12-3).

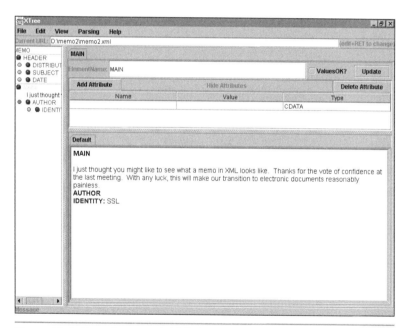

Figure 12-2 *Browsing generic XML in Jumbo*

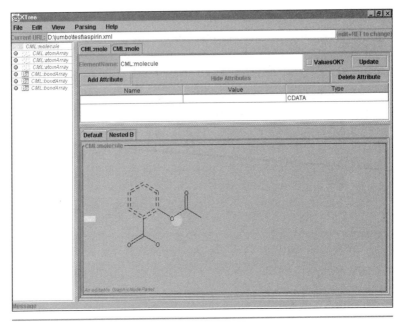

Figure 12-3 *Specific processing for particular elements in Jumbo*

Jumbo is an experimental browser, not a commercial tool, but its foundations have significant promise. Jumbo's architecture strongly suggests ways that XML could be used with current architectures to supplement or replace the existing plug-in and object mechanisms for displaying content. Right now, all content that doesn't consist of images or markup must be declared using special tags — EMBED, APPLET, or OBJECT. Adding plug-ins to a browser isn't as easy as it should be. All of these methods (with the possible exception of applets) expose users to the risk of damage from poorly written or malicious code. A more flexible architecture might allow users or documents to associate applets (or similar programs) with XML elements, providing element-specific processing either in the browser window or in separate pop-up windows. In this way, elements that just contain text can be displayed with the tools available for handling markup, while elements meant for further processing can receive it using tools they specify, as shown in Figure 12-4.

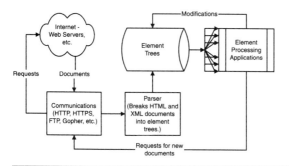

Figure 12-4 *The open browser enables elements to be processed by multiple tools.*

Implementing this architecture in the current browsers will undoubtedly create yet another arena in which the competing browser developers can build incompatible standards, such as APIs that refuse to interoperate, and code that works only with a particular browser. Still, XML itself includes a few features that could be useful for parts of this, like the NOTATION declaration. Even though using NOTATION to specify external viewers is rather obsolete in the age of the integrated browser, it may still have some use for XML as a means of specifying external processing. A NOTATION declaration that links to a Java applet could be connected to an element with a #FIXED attribute, announcing to the browser that this element needs its own specified processing tool. In combination with other attributes specifying whether the element needs its own window or should be presented in-line, this could significantly ease the first steps of XML integration. The hard part will be developing an API that allows the developers of those in-line presentation vehicles to negotiate size and location and to redraw with the browser.

Note

Jumbo even goes so far as to allow users to pick their parser! This level of modularity promises enormous flexibility.

Adding this kind of support for processors handling particular XML elements may have an unexpected side effect on the browser. Opening the browser to external, in-line applications like this is a much more dramatic move than the earlier additions of plug-in architectures, or even applets. The browser could become much less integrated, reversing the trend of piling more and more applications into the same browser space. In this scenario, the browser is reduced to a communications engine and a parser, along with a framework that enables different applications to communicate and modify the element tree. The browser could still provide the interface services, if needed, and a basic set of tools for displaying text, but even those could be outsourced to other applications. Branding this browser and selling it would be a far harder task than marketing the current batch of integrated browsers, but it may be the logical final destination of browser development.

In this possible browser future, the presentation and interface aspects of the browser would be taken over by other applications (even mini-applications) that process elements. They would have their own presentation and interface structures, which the browser might continue to coordinate. Much of the functionality that used to be in the browser would be distributed across applications devoted to the processing of particular elements. They could all share a parser, a communications engine, and perhaps the same element tree, but the browser as a unit becomes unnecessary. The parser, engines, and element tree interface become browser services, rather than a distinct unit.

At this level, the much-discussed integration of operating system and browser is possible, although both disintegrate to a certain extent. An operating system is still needed to provide an environment for running these services, and several parts of the browser become even more important than they had been previously, but the element processing applications and the services for keeping them in sync provide a new area for applications and API development. The applications could be Java applets, ActiveX controls, or even COBOL programs — it doesn't really matter, as long as they can communicate with the element trees and with each other. The processing applications could use Java's Abstract Windowing Toolkit or the Java Foundation Classes, Microsoft's Win32, or the Mac OS

Toolbox. The model could work as well in any of those systems, or even an entirely new system, provided it allowed for the communication and coordination between the growing number of parts.

Why would anyone want this Hydra-headed replacement for the friendly browser? It offers a number of advantages. First, although it is actually built out of a large number of different parts, it doesn't need to look any different to the user. A single browser window could still coordinate all of these parts (and provide a nice home for a company logo). Second, it provides parsing services to a large number of potential processing applications without requiring every application to include its own parser. It provides a single interface for parsing services, enabling developers to build to a browser services API (Applications Programming Interface) rather than choosing a parser, licensing it, and writing code that fits the parser.

This may muddy the operating systems/graphical user interface/browser waters even more than Microsoft already has, but their systems work on a somewhat different model. At present, Windows programs can use Internet Explorer as an ActiveX control, and Internet Explorer can provide a home for ActiveX controls and their data. This could, if developed further by Microsoft, develop into the shared browser services model described previously, but for now Internet Explorer remains, in practice, a collection of programs that communicate internally with each other as pieces, but communicate to external programs as a unit. Microsoft certainly seems intent on piling as much of its browser into the operating system as possible, so this may change rapidly. Microsoft's clients grow ever larger, demanding more resources by the year.

Browser services, as defined in this abstract model, are, in my opinion, better suited to a less overgrown environment than Windows, an environment built on a set of standard set of shared and manipulable class libraries rather than a set of APIs. As Jon Bosak of Sun Microsystems has stated in his white paper, "XML, Java, and the Future of the Web" (available at `http://sunsite.unc.edu/pub/sun-info/standards/xml/why/xmlapps.htm`), "XML gives Java something to do." Java is already built on a standard set of class libraries, complete with network interfaces that already provide the functionality of the communications engine shown previously. The JavaBeans standard that arrived with Java Developer's Kit 1.1 provides mechanisms for applications and applets to communicate, providing direct channels of communication between large numbers of objects.

 Cross-Reference

For a lot more information on creating XML processing applications with Java, see *Building XML Applications* by Simon St.Laurent and Ethan Cerami (McGraw-Hill, 1999).

Editors

Creating an XML editor is a greater challenge in many ways than creating a browser. Creating an XML editor that can compete with the dominant WYSIWYG (what-you-see-is-what-you-get) word processors on their terms is a difficult proposition, requiring the creation of an interactive browser that gives users the tools they need to create document structures, not just formatted text. Managing the creation of structures while presenting information in forms that users are accustomed to is a complicated job, and keeping the interface to such a tool simple, will be a difficult task. Building such an editor as a generic tool, rather than one focused on a particular XML vocabulary, is especially difficult. As a result, the editors available at the time of this writing tend to be very simple, mostly tree-based editors that provide validation services.

One approach to creating XML documents, though not necessarily the best way to edit them, is through an interview model. An application can take an XML DTD, or schema, when they become available, and present it to the user as a set of possibilities, starting at the root element. DTDs don't identify which elements may be used as root elements, so the application will need to have some additional information to present the user with an intelligent set of possibilities. The user can make choices based on the DTD, as presented by the editor. The editor can enforce constraints and keep users from creating invalid documents, letting them move forward only when the present element is acceptable. For many situations, like the project manager debriefing discussed in Chapter 8, this approach is appropriate, and enables the authors to dump all their information at one sitting. More complex documents may need a pause function for stopping in the middle, and full-scale editors will need to go far beyond this. Interviews are a good approach for information that can be entered in a single pass, but aren't very helpful for navigating previously entered information and making changes quickly.

Cross Reference

If you need to put together an editor for a particular XML DTD quickly, take a look at IBM's alphaWorks XML Editormaker (`http://www.alphaWorks.ibm.com/formula/xmleditormaker`). It takes a DTD and creates a small editor based on that DTD.

The first generation of generic XML editors, notable Microsoft's XML Notepad (shown in Figure 12-5) and Vervet Logic's XML Pro, has tended to go the tree-navigation route, presenting the document structure explicitly and having users insert and delete elements (and element content) as appropriate. For some documents, especially simple and highly structured documents, this approach works well, but for large documents or documents where users tend to confuse formatting and structure, these editors are unwieldy at best. While these editors do a good job of presenting a close-up view of XML documents, many users would prefer a more familiar, less hierarchical approach to the documents they use every day.

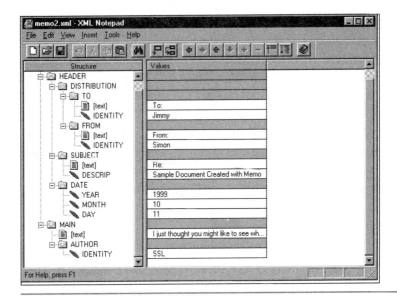

Figure 12-5 *Editing an XML document in Microsoft's XML Notepad*

Cross Reference

XML Pro is available from Vervet Logic at `http://www.vervet.com`. Microsoft's XML Notepad is available from `http://www.microsoft.com/xml/notepad/intro.asp`. XML Notepad requires users to have Internet Explorer 4.0 or 5.0 for Windows installed, as it uses the parsers supplied with those browsers.

More editors are on the way. SoftQuad, maker of the popular HotMetal HTML editor, has announced plans for XMetal, an XML editor using a similar interface. Some layout programs, notably Adobe's FrameMaker and Corel's WordPerfect, now include XML exporting. (Microsoft's Office 2000 will use XML to some extent, but not as a direct export format for documents. HTML with embedded XML seems to be Microsoft's Web format of choice.) The advent of XML may prove to be an opportunity for developers, spawning a new community of tool-builders the way HTML did.

Integration

There are plenty of parts available for using XML, some still in development and others fully grown. Making these parts work together—especially parts that were originally designed for XML's predecessor technologies, SGML and HTML—can be a challenge. If necessary, integrators can always build their own glue and their own parts, as described in the next section, but for now we'll explore less drastic options that use existing technologies. In the simplest case, shown below in Figure 12-6, a browser that can present XML (using CSS or XSL) connects to a Web server, which retrieves an XML file and style sheet and sends them on to the browser. Files are added to the Web server using traditional file server and FTP mechanisms.

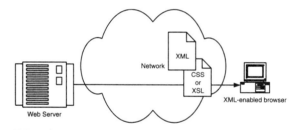

Figure 12-6 *Viewing XML documents over the Web*

Note

Although a browser is the client of this XML transmission, any gateway – a recipient database, a set of instruments, an e-mail system, or something completely new – could be at the end of the connection. XML clients are by no means limited to browsers. (Browsers do, however, provide a familiar set of mechanisms that simplify discussion of the features.)

Caution

None of the XML browsers currently available support XLink. (After all, it's still only a Working Draft.) This makes building sites that contain multiple XML pages pretty much an impossibility, as links don't appear. The discussion that follows makes the assumption that XLink support will appear in browsers at some point in the not-too-distant future.

In another case likely to be typical of XML document distribution over the Web, a processor on the Web server translates the XML into HTML for presentation, as shown in Figure 12-7.

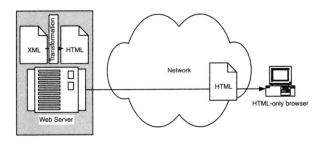

Figure 12-7 *Using server-side processing to convert XML documents into HTML for transmission over the Web*

Caution

If you use server-side processing (with XSL or another tool) to convert your XML to HTML, be sure to have some kind of caching mechanism so you don't have to perform the conversion every time a document is downloaded. Site performance may be drastically impaired unless you take steps to enhance efficiency.

Server-side processing may not be about transforming XML into another format; it may simply involve the conversion of information stored in a non-XML format (a database, for example) into an XML document. This could be done with traditional CGI processing, servlets, Active Server Pages, or whatever seems appropriate, as shown in Figure 12-8.

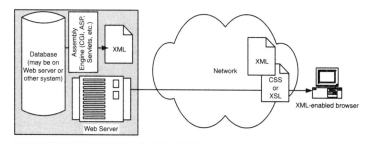

Figure 12-8 *Using server-side processing to assemble XML documents*

Additional processing (security management, caching, further transformations, and so on) can take place at any point between the repository and the viewer/editor. If this happens repeatedly, as shown in Figure 12-9, it may be time to find a more efficient approach for transmitting XML than HTTP, a least to the point at which (if necessary) HTTP carries the information to the client computer.

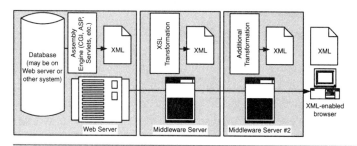

Figure 12-9 *Processing XML between the repository and the viewer*

Because of XML's readily processed structures, a variety of solutions for simplifying these complex models is available. If the processing is taking place within a single environment, the laborious task of parsing and re-assembling can often be skipped. Processing, especially generic processing, like XSL transformations, can be done at the server, at the client, or anywhere in between, as appropriate. (It also depends on the environments used to support that processing, of course.) The same set of processes shown above in Figure 12-9 could be handled by a smaller set of systems, as shown in Figure 12-10.

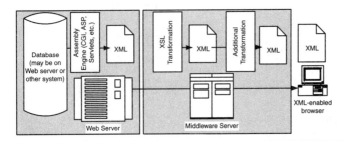

Figure 12-10 *Combining XML processing to reduce the number of parses and transmissions needed to process XML*

XML's flexibility creates perhaps as many questions as it solves, but the ease of XML processing makes it an excellent tool for integration, in whatever processing sequence you find most efficient and most appropriate to your needs.

Building Custom Applications for XML

Although we've taken as much advantage as possible of XML's ability to keep documents human-readable, the real reasons that make XML exciting have to do with machine-readability. Markup is designed to be easy to program, using a nested structure that works well with both recursive functions and object-oriented programming. Although parsing valid XML documents is not a light task, neither does it present the enormous challenges faced by programs that must parse other formats. The developers of the XML specification made creating XML applications much easier by tightening the rules for XML document structure syntax, while at the same time reducing the need for a lot of processing by adding the well-formedness option. XML's firm requirement that all elements have complete start- and end-tags, or indicate that they are empty by closing the tag with />, makes it far easier to write a parser. Both SGML and HTML allowed elements to skip end tags, which required significant code effort to determine where exactly the end of an element was supposed to be. (Converting from these formats to XML is hit-or-miss as a result.) SGML also allowed abbreviated element names, adding an extra level of lookup to the parsing process. XML's basic structures, expressed in the criteria for well-formed documents, ensure that parsers can be reasonably simple programs that won't add incredible amounts of processing overhead to document processing.

 Note

While XML has made it much easier to write a parser, it's still a lot of work. Most applications rely on parser modules built by other developers, rather than building their own parsers.

Validating XML documents, as opposed to checking them for well-formedness, remains something of a challenge, thanks to parameter entities and the need to check element structures against the DTD. DTDs can be incredibly complex documents to interpret, especially DTDs that extend back through several files because of multiple parameter entities and DOCTYPE declarations (not to mention IGNORE and INCLUDE sections). Applying large DTDs to small files can waste processor cycles while the parser interprets extra information it will never apply and adds overhead to every element lookup. Still, validating documents is a critical part of much XML processing, simplifying the processing that is left to applications. Validation may occur at several different points in the lifetime of a document, from its initial construction to its final presentation.

Many XML applications are probably going to end up using parts of XML, working with parsers that straddle the distinctions between well-formed and valid. Applications that can handle XML linking will probably need to do some validating, unless programmers want to present the attributes needed to create links in every single element instance. Documents that use entities extensively might not need a DTD that defines their elements and attributes, but they do need a parser that can expand their entity references. How far practice will diverge from the twin standards of valid and well-formed remains to be seen, but more levels are likely to appear.

There are many situations for which full DTDs may not be appropriate. Combining the extreme flexibility of well-formed documents with the powerful tools available in valid documents and the new complexities of namespace processing will likely cause some problems for developers. Managing the flow of information between systems that need maximum efficiency and those that need maximum reliability will be a challenge for a while.

 Cross Reference

The XML-Dev mailing list is a key forum for developers creating parsers and XML applications. The archives for the list and information on joining are available at `http://www.lists.ic.ac.uk/hypermail/xml-dev/`. When communicating on this list, keep in mind that it is a mailing list aimed at high-level development, not XML tutorials. Three other lists of particular note to developers are xml-app, java-xml-interest, and Perl-xml. A handy form for subscribing to these (and many other) mailing lists is available at Elliotte Rusty Harold's Cafe Con Leche site, at `http://metalab.unc.edu/xml/mailinglists.html`.

Tools for Programming XML

XML is not a programming language; nothing in XML limits the development of XML-centric applications to a simple development environment or language. Although the W3C's Document Object Model (DOM) specifies bindings for Java and JavaScript (as well as a CORBA IDL binding), plenty of other environments, from C++ to Perl to Delphi to Visual Basic to Lisp may be appropriate for your needs, depending on the experience you (or your organization) have. (I keep looking for a COBOL parser, but no one has announced one publicly yet.) XML can even be used as the glue between multiple applications written in completely different environments, enabling them all to trade data back and forth without having to build interfaces between specific components. As long as they can all process XML, they can use it as a common data format.

At this point, the leading contender for XML development appears to be Java. Java has a significant advantage over other languages and development tools for a very simple reason: like XML, it was built for Unicode from the ground up. The requirement that parsers be able to handle the full 2-byte Unicode canonical encoding causes problems for C and C++ (although there are many ways around it), older versions of Perl (where key parts of the language have received significant upgrades and extensions), and all other development tools that expect characters to occupy a single byte. As a result, much of the work currently under way in XML development is being done in Java. Java's structures are also a good match for XML, with hierarchies that are easily compatible with XML. Java also provides easy interfaces between classes and objects, making it very simple to add a generic parser to a data processing application. Even though Java's facilities for handling text are not the most advanced, they are more than a match for the level of processing required by XML parsing. Java applets also fit well with several of the Web-based possibilities for XML. Java applets provide a convenient mechanism for presenting XML content in browsers that don't themselves understand XML, filling an important gap.

Java has several other significant advantages, including a community actively developing frameworks. In addition to the DOM and its Java bindings, the Java-based SAX API (`http://www.meg-ginson.com/SAX`) for expressing XML documents as event streams provides a standard foundation for many XML tools. SAXON (`http://home.iclweb.com/icl2/mhkay/saxon.html`) and MDSAX (`http://www.jxml.com/mdsax`) provide two (different) frameworks developers can use to extend SAX to build Java applications for processing and presenting XML. (Coins, available at `http://www.jxml.com/coins/`, extends MDSAX further.) IBM's alphaWorks (`http://www.alphaWorks.ibm.com`) is constantly churning out new releases of Java tools for parsing and processing XML.

C++ is also a very viable environment for XML development. Like Java, its object structures can embrace nested element structures quite easily. Even though adding classes to a C++ project is somewhat more complex than it is with Java, there is no lack of powerful C++ tools. C++ is already in use for a wide variety of data processing projects, including markup processing; and libraries are available. Unfortunately, most of the C++ world still expects to see single-byte characters, making it fairly difficult to work with Unicode. Documents encoded in UTF-8 (and which use its ASCII subset) should work well with most standard flavors of C++, and more tools for C++ Unicode development are appearing.

 Note

Does Unicode matter anyway? The answer depends on your needs and the platforms you work with. Unicode has been slow to take off because of limited application support. However, both XML and Java provide support for processing Unicode characters (not necessarily displaying them, which is more a matter of the operating system and the available font sets) at their foundations. Unicode has begun picking up steam, however, with native support available in both Microsoft's Windows NT and Sun Solaris 2.6 operating systems. Java and XML are two key components for the future of document processing, so expect to see more action in the Unicode field.

Perl has been the text hacker's choice for years, helping developers blast through seemingly impossible barriers with a few lines of code. Perl's rich support for regular expressions has helped thousands of programmers create CGI scripts, writing HTML and interpreting the data sent back by forms. At the same time, Perl has helped developers implement changes across entire sites, addressing challenges like changing all the legal notices on a site overnight with elegance and ease. Perl use is hardly limited to HTML, SGML developers have used Perl to find problems in their documents and fix them as automatically as possible. Perl relies on external parsers to feed it XML information. The original Perl module for XML parsing, XML::Parser, was written by Larry Wall (Perl's creator) and Clark Cooper, uses James Clark's C-based Expat parser, and has been available since October 1998. In addition to XML::Parser, new modules are constantly under development, connecting Perl to more aspects of XML processing. For the latest, check the CPAN archives at `http://www.perl.org`.

Python, another scripting language with roots in UNIX, has been a popular tool for XML scripting. Resources including a Python parser (xmlproc), an implementation of SAX, and various other tools are available through `http://www.stud.ifi.uio.no/~larsga/download/python/xml/index.html`. Python is the language of choice of a significant number of developers working on XML and even within the XML working groups, so the number of tools available for Python should increase significantly in the near future.

 Cross Reference

Need to find some tools for working with XML in your favorite development environment? Visit `http://www.stud.ifi.uio.no/~larsga/linker/XMLtools.html` for a list of free tools, updated regularly, or `http://xmlsoftware.com` for a listing of tools that includes commercial products.

Chapter 13

XML and the Future: XML's Impact on Ever-Expanding Webs

Even though it's clear that the adoption of XML will require some significant changes to the basic infrastructure of the Web, its impact on the structures of sites remains less clear. The W3C's positioning of XML in the Architecture Domain leaves many questions about what XML is really for. So far, XML has mostly seen use as a standard used to define other standards, which in turn define other files, and not as a general document format. XML's eventual position in the world of the Web and how it will expand Web technology into new fields is not yet clear, though the W3C's move to rebuild HTML as a set of XML modules presents one possibility. Concluding our exploration of XML's potential, we'll survey its implications for the development of Web sites and similar document-based information distribution architectures.

Current Web Site Architectures

When the Web first appeared, sites had extremely simple structures, modeled after the hierarchical models of its predecessors, FTP and Gopher. All requests for files referred to actual files, stored in the file system of the server. URLs corresponded to a subset of the file structure on the server, and answering requests was a matter of finding the right file, adding an appropriate header, and sending it back to the browser that requested it. Hyperlinks contained the URL information, enabling developers to create crazy quilts of HTML without having to create crazy quilt file structures. Directory structures were the most commonly used organizational tool in the early days, which enabled developers to create somewhat structured sites.

As the demand for more up-to-date information has exploded across the Web, many sites have turned to database-driven sites. Tools like CGI, Cold Fusion, Java servlets, and Active Server Pages (ASP) put attractive front ends on information stored in relational database systems and even legacy mainframes. Database-generated pages make sites like the FedEx tracking page possible, but are also used for many pages that seem like ordinary HTML to users. Visitors to the Microsoft site, for example, will encounter many pages created with ASP. Microsoft uses a database system in the background to manage data used on many of its pages, enabling it to make changes quickly.

Database-driven sites power many intranets as well, enabling employees to tap into data sources once locked in cold rooms guarded by protective MIS staff. Groupware and communications software have metamorphosed into Web applications. Lotus Domino's transition from Notes server to Web server was a notable change, providing instant translation of Notes-formatted documents into Web pages. The complex data structures behind Notes have applications on the public as well as the private Web, and Domino has moved out from behind the corporate firewall to power a few Internet servers.

There are several problems with database-driven sites, however. First, they tend to require more horsepower to overcome the overhead of connecting to a database; or the database server may need more horsepower to handle the increased demand placed on it. Second, database-driven sites are rarely search engine-friendly; most of them in fact put up "Do not enter" signs with the robots.txt file discussed in Chapter 7. Although the information contained in the database is probably well-structured and easily searchable, there's no easy way for a search engine to connect to a database and collect structured data. (It would probably indicate an enormous security hole as well.) Finally, complex database-driven sites usually require a fairly dedicated team of developers to build applications that can manage the database in addition to the usual team of HTML developers, adding considerable expense to a Web project.

The slow spread of Cascading Style Sheets and dynamic HTML has also had an impact on site architecture. It's becoming more common for certain aspects of Web design to become centralized. Style sheets in this model can be controlled at one location, enabling the company to provide a basic look for their sites that can then be modified. Dynamic HTML interfaces can be stored as JavaScript code files or as Microsoft's new scriptlets, which combine scripting with HTML to create reusable interface controls. HTML documents today are far more than text with markup. Currently, the roster of items that can appear in Web pages includes:

- HTML
- Images (GIF, JPEG, PNG, XBM, and so on)
- Sounds (AIFF, AU, WAV, and so on)
- Video (QuickTime, MPEG, AVI, and so on)
- Specialized Plug-in Content (Splash, Shockwave, Acrobat, and so on)
- JavaScript
- VBScript (Internet Explorer only)
- Java applets
- ActiveX controls (Internet Explorer only)

The Web is already a rich programming environment, with constantly improving tools for programming and presentation. Many people, including Web developers, would argue that the Web is complex enough as it is without adding another layer of complication. Adding XML (and all its associated standards) to the Web may be, from this perspective, unnecessary.

Transitional Architectures

Adding XML to the existing Web architecture isn't especially difficult, as was outlined in the previous chapter. Existing Web servers and the HTTP protocol can handle XML just as they handled HTML, without needing to know about the files they are transferring. Much of the application architecture surrounding HTML can be reused for XML, requiring closer attention to the syntax and vocabulary of the documents produced, but not many other changes. Although this scenario sounds fairly rosy, there remain some key problems. The browsers that have been "officially" released are only beginning to show support for XML and still have inconsistent implementations of Cascading Style Sheets. Making the transition from HTML to XML (if it is to happen) will require some component in the process to learn about XML — the browser presenting the information, or the server sending it.

Note

As was noted in the previous chapter, the lack of an XLink recommendation is another serious impediment to XML's use on the Web. The W3C is pushing forward with several proposals (like Scalable Vector Graphics) that only use the simple link mechanism, suggesting at least one road ahead.

Both Netscape and Microsoft are revising their browsers to accommodate XML. As of this writing, both companies have released software capable of displaying XML documents using Cascading Style Sheets, though Netscape's is currently a preview releases, not yet ready for widespread distribution. Netscape's Gecko preview release focuses on presenting HTML and XML information with the assistance of Cascading Style Sheets. Microsoft's Internet Explorer 5.0 includes an early implementation of XSL in addition to its Cascading Style Sheet support for XML, plus a rendering engine for vector graphics stored in its XML-based Vector

Markup Language (VML). The third graphical browser vendor, Opera, hasn't yet announced XML support. (How text-based browsers like Lynx will respond to XML remains a question.)

Even as these browsers are released, users will take a number of years to upgrade (if, indeed, they ever do). It may take several years before developers can assume that most of their audience is using tools that can cope with information in an XML format. In the meantime, developers who want to move forward into XML for reasons beyond presenting data to Web users (like efficient management and storage) will have to provide tools for presenting information stored in XML formats to users whose software lacks XML support. The transition architecture will probably be the one shown in Figure 12.7, in which a processor on the server examines the information a browser sent with the request that identifies its capabilities, and transforms the XML document into an HTML equivalent when necessary. In addition to the extra processing cycles this can consume, it means that developers and designers are going to need to create a mapping between XML elements and their HTML equivalents. This can be done with XSL or it can be done with a custom software tool, but in either case it means extra information about the documents that needs to be created.

Designers who've worked with HTML for years have seen this pattern before, where sites had to have multiple faces for different browser versions. Every new technology added to the Web left behind users who didn't upgrade until the costs of not having support for that technology become sizable enough to drive them to the effort of downloading (or getting a new computer). Frames, scripts, applets, and even tables all caused problems at one time or another. XML has the advantage over these older technologies of being easily processed, enabling developers to automate the process of presenting two "faces" (new XML and old HTML), but there will still, as always, be some transition costs.

Transitioning HTML: Moving to XML Syntax

While developers are faced with the task of converting XML to HTML, the W3C is going the other direction, rewriting HTML as a set of modules using XML syntax. Although the W3C is moving toward XML-based standards in general (like Synchronized Multimedia Integration Language, SMIL, and Structured Vector Graphics, SVG), moving HTML to an XML vocabulary involves much more than just achieving syntactical consistency within the W3C. HTML has grown enormously over the years, moving from a simple set of tags with a few attributes to a gigantic collection of elements and attributes using an SGML DTD. The sheer bulk of HTML makes it hard to create new HTML browsers — supporting the entire standard requires a lot of coding, and designers have enough trouble building documents for the few browsers that dominate the market without having to worry about new subsets appearing in newly developed browsers. Non-PC devices, like cell phones and personal digital assistants, don't have the displays or the processing facilities needed to implement a "full" version of HTML or to successfully process the wide variety of syntaxes used in current HTML development. (Full-size PC browsers don't mind missing end tags or unquoted attributes, but it takes extra processing cycles to compensate.) To address these needs, the W3C HTML Activity is moving toward the next version of HTML, code-named "Voyager." Rather than adding new features, as in past versions, the Working Group is breaking HTML into a group of smaller vocabularies (modules) and shifting toward an XML vocabulary. An RDF-based profiling system will also help devices identify their capabilities to servers, making it possible for servers to customize content to meet the capabilities of a given device, making the modules more useful.

Cross-Reference

Material in this section is subject to significant change as the Voyager specification develops. For the latest top-level view of what the W3C is doing with HTML, visit http://www. w3.org/MarkUp/Activity.html. For the latest working draft, which actually spells out the new model and its implications for document creation, visit http://www.w3. org/TR/WD-html-in-xml/. (Eventually a recommendation should arrive, which will replace the working drafts.)

The Working Draft describes the syntactical changes HTML developers will need to learn to acclimate to the new XML-based model. For the most part, all of them have been covered in this book, with the significant exception that HTML element and attribute names are all going to be lowercase from now on. (Assuming the current working draft's proposal sticks, of course.) Documents will need to be well-formed, requiring that script and style elements either resort to CDATA sections (if they include <, >, or & charactersor use external scripts). Empty elements must use the /> syntax, though the specification recommends using a space before the slash (like br />) for compatibility with older browsers. Some elements (notably title and base) will need to appear in a particular sequence to conform with the Voyager DTDs. Voyager uses XML namespaces to inform processors of which vocabulary is in use, relying mostly on the default namespace, which doesn't require a prefix, to maintain compatibility with older browsers. HTML built using Voyager should be usable in both HTML browsers and Generic XML Processors, using style sheets for much of its formatting. The current working draft identifies 16 modules, listed below in Table 13-1.

Table 13-1 *The 16 Voyager Modules*

Module	Elements in Module
Base	html, head, title, base, meta, link, body, h1, h2, h3, h4, h5, h6, p, br, a, bdo, span, div.
Transitional	Basefont, font, center, s, and u. (also contains border, align, and noshade attributes)
Style	style, link (for use with style sheets), and style attribute.
Script	Script, noscript.
Font	tt, b, I, big, small
Phrase	abbr, acronym, address, blockquote, cite, code, dfn, kbd, q, samp, var.
Inflection	em, pre, strong, sub, sup, hr
Editor	del, ins.
List	dd, dl, dt, li, ol, ul.
Forms	Button, fieldset, form, input, isindex, label, legend, optgroup, option, select, textarea,.
Table	table, caption, col, colgroup, thead, tbody, tfoot, th, tr, td.
Image	Img
Image Map	map, area.
Object	Object, param.
Applet	Applet, param.
Frames	Frameset, frame, iframe, noframes.

Like HTML 4.0, Voyager defines multiple profiles for conformance. The Voyager-strict profile matches the HTML 4.0 strict profile, while Voyager-loose is for use with documents converted from HTML 4.0 transitional and Voyager-frameset is for use with documents from the HTML 4.0 frameset. DTDs for all of these are available in the Working Draft. Once HTML has been modularized, additional XML modules—like MathML, MusicML, or

Structured Vector Graphics — should have an easier time fitting into HTML documents. Combined with the device profiling that is a separate (but important) part of the progress toward modularity, HTML's latest developments may make it a suitable container for many types of XML information.

Implications of XML on the Web

Whether or not Web browsers and Web servers undergo the dramatic transition I suggested in the previous chapter, the advent of XML document presentation in the browser will likely change the underlying architectures of many sites. The XML syntax itself and the XLink specification will drive these changes in architecture and design, although in different ways. XML syntax promises to bring a Web where content, presentation, and scripts are separated from each other more distinctly than they have been in HTML, while XLink will distinguish itself by providing richer interfaces and a fragment model for document retrieval.

XML continues the trend to separate content from formatting that already gained some momentum in the HTML world with the appearance of the Cascading Style Sheets recommendation and the key role it plays in both Netscape and Microsoft's implementations of dynamic HTML features. The most appealing aspect of Cascading Style Sheets to many designers is its ability to centralize style information, avoiding much of the repetitive work needed to create and update HTML pages. Style sheets are an automated version of the graphic designer's spec book, providing a smooth path for formatting to flow into documents without constant hand-tweaking. CSS's also has advantages for application development, providing a basic structure for formatting that can be applied to elements without as much concern for what kind of element the target of an operation is.

Note

An interesting counterpoint to this "separation of structure and formatting" argument is the use of XML for markup that purely indicates formatting, like the formatting objects of XSL. The ease with which XML documents can be transformed from structured documents to these formatting documents, however, still makes for a strong argument for using formats that reflect the content structure of a document as base formats. These structures can then be annotated with styles (with CSS) or transformed into a formatting-oriented markup language (like XSL's formatting objects, or a vector graphics markup language).

CSS2, the newest version of Cascading Style Sheets, brings HTML developers used to working with its predecessor (CSS1) much more power, including support for tables, positioning, and other layout tasks. CSS2 provides a tutorial for using it with XML, not just HTML, and promises to be the primary tool for lightweight styling on the Web. XSL (which claims not to be a competitor to CSS, just a different way of doing things) is much more complicated, but offers much more power, especially in transforming documents between formats. XSL's rule-based transformations open up entirely new horizons for browsers, enabling authors to create different sets of rules for different situations and make better use (and reuse) of the information stored in XML documents.

The relationship of XML to scripting is more complex. SGML purists seem puzzled, and occasionally offended, by the common mixture of scripts with markup that is common practice in the HTML world. Because of its use as an interface as well as a document presentation format, HTML has needed stronger, more flexible tools than are commonly used in SGML environments. The introduction of the SCRIPT tag in Netscape 2.0 opened the floodgates for millions of documents that combine some amount of scripting with document information. The appearance of dynamic HTML has led to the creation of documents that contain complete interface structures (for example, a program to handle opening and closing headings on an outline) as well as the content they display. More and more of these documents, in fact, are becoming incomprehensible without the scripts needed to make them work. Because of the often close relationship between a script and the structure of a particular document (and the odd problems that can happen when transmission difficulties prevent the scripting file from loading properly), HTML scripters have tended to combine as much information as possible in a single file. Scripts are sometimes stored in separate files (using the SRC attribute or server-side includes), but usually this degree of separation is reserved for scripts that are used by multiple documents. Library files containing code used by multiple HTML documents are easier to manage than duplicate copies of code stored in 50 different files.

XML's advent will probably push many developers to begin separating code from content. XML's syntax is not friendly to SCRIPT elements, requiring CDATA-marked sections for any code that includes markup characters, as discussed in Chapter 7. Even if developers can cope with these requirements, XML's status as a potential universal file format may further promote the separation of code from content. Probably not all processing applications will be script-enabled, and some will need to ignore scripting content anyway. Separating script from content will reduce the load on these applications. Changing from HTML's integrated model to XML's modularized architecture will cause some problems at first, although HTML developers have certainly had to learn to keep track of all the images, applets, controls, and other content material linked into documents. The change will require close examination of documents and their structures to determine what can profitably be shared across multiple documents. In an ideal case, a set of HTML documents that was stored as shown in Figure 13-1 could be reorganized using XML's tools as shown in Figure 13-2.

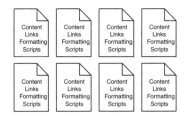

Figure 13-1 *HTML's original integrated model tends to keep content, links, formatting, and scripting in the same document.*

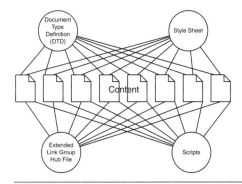

Figure 13-2 *XML's linking structures and encouragement of modularity can break documents down into content and a set of shared components.*

Keeping track of these relationships and making them work efficiently will require another generation of tools. At present, the Web-building tools available can keep up with HTML documents, graphics, and a few components, but few of them can manage scripts or style sheets this way, and extended linking groups have added an entirely new dimension to the task. Until the tools catch up, it's likely that developers will continue to mix and match content, format, script, and links, if only because it avoids the need for a librarian to keep track of all the parts. Java applets and ActiveX controls can still play similar roles to the parts they play now, although they may be activated quite differently, as we saw in Chapter 12. Images, sounds, and other data files will also remain separate. The need for site organizers is, as always, on the rise.

XLink's long-term impact on site architectures will probably be even greater. XLink makes it possible to split and combine documents in ways that get developers past the limitations of conventional file structures. Although taking full advantage of these abilities will require the repository developments outlined in Chapter 12, fragments (identified with XPointers) and linking offer developers a new way of thinking about their documents that makes the file-based systems of HTML seem as quaint as the terminal interfaces of yesteryear. Because of their grounding in file systems, HTML documents have had to appear as complete units. Half an HTML file might occasionally be readable (as long as it isn't a table), but there's no way to download portions of files. As a result, most developers have leaned toward creating sets of smaller documents, which load more quickly but can become difficult to manage. Anyone who has had to print out documentation that was spread out over hundreds of HTML pages has encountered the limitations of this method firsthand.

Fragments and linking make it possible to refer to parts of documents and embed them in other documents to create new documents. Fragments and linking have the potential to unseat some of the database-driven applications currently available, by making it easy for developers to reuse data and include it in multiple documents without needing to write custom applications. A catalog, for example, could store all its information in an enormous document that does nothing but keep track of items. The "pages" of the catalog could reference that catalog with XPointers to retrieve chunks based on attributes and content. As a result, templates could link to all the items on sale, all sporting goods, a particular deck of cards requested by a customer, or even all the items in the catalog by making the appropriate request. If the server was capable of handling fragments efficiently, all of this information could be transferred appropriately, with only the needed items being sent.

Making fragmenting and linking work to full effect requires a whole set of enabling technologies: servers than can process XPointers efficiently to return appropriate fragments, browsers that can cope with the XLink specification to enable embedding of linked content, and authoring tools that will help site managers keep track of the data stored in these new document structures. The revolution this can make possible is probably a few years off, if the speed at which HTML tools have been developed is any indication.

Web Structures as Application Architecture

Even though Web browsers have rapidly grown into a popular interface, they haven't yet been able to offer the kinds of services that users expect of their computers. The latest rounds of improvements to Web browsers and servers have beefed up the Web's claim to being a universal interface for all kinds of data. Although Java arrived several years ago, Java development is finally reaching the point where applets and Java applications are capable of competing with full-blown operating system-specific applications. Dynamic HTML and the Document Object Model (DOM) have made it possible to create polished interfaces inside of a Web browser that offer considerably more functionality than form fields, drop-down boxes, and clickable buttons and images. The scripting languages, particularly JavaScript, have grown up, acquiring object-oriented extensions and other improvements along their path from form validators to interface managers. In the midst of this explosive growth, XML has appeared to clean up the messes created by six years of rapid development and provide a firm foundation for all of these technologies.

XML offers the Web real potential to become both a tool for exchanging information and for managing documents — not just in the familiar context of Web sites, but also in the realms of Electronic Data Interchange (EDI) for business-to-business communications, and the possible replacement of the familiar file system by new systems better capable of sharing documents with multiple users, keeping track of versioning, and managing the connections between them. In both cases, there are some definite gains to be had for the Web users and the EDI, and document management systems users. For the Web, it would signal that the patchwork system connecting megabytes of information had matured into a powerful family of standardized and reliable protocols, giving vendors with Web experience new opportunities to enter additional markets. For EDI and document management, it would mark a dramatic shift from custom-built (and often proprietary) systems to a world of commodity components, where building these systems becomes a matter of connecting readily available tools rather than hand-coding complex applications. The architectures described in the previous chapter — repositories, processors, and gateways — have applications that extend well beyond the traditional Web space into all forms of distributed computing. These architectures are appropriate foundations for an enormous number of different applications.

XML does have its limits, however. XML is not likely to make the browser a better interface for creating graphics editors or video games. XML is not the solution for every problem by any means. Long strings of binary data, like sound, bitmapped graphics, and video are very bad candidates for the creation of XML formats. (Base64, an encoding that could be used to slip binary information into XML files, is much more verbose than the data it represents.) Still, XML is a better solution for projects handling structured information from CAD/CAM (where it lets users exchange information across platforms and companies) to document management to presentations to possibly even the worlds of word processing, spreadsheets, and (to a certain extent, taking full advantage of repository technologies) databases. XML's structures are flexible enough to store hierarchies, tables, spreadsheet information, and complex documents. Developing interfaces that will make writing XML documents as easy as reading them will take years of development and improvements in other key standards. Moving the Web from presentation engine to workhorse will require many more steps, and probably years of development. XML may find a "killer application" that moves it quickly to the fore, or it may need years of quiet infiltration.

XML and the Future of the Web

The scenarios portrayed here demonstrate a few of many possibilities. Even though many HTML developers might prefer that XML stay in a separate world of Web services — if only to avoid yet another learning curve — and although some of the XML community seems hostile to the tools used on the Web today, it doesn't seem likely that XML will stay off the Web for long. XML is a drastic change from the HTML model, but it remains close enough to seem familiar. HTML developers who have spent years trying to interpret the latest tags from Netscape and Microsoft can now focus on creating their own tag systems and accompanying style sheets without needing to be as tightly bound to a single set of rules. Client-server developers who have struggled with complex tools but haven't been able to make the Web do what they need may see XML with the accompanying document object model as their best option. XML, style sheets, and Java all have their own sets of rules, but the additional flexibility they allow should convince several different groups to converge on this new standard for data interchange. With any luck, XML will drive changes in the tools we use to read, write, process, and share that data as well.

Despite the challenges it faces, XML seems likely to succeed. The SGML community has provided an initial base of applications (including open source components and software) and support, and the interest of key players like Microsoft, Netscape, and Sun promises it a bright future. So far the W3C has provided XML with a strong center, a place where these competitors can participate in discussions leading to common standards, and prepare for their implementation. If XML continues to develop as it has, it should quickly find favor as the architecture that enables the Web to finally deliver on its promises of convenient, friendly, cheap, and interactive information access.

Glossary

Active Server Pages

A server-side tool created by Microsoft that combines scripting and objects with markup, used to create dynamic Web sites.

ancestor

An element that contains another element, even when other container elements are in between. The root element, for example, is the ancestor of all of the elements in an XML document. In <FIRST><SECOND>-<THIRD/></SECOND></FIRST>, the FIRST element is the ancestor of both the SECOND and THIRD elements.

application programming interface (API)

A specification that programmers can use to create interoperable software.

application

Either a program that does something (views, formats, sorts, imports, and so on) with XML or a set of markup tags created with XML. HTML, for example, is an application of SGML, definable with an SGML DTD (and soon to be an application of XML!).

ASP

See Active Server Pages.

attribute declaration

A declaration within the document type definition that identifies that a particular attribute may be used with a particular element, which may also identify its type, provide default (or fixed) values, and limit its permitted values.

attribute

A source of additional information about an element. Attribute values may be fixed in the DTD or listed as name-value pairs (name="value") in the start-tag of an element.

C++

An object-oriented language commonly used to build high-performance software.

Cascading Style Sheets (CSS)

A standard that provides formatting control over elements using information contained in <STYLE> tags and STYLE attributes. Less powerful than XSL, it nonetheless looks like it has a bright short-term future as the only style mechanism already recommended by the W3C and (partially) implemented in major browsers.

case-sensitive

Case-sensitivity means that characters must match exactly. Non-case-sensitive applications typically transform lowercase and uppercase characters into a single case, and treat THIS and this as identical. Almost everything in XML (except xml:lang attribute values) is case-sensitive.

CDATA

See character data.

CDF

See Channel Definition Format.

CGI

See Common Gateway Interface.

Channel Definition Format (CDF)

An XML-based "push" standard that describes documents containing URL information along with descriptions, icons, and information on when the material should be automatically retrieved.

character data (CDATA)

CDATA has two very different meanings in XML. First, CDATA is used in attribute declarations to indicate that an attribute may contain character (non-enumerated text) content, including entities that should be expanded. Second, CDATA sections use markers (<![CDATA[and]]>) to indicate text within documents that is *purely* character data, containing no elements or entities. CDATA sections provide an "escape" mechanism for authors whose documents contain characters (typically <, >, and &) that would interfere with normal processing.

child element

An element nested inside another element. In <FIRST><SECOND/></FIRST>, the SECOND element is the child element of the FIRST element.

Common Gateway Interface (CGI)

An interface commonly used by Web servers to connect user requests to programs running on the server for processing.

content

The text and markup within an element or attribute.

content model

A set of rules describing the content that may appear inside of an element, typically specified using element declarations.

CSS

See Cascading Style Sheets.

descendant

An element that is contained by another element, even when other container elements are in between. All of the elements in an XML document are descendants of the root element, for example. In <FIRST><SECOND><THIRD/></SECOND></FIRST>, the THIRD element is the descendant of both the SECOND and FIRST elements.

document object model (DOM)

A means of addressing elements and attributes in a document from a processing application or script. The W3C Document Object Model Working Group is developing a standard model for HTML and XML documents. Level One is a W3C Recommendation; Level Two is in development.

Document Style Semantics and Specification Language (DSSSL)

A transformation and style language for the processing and formatting of SGML documents. A predecessor to XSL.

document type declaration

In valid documents, the declaration that connects a document to its document type definition. The declaration may connect to an external file or include the definition within itself.

document type definition (DTD)
A set of rules for document construction that lies at the heart of SGML development and all valid XML document construction. Processing applications and authoring tools rely on DTDs to inform them of the parts required by a particular document type. A document with a DTD may be validated against the definition.

document
A "textual object". In HTML, documents (or "pages") were single files containing HTML. In XML, documents may contain content from several files (or other sources) and should include markup structures that make it valid or well-formed.

DOM
See Document Object Model.

EBNF
See Extended Backus-Naur Form.

ECMAScript
The standard for JavaScript syntax, as laid down by the European Computer Manufacturers Association in ECMA-262.

element declaration
A declaration (appearing in the document type definition) identifying an element's name and describing its content model.

element
The fundamental logical unit of an XML document. XML documents contain a few opening declarations (the XML declaration and prolog) followed by a root element, which may in turn contain other elements and content.

empty element
An element that has no textual content. An empty element may be indicated by a start-tag and end-tag placed next to each other (<EMPTY></EMPTY>) or by a start-tag that ends with /> (<EMPTY />). Empty elements may contain attributes only.

encoding declaration
The encoding declaration is made in the XML declaration at the start of an XML document, and specifies which mapping of numerical values to characters is used for that document.

end-tag
A tag that closes an element. An end-tag follows the syntax </*Name*>, in which *Name* matches the element name declared in the start-tag.

entity
A reference to other data that often acts as an abbreviation or a shortcut. By declaring entities, developers can avoid entering the same information in a document or DTD repetitively.

event-based model
A model for processing XML documents in which the content of the document is expressed as a series of method calls whose type and content describe the document. Event-based models are lightweight and easily chained, making it easy to create filters and small applications. Many parsers provide event-based interfaces, and SAX is the most commonly used standardized event-based interface.

Extended Backus-Naur Form (EBNF)
The formal notation used in the XML 1.0 specification to represent XML grammar. EBNF is also used to describe standards where XML DTD notation is inappropriate, like the Resource Description Framework.

extended link group
A group of documents whose contents are analyzed for links to help establish two-way links without requiring their declaration in every document.

extended link
A link that contains locator elements rather than a simple HREF attribute to identify the targets of the link.

Extensible Markup Language (XML)
A standard created by the W3C that provides a much simpler set of rules for markup than SGML, while offering considerably more flexibility than HTML.

Extensible Protocol

A proposal under development at the Internet Engineering Task Force (IETF) that would apply XML to a generic protocol for communications over a network.

Extensible Style Language (XSL)

A style sheet standard under development at the W3C. XSL enables developers to specify formatting far more precisely than Cascading Style Sheets permit. XSL seems promising, but is not yet a W3C Working Draft or Recommendation.

external DTD subset

The portion of a document type definition that is stored outside of the document. External DTDs are convenient for storing document type definitions that will be used by multiple documents, enabling them to share a centrally managed definition.

external entity

An entity whose declaration contains a reference to an external resource, rather than the content of the entity itself.

fatal error

A violation of the well-formedness constraints. Parsers should stop processing the document and report an error to the application. (Note that a fatal error for the parser is not necessarily a fatal error for the application.)

filter

A small piece of software typically used with event-based interfaces that processes or transforms document events before passing them to the application.

formatting object

In XSL, the set of tools used to describe presentation. A source XML document is transformed into a set of formatting objects, which are then displayed or otherwise processed.

fragment

A portion of a document identified by an XPointer or other query mechanism. A fragment may refer to one element and all its content (including subelements), a group of elements, or even a selection based on content. The W3C XML Activity has a working group focusing on fragment handing.

general entity
An entity for use in document content. When used in documents, the name of a general entity must be preceded by an ampersand (&) and should be followed by a semicolon (;).

Generalized Markup Language (GML)
The predecessor to SGML, developed in 1969 by IBM in efforts led by Charles Goldfarb. GML originated the use of <, >, and / for markup and is still in use for document applications.

group element
An XLink element containing a set of additional XML files that are considered potential candidates for multidirectional linking.

Hypermedia/Time-based Structuring Language (HyTime)
A set of multimedia and linking extensions to SGML, formalized as ISO/IEC 10744-1992. HyTime is one of the foundations for XML-LINK.

HyperText Markup Language (HTML)
The most popular markup language in use today, HTML is an application of SGML. HTML is one of the foundations of Web development, providing formatting and basic structures to documents for presentation via browser applications.

HyperText Transfer Protocol (HTTP)
The protocol that governs communications between clients and servers on the World Wide Web. HTTP enables clients to send requests to servers, which reply with an appropriate document or an error message.

in-line link
A link in which the element making the linking declarations is itself a part of the link.

instance
The actual use of an element or document type in a document, as opposed to its definition. An instance may also refer to an entire document; a document may be an instance of a DTD if it can be validated under that DTD.

internal DTD subset

The portion of a document type definition that appears inside the document to which it applies. Internal DTD subsets can be hard to manage, but provide developers an easy way to test out new features or develop DTDs without disrupting other documents.

internal entity

An entity which contains its content inside the declaration rather than referring to an external resource.

ISO

The International Organization for Standardization, which sets industrial standards relating to everything from measurement to character sets to shipping containers to quality processes to SGML.

Java

An object-oriented language optimized for use over the Internet.

JavaScript

A scripting language typically used in Web browsers, though it can also be used on the server as part of Active Server Pages or other development environments. Apart from some surface similarities, JavaScript is definitely not Java, or even a "lite" Java. JavaScript is standardized as ECMAScript.

markup declaration

The contents of document type declarations, which are used to define the elements, attributes, entities, and notations. They specify the kinds of markup that will be legal in a given document.

markup

Structural information stored in the same file as the content. Traditionally, structural information is separated from the content and isolated in elements (defined with tags) and entities.

Mathematical Markup Language (MathML)

An XML application developed by the W3C for the presentation and communication of mathematical structures, particularly equations.

Meta-Content Framework (MCF)

A standard developed by Apple and continued by Netscape that represented metadata as a multidimensional space for user navigation. MCF is one of the many inputs to the Resource Description Format (RDF).

mixed content

Content within an element that includes text, possibly including other child elements. Mixed content models have limited options for constraints in XML; once an element contains text, additional elements declared within that content model may appear as few or as many times as the author likes, in any order.

name characters

Letters, digits, hyphens, underscores, colons, and full stops. (Full stops in Latin character sets are periods.) Colons are reserved for use with namespaces by the namespaces in XML recommendation, so don't use them unless you're supporting namespaces.

name token

Any string composed of name characters.

name

A name must begin with a letter and may only contain name characters.

namespace

An additional layer of naming information that uses Uniform Resource Identifiers to provide unique names for elements. Useful when information defined in multiple DTDs is combined.

notation

An XML structure that identifies the type of content contained by an element by providing an identifier for the content type.

open source

Typically used to refer to software that is released with source code and a license that permits modification of that source code. A variety of licenses are available, with different constraints on modification and redistribution.

out-of-line link

A link in which the element defining the link is not itself a member of the set of targets defined by the link. Out-of-line links enable developers to declare links separately from the content of the document; out-of-line links may even appear in separate files.

parameter entity
An entity used to represent information within the context of a document type definition. Parameter entities may be used to link the content of additional DTD files to a DTD, or as an abbreviation for frequently repeated declarations. Parameter entities are distinguished from general entities by their use of a percent sign (%) rather than an ampersand (&).

parent element
An element in which another element is nested. In <FIRST><SECOND/></FIRST>, the FIRST element is the parent element of the SECOND element.

parsed character data (#PCDATA)
Parsed character data is text that will be examined by the parser for entities and markup. Parsed character data should not contain any &, <, or > characters; these need to be represented by the & &lt, and > entities, respectively.

parser
An application that converts a serial stream of markup (an XML file, for example) into an output structure accessible by a program. Parsers may perform validation or well-formedness checking on the markup as they process it.

Perl
A scripting language, first developed for Unix, that has become a key part of many CGI applications as well as a general-purpose text-processing utility language.

processing application
An application that takes the output generated by a parser (it may include a parser, or be a parser itself) and does something with it. That something may include presentation, calculation, or anything else that seems appropriate.

processing instruction
Directions that enable XML authors to send instructions directly to a processing application that may be outside the native capacities of XML. A processing instruction is differentiated from normal element markup by question marks after the opening < and before the closing > (i.e. <? instruction ?>). The XML declaration is itself a processing instruction.

processor

In the XML 1.0 specification, another term for the software commonly referred to as a parser.

prolog

The opening part of a document, containing the XML declaration and any document type declarations or markup declarations needed to process the document.

Python

A scripting language popularly used for XML applications.

recursion

A programming technique in which a function may call itself. Recursive programming is especially well-suited to parsing nested markup structures.

Resource Description Framework (RDF)

A standard for storing metadata (information about information) under development by the W3C that uses several XML syntaxes.

root element

The first element in a document. The root element is not contained by any other elements (though the prolog may come before it) and forms the base of the tree structure created by parsing the nested elements.

SAX

See Simple API for XML

servlet

A server-side Java component, typically used to generate markup for transmission over the Web.

sibling

An element with the same parent element as another element. In <A><B/><C/></A>, the B and C elements are siblings because they share the parent A element.

Simple API for XML

An event-based API for connecting Java parsers to applications, also used to create filters between the parser and the application. Most Java parsers provide SAX support.

simple link
A link that includes its target locator in an HREF attribute.

SMIL
See Synchronized Multimedia Integration Language

standalone
A declaration that indicates whether a document references external resources.

Standard Generalized Markup Language (SGML)
The parent language of HTML and XML. SGML provides a complex set of rules for defining document structures. HTML uses structures defined under that set of rules, whereas XML provides a subset of the rules for defining document structures. SGML is formally standardized as ISO/IEC 8879-1986, although a series of later amendments have continued its development.

start-tag
The opening tag that begins an element. The general syntax for a start-tag is *<Name attributes>*, where Name is the name of the element being defined, and attributes is a set of name-value pairs. All start tags in XML must either have end-tags or use the empty element syntax, *<Name attributes/>*.

Structured Vector Graphics
A W3C standard under development for describing easily scaled and processed vector graphics that uses an XML vocabulary.

style sheet
A formatting description for a document. Style sheets may be stored in separate files from the documents they describe.

SVG
See Structured Vector Graphics

Synchronized Multimedia Integration Language
A W3C recommendation providing an XML vocabulary that provides references to resources and organizes them into presentations based on both spatial and time-based layout.

tag

A component of markup used to delineate element beginnings and endings. In <A><B /></A>, <A> is the start-tag for the element A, </A> is the end-tag for the element A, and <B /> is an empty tag representing the element B.

tree-based model

A model for processing XML documents in which an object tree representing the document is constructed and then processed. Once the tree is built, the entire document content is available at any time. The Document Object Model (DOM) is a commonly used tree-based document model.

UCS-2

The standard encoding for Unicode characters, presenting the complete 2-byte representation for every character.

Unicode

A standard for international character encoding. Unicode supports characters that are 2 bytes wide rather than the 1 byte currently supported by most systems, enabling it to include 65,536 characters rather than the 256 available to 1-byte systems. Visit http://www.unicode.org for more information.

Uniform Resource Identifier (URI)

An identifier for a resource that may contain either a Uniform Resource Locator or a Uniform Resource Number.

Uniform Resource Locator (URL)

An identifer for a resource that provides a pathway for retrieving the resource. A complete URL identifies a protocol, a computer to contact, and the location of the resource on that computer.

Uniform Resource Number (URN)

A number that an application may resolve to reference a resource. Because of the lack of cataloging systems, URNs have received much less use than URLs.

unparsed entity

An entity that refers to an external resource (typically a binary file). Unparsed entities are passed to the application, which may then process the entity however it likes.

URI

See Uniform Resource Identifier.

URL

See Uniform Resource Locator.

URN

See Uniform Resource Number.

UTF-8

An encoding that provides access to the Unicode character set but uses an algorithm to enable the presentation of characters with values less than 128 in a single byte (very useful for English), while requiring two or three bytes for characters in other ranges above 128.

valid

A document is valid if it conforms to a declared document type definition (DTD) and meets the conditions for well-formedness. All elements, attributes, and entities must be declared in the DTD, and all data types must match their definition's requirements.

validity constraint

A rule that only validating parsers are required to enforce. Violations typically indicate that a document doesn't match up to the rules set forth in its document type definition (DTD).

VBScript

A scripting language created by Microsoft based on its Visual Basic language. VBScript works in the Internet Explorer browser, Active Server Pages, and some Microsoft applications.

Voyager

The W3C HTML Activity's project to describe HTML as a set of XML modules.

W3C

The World Wide Web Consortium, the standards body responsible for many of the standards key to the functionality of the World Wide Web, including HTML, XML, HTTP, and Cascading Style Sheets. The W3C site includes the latest public versions of their standards as well as other information about the Web and standards processes. Visit http://www.w3.org for more information.

well-formed

A well-formed document may or may not have a DTD. Well-formed documents must begin with an XML declaration and contain properly nested and marked-up elements.

well-formedness constraint

A rule that all XML parsers are required to enforce. If a document doesn't meet the well-formedness constraints (which lay out basic document syntax), the parser is required to stop and present the application with a fatal error.

XLink

The W3C's set of rules for establishing links among XML documents. Still in the Working Draft stage at the time of this writing.

XML declaration

The processing instruction at the top of an XML document. It begins with <?xml, includes a version identifier, required markup declaration, and encoding identifier, and closes with ?>. (The XML declaration is case-sensitive. Although the standard is referred to as XML, the XML declaration must open with <?xml.)

XML

See Extensible Markup Language.

XML-RPC

An XML standard for making Remote Procedure Calls (RPC) among computers on a network.

XP

See Extensible Protocol.

XPointer

A reference to a fragment of a document. XPointers use a syntax derived from the Text Encoding Initiative, modified to take into account the needs of the HTTP protocol for encoding URLs. Also used to describe the W3C's set of rules for creating XPointers. Still in the Working Draft stage at this writing.

XSL

See Extensible Style Language.

Index

my2cents.idgbooks.com

Register This Book — And Win!

Visit **http://my2cents.idgbooks.com** to register this book and we'll automatically enter you in our fantastic monthly prize giveaway. It's also your opportunity to give us feedback: let us know what you thought of this book and how you would like to see other topics covered.

Discover IDG Books Online!

The IDG Books Online Web site is your online resource for tackling technology — at home and at the office. Frequently updated, the IDG Books Online Web site features exclusive software, insider information, online books, and live events!

10 Productive & Career-Enhancing Things You Can Do at www.idgbooks.com

1. Nab source code for your own programming projects.

2. Download software.

3. Read Web exclusives: special articles and book excerpts by IDG Books Worldwide authors.

4. Take advantage of resources to help you advance your career as a Novell or Microsoft professional.

5. Buy IDG Books Worldwide titles or find a convenient bookstore that carries them.

6. Register your book and win a prize.

7. Chat live online with authors.

8. Sign up for regular e-mail updates about our latest books.

9. Suggest a book you'd like to read or write.

10. Give us your 2¢ about our books and about our Web site.

You say you're not on the Web yet? It's easy to get started with IDG Books' *Discover the Internet,* available at local retailers everywhere.